IMAGES
of America

SWEETWATER

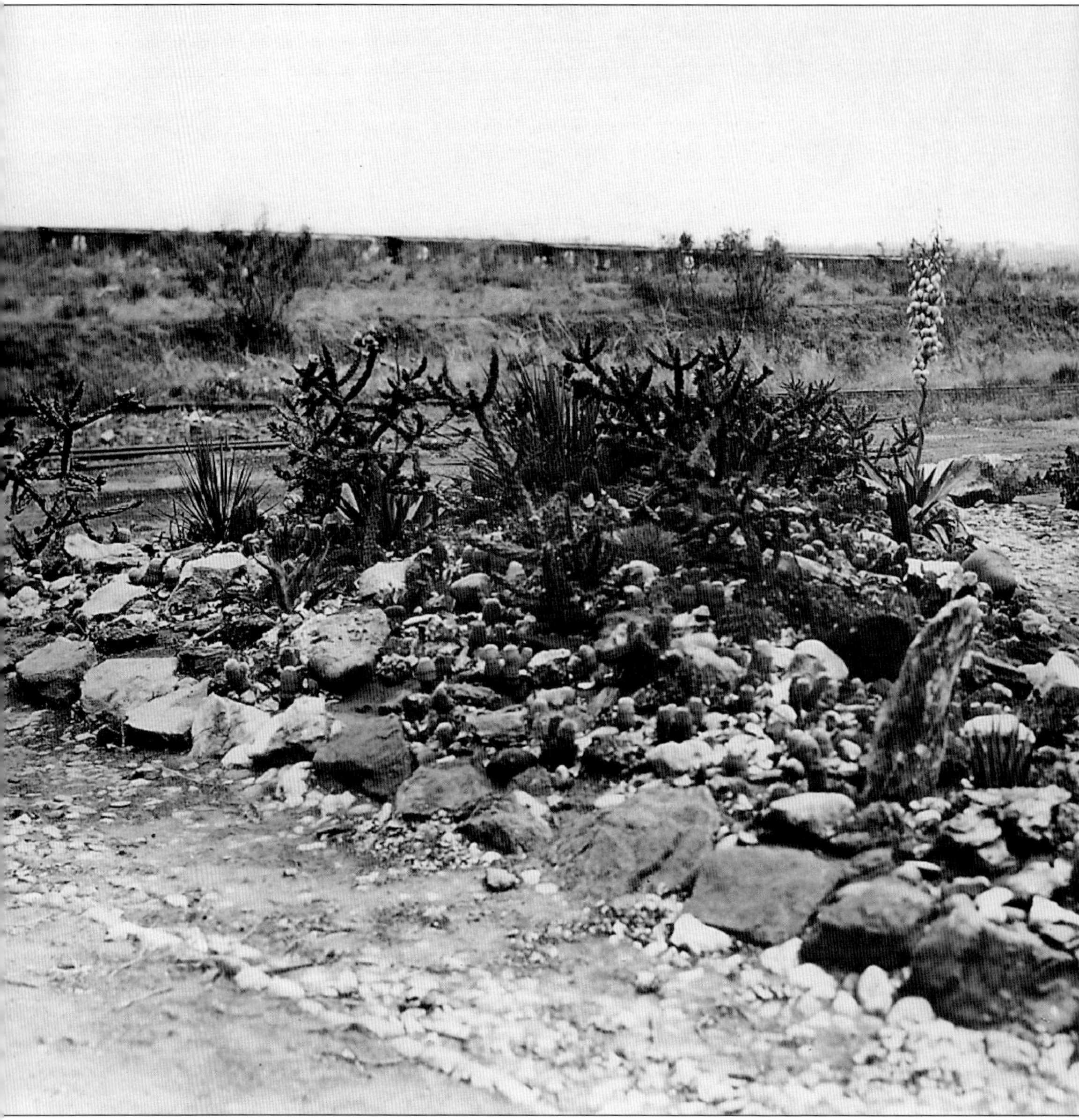

Tree cholla or walking stick cholla greeted early Native Americans, buffalo hunters, pioneers, and cowboys. This cactus is both a blessing and a curse—it serves as a wonderful food and water source in times of famine, but the burning wounds caused by its rough spines have earned it the nickname "hell on a stick." Cholla can be found in Newman Park, which was then called City Park.

On the Cover: This view of the north side of the square, which surrounds the Nolan County Courthouse, was photographed in 1949. Montgomery Ward is shown in what is now called Tara on the Square near the corner of Locust and Third Streets; currently, the Hall Law Firm is located in the building.

IMAGES
of America

SWEETWATER

Melonnie Hicks, Betty Turner, and
the Pioneer City County Museum

ARCADIA
PUBLISHING

ISBN 978-1-4671-3096-7

Published by Arcadia Publishing
Charleston, South Carolina

Printed in the United States of America

Library of Congress Control Number: 2013951895

For all general information, please contact Arcadia Publishing:
Telephone 843-853-2070
Fax 843-853-0044
E-mail sales@arcadiapublishing.com
For customer service and orders:
Toll-Free 1-888-313-2665

Visit us on the Internet at www.arcadiapublishing.com

Melonnie would like to dedicate this book to her daughter, Emorie, for being endlessly patient while mommy worked on her book, and to her parents for their babysitting services as well as encouraging all their friends to share their stories.

Betty would like to dedicate this book to Franzas Cupp and Kent Boatright for giving her the opportunity to be so immersed in the history of Nolan County in general, and Sweetwater in particular.

Contents

ACKNOWLEDGMENTS

We would like to specially thank the people of Sweetwater, both past and present, for sharing their memories through photographs and stories with the Pioneer City County Museum. We are grateful to the Nolan County Historical Commission, Travis Monday, Laura Sheridan, Carlos Alvarado, Roy Crane, Sweetwater Junior Historians, and many others for their past dedication to researching Nolan County's history. Thanks go to E.A. and Gladys Harkins, E.L. Duncan, and Mrs. E.F. Barton for developing a history museum and to both Henri Elizabeth "Hank" Pepper and Franzas Cupp for their tireless dedication to preserving Nolan County's history and sharing our curious story with children of all ages. This book has revived an interest in our community's history, and we thank you all for your support. Unless otherwise noted, all images appear courtesy of the Pioneer City County Museum and Nolan County Historical Society.

INTRODUCTION

In 1877, Billie Knight set up a dugout trading post on Sweetwater Creek to serve buffalo hunters. Knight's dugout sat about three miles east of the current site of Sweetwater. At the time, the store was called the Blue Goose trading post because, according to legend and Judge R.C. Crane writing in "Early Days in Sweetwater," "some newly arrived cowboy from the east killed a blue crane. The cowboys told him it was a blue goose and he cooked and ate it accordingly." This type of horseplay was common among the area's earliest inhabitants; Judge Crane tells of an evening in Knight's trading post when some rambunctious cowboys began "throwing cartridges into the fire. Knight [trying] to get them to quit . . . got up from his seat on a powder keg and said, 'Boys, if you insist on shooting things up we will make a complete job of it,' with that he swung the powder keg toward the fire and everyone in the dugout broke for the door . . . What Knight knew but the boys did not is that the keg was empty."

Knight sold the trading post to Amos Bochee and then moved to Buffalo Gap. Bochee soon sold the store to a man named Kelso, who, according to Judge Crane, "built a shack out of cedar poles for the store." Kelso did not own the store long and sold to James Manning, the district surveyor for Shackelford County. By March 27, 1879, enough people had moved into the area that a post office was set up in Manning's store under the name Sweet Water. The name was taken from the Kiowa, who called the creek Mobeetie, meaning "sweet water" in English. Several towns along the creek have shared the moniker, but only Sweetwater kept this version of the name.

In June 1880, about 630 people lived in what is now considered Nolan County. Many of the residents worked for the Texas & Pacific Railroad, which was then under construction. In December 1880, an election, spurred by Tom Robard, the first teacher in Nolan County, was held at the post office. On January 10, 1881, the Commissioners Court of Shackelford County declared the election results, and the Sweet Water Post Office was declared the temporary Nolan County seat until a permanent one could be determined. The election for the permanent county seat was held March 31, 1881, and on April 12, 1881, the Commissioners Court of Nolan County declared the result of the election. Sweetwater was named the official county seat with, according to Judge Crane, "not a building on the site constructed of wood, rock, or brick." This election was fraught with controversy as a blizzard caused the majority vote for an alternate site to be thrown out.

The site chosen for the county seat was Section No. 47, Block No. 22, which was owned by the Franco Texas Land Company. One of the original matters considered in the election was a $10,000 bond the land company set aside for the building of a courthouse and a suitable lot for a jail. For whatever reason, there is no record of the company upholding this pledge. On March 18, 1882, the Texas & Pacific Railway Company bought 480 acres and began its plat of Sweetwater. The first lot sold was to J.S. Johnson, an early sheriff of the county and sheep rancher, on the southeast corner of Oak Street and Broadway Avenue, where Azteca is now located, for the sum of $100.

The first house "built of lumber" was constructed between July 18, 1881, and September 1, 1881, on the third lot of land sold to R. West Starr for the purpose of a saloon. By March 1883, there were five saloons in Sweetwater within one block of the Texas & Pacific depot; three were on the west side of the street with the other two on the east side. This street very early on earned the name Rat Row, both for the rats that lived under the raised wooden sidewalks as well as the rowdy people who frequented the block. Rat Row is the part of Oak Street that sits between First Street and Broadway Avenue. After this first saloon was established, the growth of Sweetwater was painful and slow going.

The story of Nolan County's courthouses reflects the growing pains experienced by Sweetwater. The shack that had served as Manning's store was moved into town and was located just south of the west end of the site of the Aycock Building; it is considered the first courthouse as it was used for all general county purposes for more than a year. In late summer of 1881, T.E. Douthit and J.W. Posey erected a two-story business house near the corner of Third and Locust Streets, and it hosted the first term of district court. It was in this courtroom that the town's first official Christmas tree was staged. Much like the rest of Nolan County's courthouses, this building too had structural problems, and the floor sank under the weight of the tree. However, thanks to the quick action of Douthit, a panic was narrowly avoided and the tree was saved. Neither of these buildings was actually referred to as a courthouse, and one was still needed. Though the first courthouse was built in 1883, it fell due to faulty construction in 1885; it would still be 10 years before an official Nolan County Courthouse was used for all county purposes.

A jailhouse, built in 1882, served until 1891. This jailhouse was a welcome relief to the prisoners in the area since they were chained to a mesquite tree prior to its construction. The jailhouse also temporarily housed county offices. Again according to Judge Crane, penal labor came into being when the commissioners court passed the order that "convicts be made to work on county improvements . . . and if he refuses . . . to be fed bread and water and not be allowed anything else until he is willing to perform good work and to be chained to a mesquite tree away from any person . . . until he works . . . to pay his fine." A closer look at county records shows that 90 percent of all law violations occurred on Rat Row, and most of these were for gaming and carrying a pistol, betting at monte, keeping gaming tables, drunkenness, and assault and battery.

Even though there were rowdy cowboys causing commotion on this street, it is said that whenever a woman made an appearance, the men were never to speak an improper word to nor about her or they would be turned "on their ear [and made to look] considerably worse than thirty cents worth of dog meat." This contrast of rowdiness and chivalry echoes the tone of the rest of Sweetwater's history; this town has rounded up rattlesnakes, survived the Depression, trained the first Women Airforce Service Pilots, became an All-America City, and is now known as the "wind energy capital of America."

One

Establishing Sweetwater

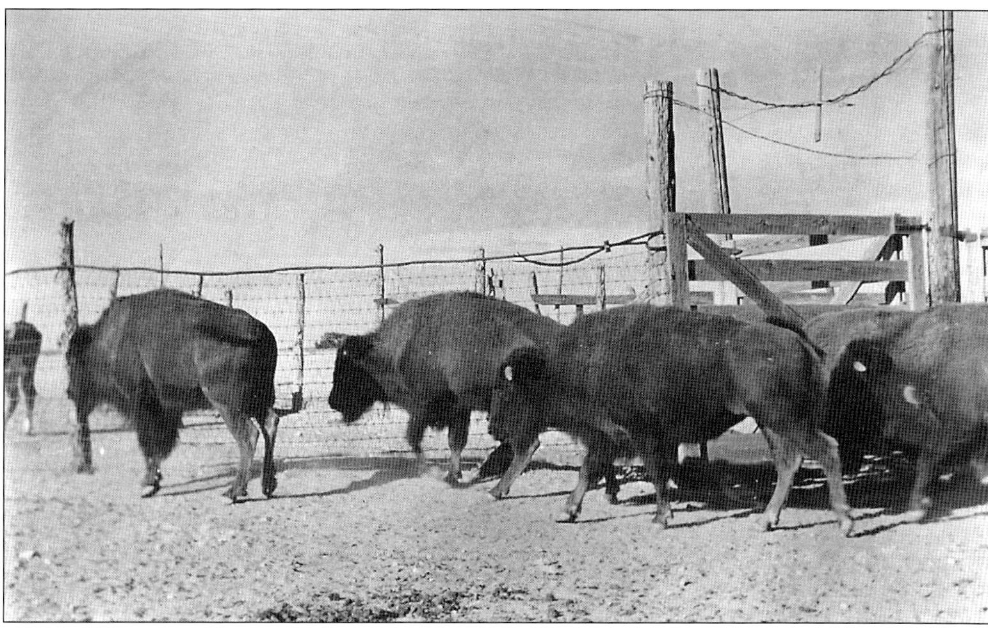

Buffalo are seen on the Double Heart Ranch. The first reports of buffalo in Texas were by Álvar Núñez Cabeza de Vaca during his journey from Florida to Mexico, in his account *La Relación*, published in 1542. The "great slaughter" in the late 19th century brought buffalo hunters to this area, which prompted Billie Knight to set up his trading post on Sweetwater Creek.

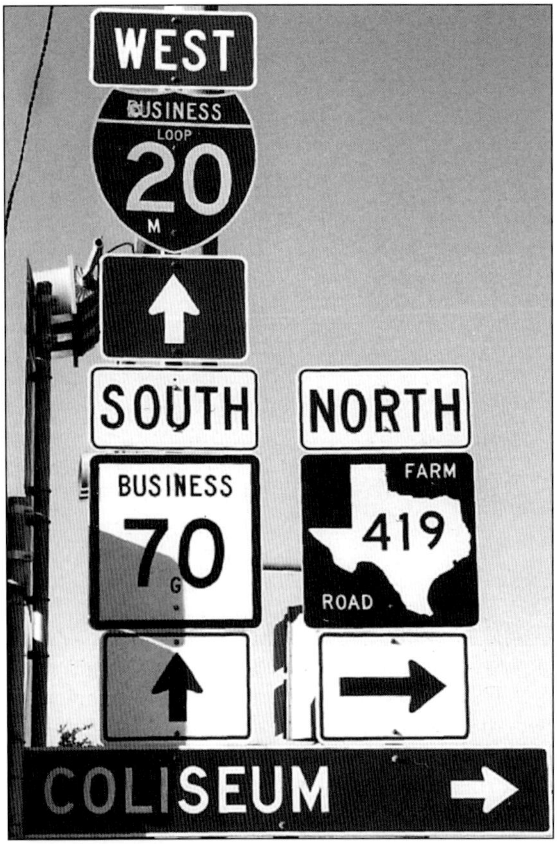

Sweetwater sits at the junction of old Highway 80, Interstate 20, running east and west, and Highway 70, running north and south. The present location of Sweetwater is its second since its inception. The original site was referred to as Blue Goose, located about three miles east near present-day Garden of Memories Cemetery.

John R. Lewis built this house in the southern part of Nolan County around 1881. The house is typical of the improvements made in early Sweetwater. This particular house was constructed in front of a log home that had been erected by Lewis several years before.

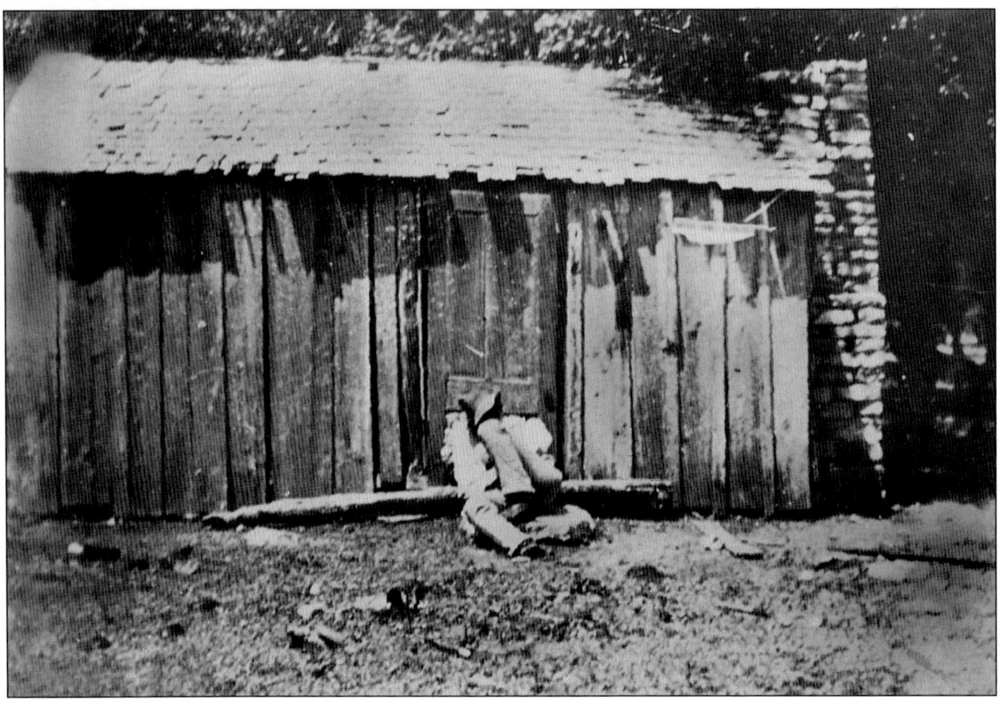

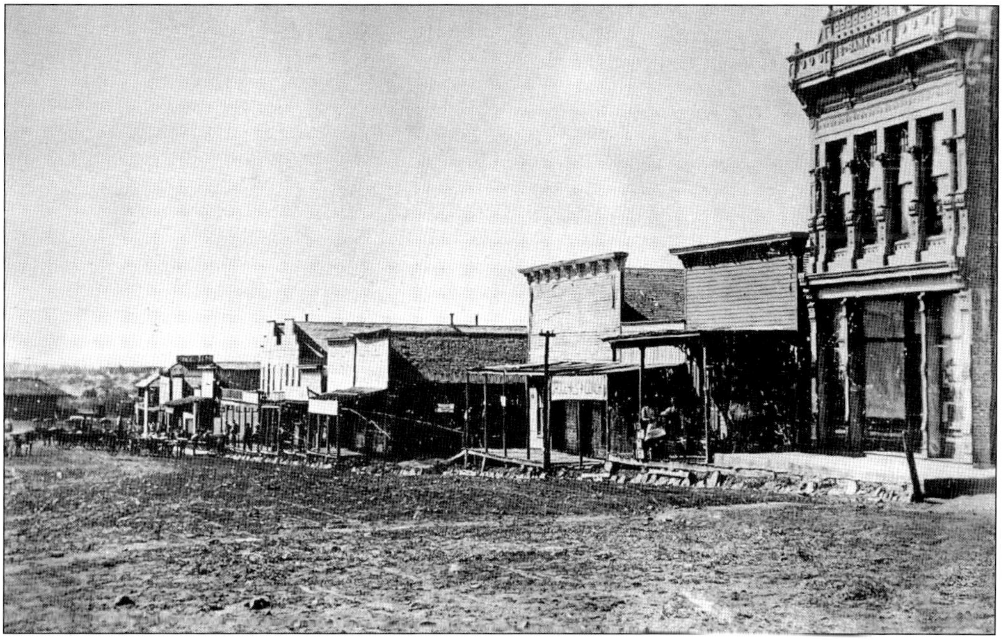

Pictured is Rat Row in 1888. City Hotel can be seen on the far left; it, along with most of Rat Row, was destroyed in one of Sweetwater's early fires. The hotel was rebuilt in 1911 as the Commercial Hotel, which operated until the 1960s. Thereafter, it became a private residence for various families, including the Stracener family. The building still stands and continues to serve as a private residence. In the foreground can be seen the Trammell Bank on the southwest corner of Oak Street and Broadway Avenue.

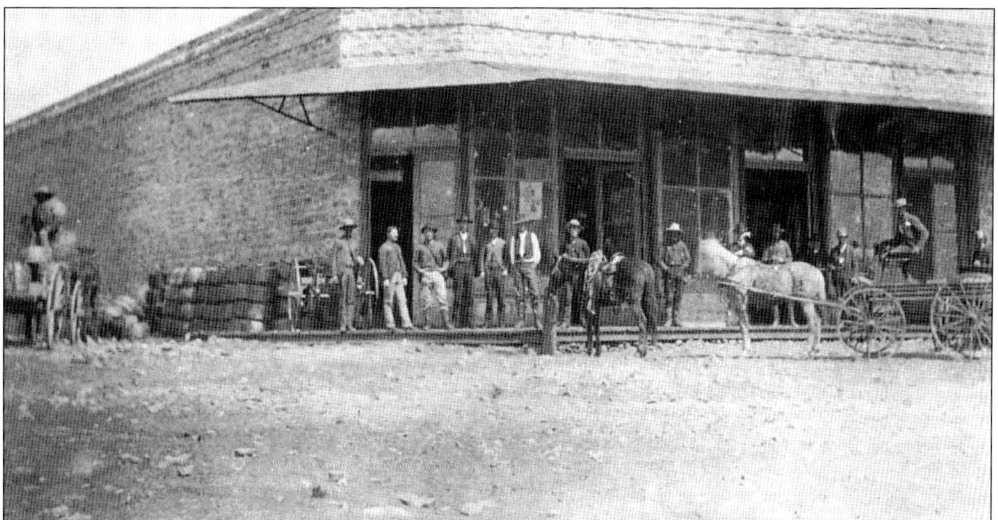

Pictured is the first brick building in Sweetwater. Constructed by N.I. Dulaney between 1885 and 1886, N.I. Dulaney and Brothers was a general mercantile store until N.I. Dulaney passed away in the early 1890s. The building has also housed the Sweetwater Producers Credit Association and Willis Art Gallery.

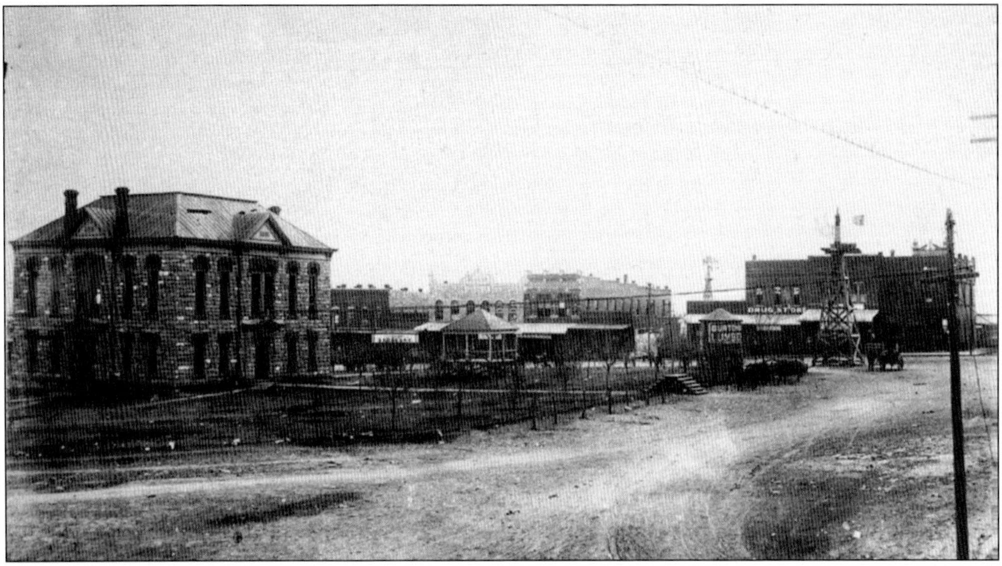

Here is courthouse square featuring Nolan County's second courthouse. The municipal band, politicians, and preachers used the gazebo on the north side of the square. The windmill on the far right sat over a drilled well and supplied water for livestock. For drinking water, people depended on underground cisterns.

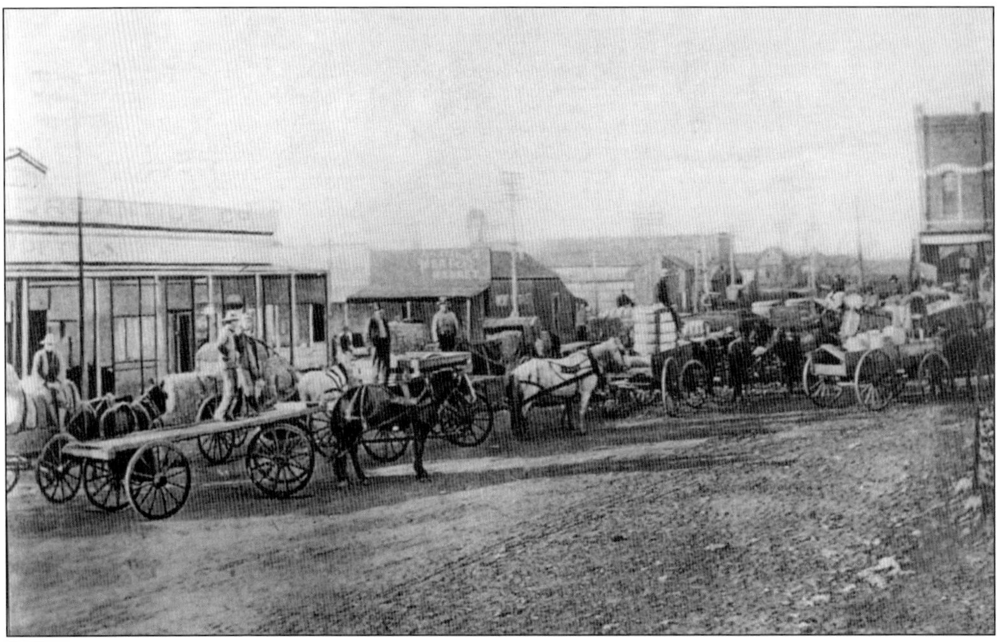

In this early 1900s street scene, wagons are loaded with bales of cotton and are ready to be taken to market. The installment of barbed-wire fences in the 1870s and the arrival of the railroads through West Texas increased cotton production and sales, spurring Sweetwater's economy.

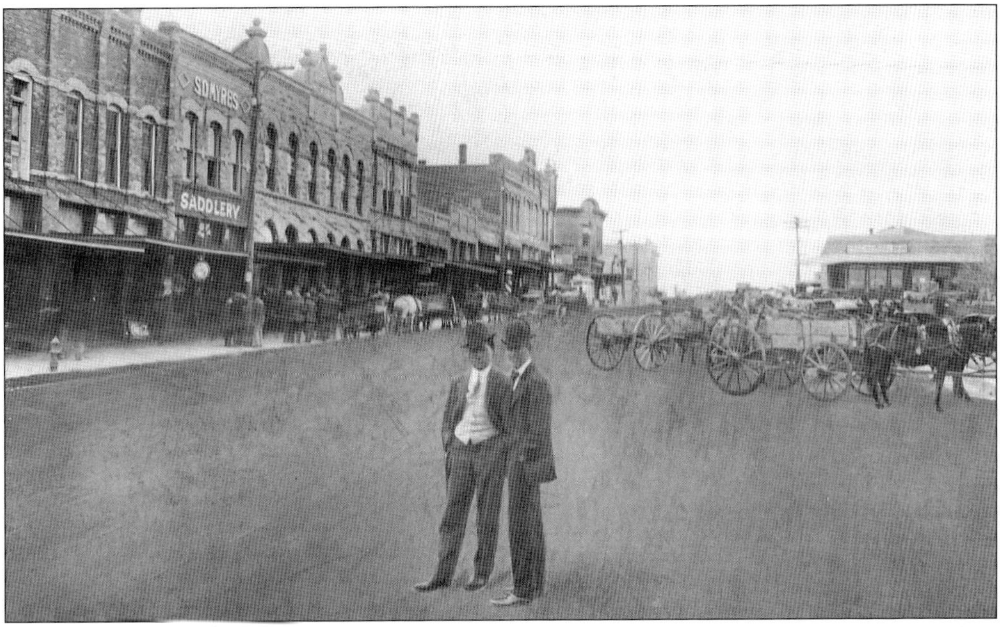

This is a view of Oak Street, facing north. Many of the buildings on this block are still standing and used for various purposes, such as Wetsel and Carmichael law firm, Morgan Real Estate, Beall Abstract and Title Company, Oak Street Salon, Cornett Computer Repair, and Latria's clothing store. S.D. Myres' Saddlery, pictured, was located in the former location of Staton's Pharmacy.

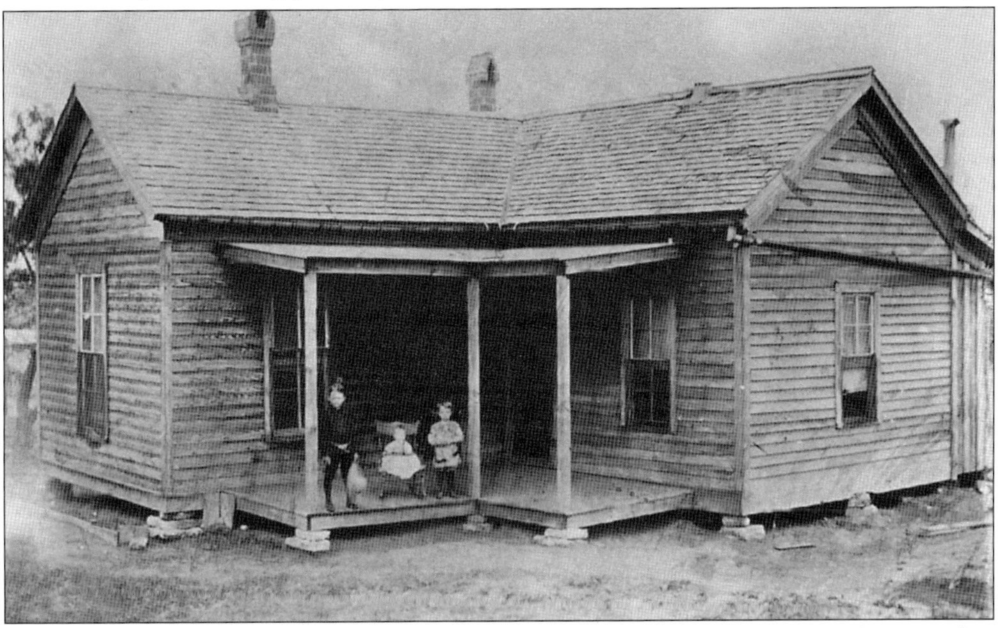

Taken in about 1906, this photograph is of the first home of S.D. Myres upon his arrival in Sweetwater. The Myreses' children Ted, Billy, and Melrose, are on the front porch. The house was located on west Third Street, where Ludlum's cycle shop now stands. Samuel Dale Myres moved to Sweetwater in 1897 and bought a saddlery in 1898; he served as mayor from 1908 to 1911 and was instrumental in many city improvements. After fire destroyed his first shop, Myres reopened a block north on Oak Street.

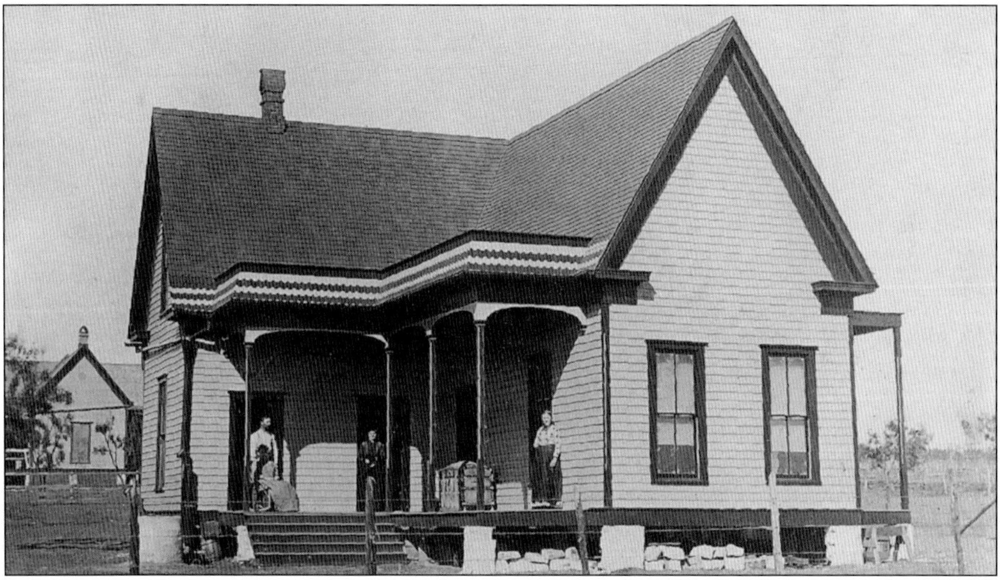

The home of Jefferson Dulaney, co-owner of N.I. Dulaney and Brothers with N.I. Dulaney, was located on the corner of Cedar and Fifth Streets and was typical of new homes in the late 1880s. Jefferson and his brothers came to Sweetwater in 1879 and owned the first store in town where they sold general merchandise and shipped in the first lumber.

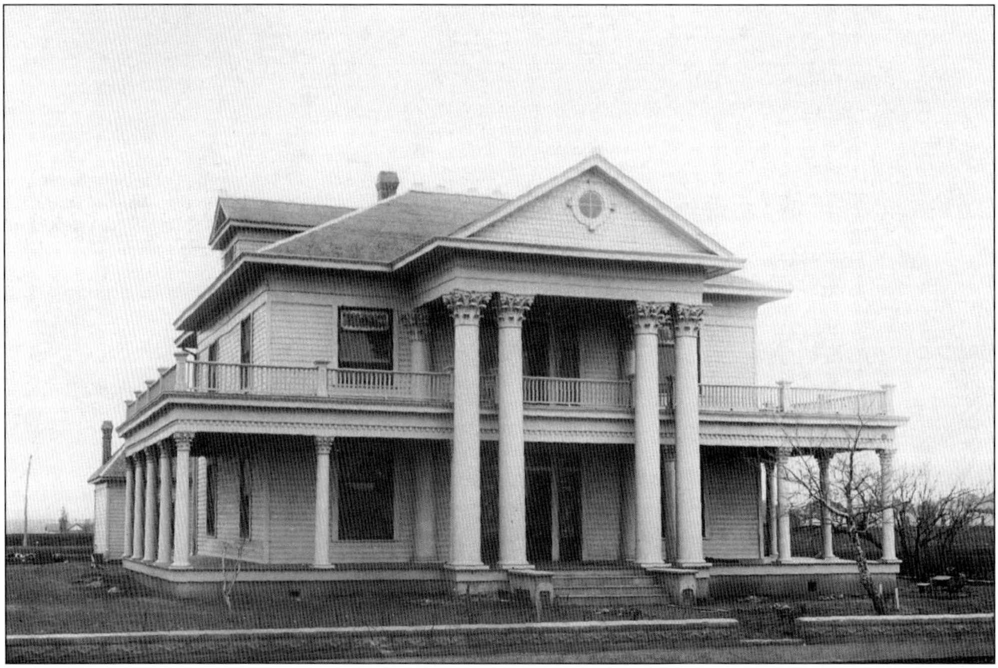

Here is the home of Ed and Hattie Bradford. Ed's father, William Martin Bradford, owned the first lumberyard in Sweetwater, hauling lumber in by wagon. In 1917, Ed organized the Texas Bank and Trust Company; he was president until his retirement in 1936. Ed is most well known for the "Superior" strain of Herefords he developed.

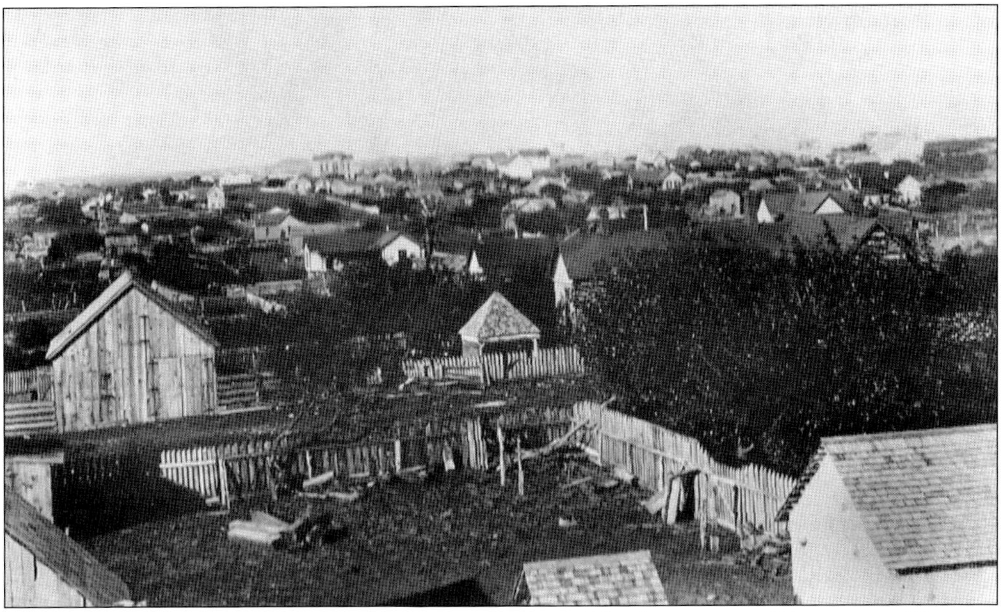

Taken from the windmill tower, this photograph is a c. 1892 bird's-eye view of Sweetwater. This spot would later become the site of J.A.J. Bradford's home. In the foreground to the left and right are the garage and home, respectively, of J.H. Beall. In the far rear is Nolan County's second courthouse.

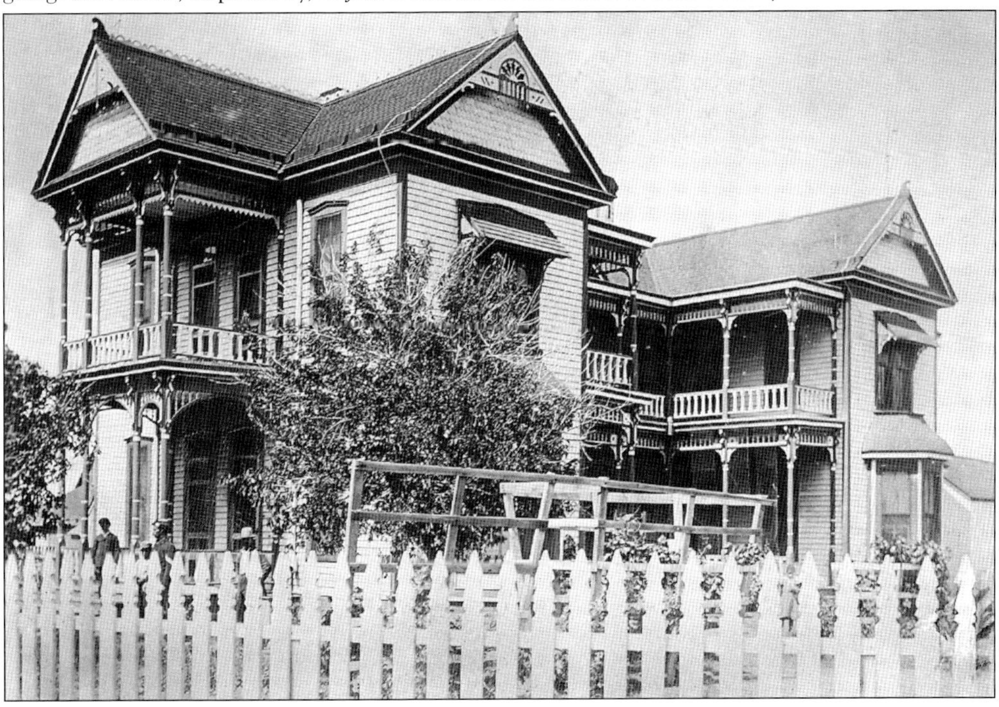

The rebuilt home of J.F. Newman, located at the corner of James and Ragland Streets, was later replaced by a redbrick home owned by B.C. "Skinny" Pace. J.F. Newman raised some of the finest races horses and polo ponies in the West; ran a bank in Sylvester, Texas (J.F. Newman and Sons Bank); helped to form the Chuck Wagon Association; served as Nolan County sheriff from 1890 to 1896; and held a deputyship in New Mexico Territory.

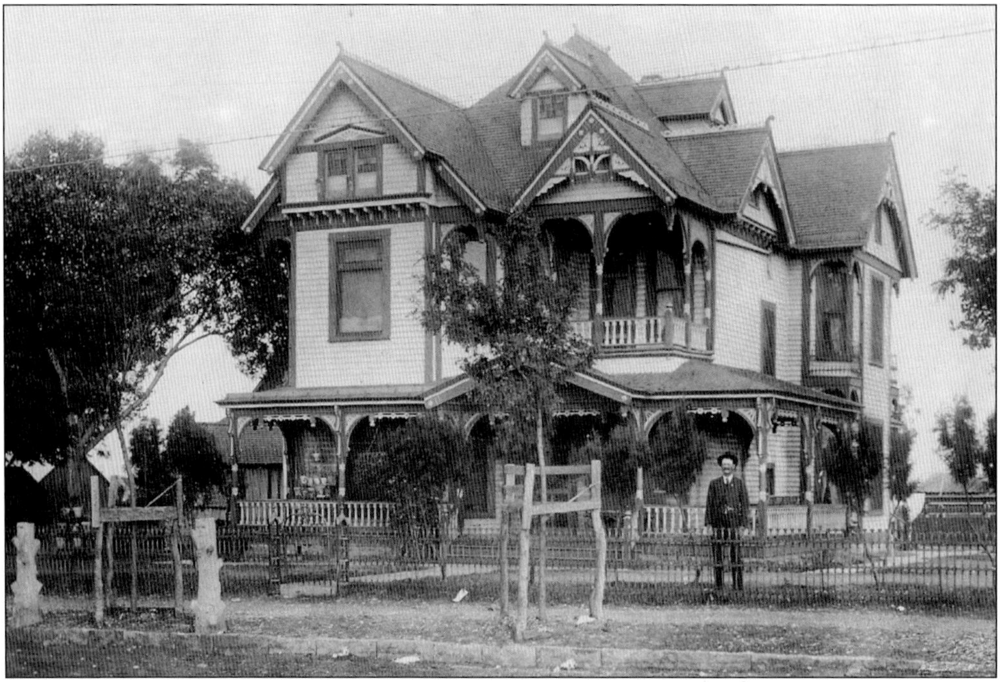

Here is the home of Thomas and Mary Jane Trammell, built in 1901; this site later became the Scott Hotel. Mary Jane was the daughter of Martin Newman and helped to found the First Baptist Church of Sweetwater. Tom founded the first bank in Sweetwater and had extensive ranching interests in Texas and New Mexico. The family moved to Nolan County in 1880 when the post office was still called Blue Goose. Thomas Trammell is standing at the fence.

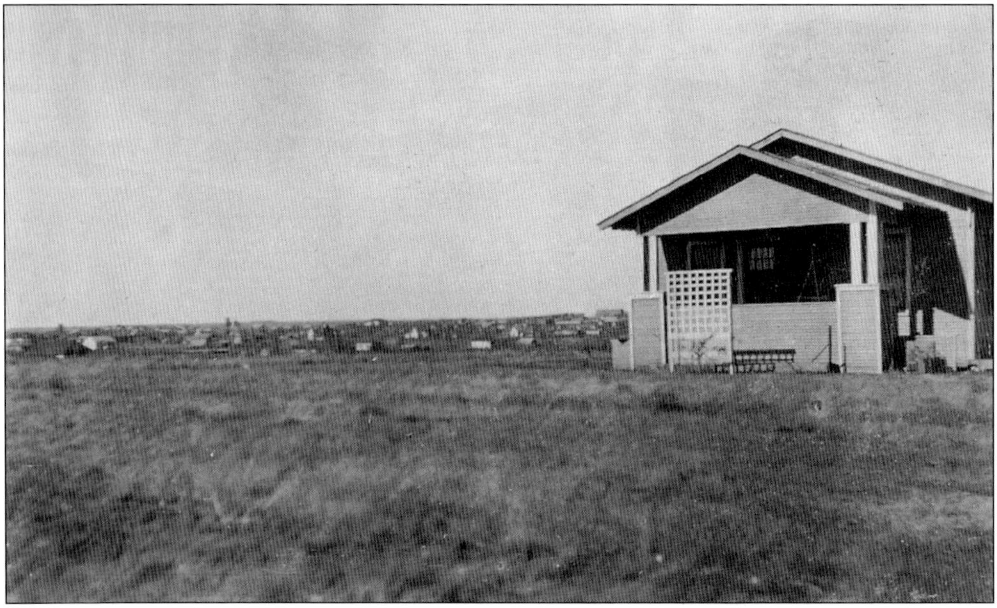

A.J. Walker's house at the corner of Oklahoma and Neff Streets was built around 1922. This house is representative of the types of family homes that citizens were building at this time. Sweetwater can be seen in the distance.

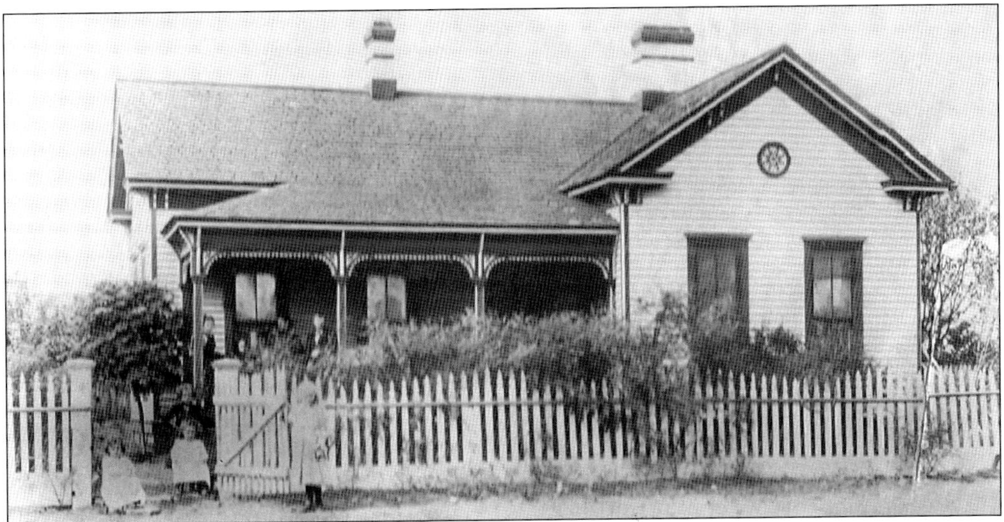

The home of Silas George is on the site previously occupied by the home of G.H. Connell, who sold it to H.G. Bardwell. H.G. Bardwell was sheriff of Nolan County and sold the property to Silas George. One of Silas George's children, pictured here, grew up and married Henry Rogers. The Rogers family is responsible for the first gin in Sweetwater.

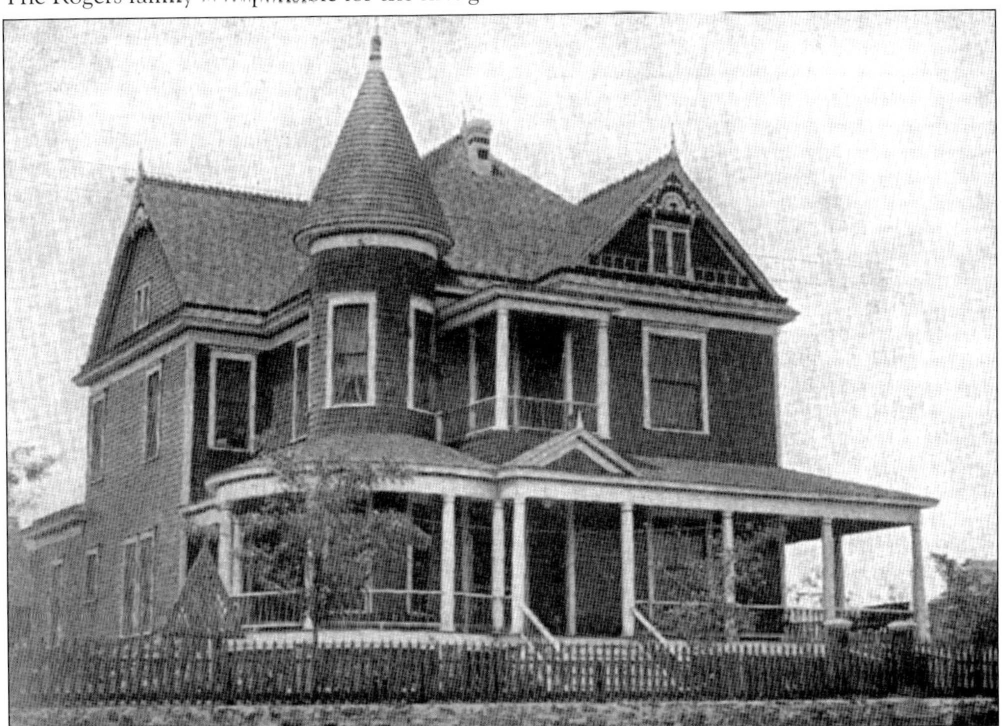

The residence of Judge James Henry Beall and family, built around 1885, was located where Broadway Baptist Church now stands. Judge Beall was the first schoolteacher at Mulberry Canyon and was appointed tax assessor of Nolan County in 1882. Law always appealed to him, however, so he studied while he taught and worked as tax assessor. He was admitted to the bar in 1884 and began practicing law in Sweetwater. He was elected county judge in 1892; today, Judge Tim D. Fambrough holds this position.

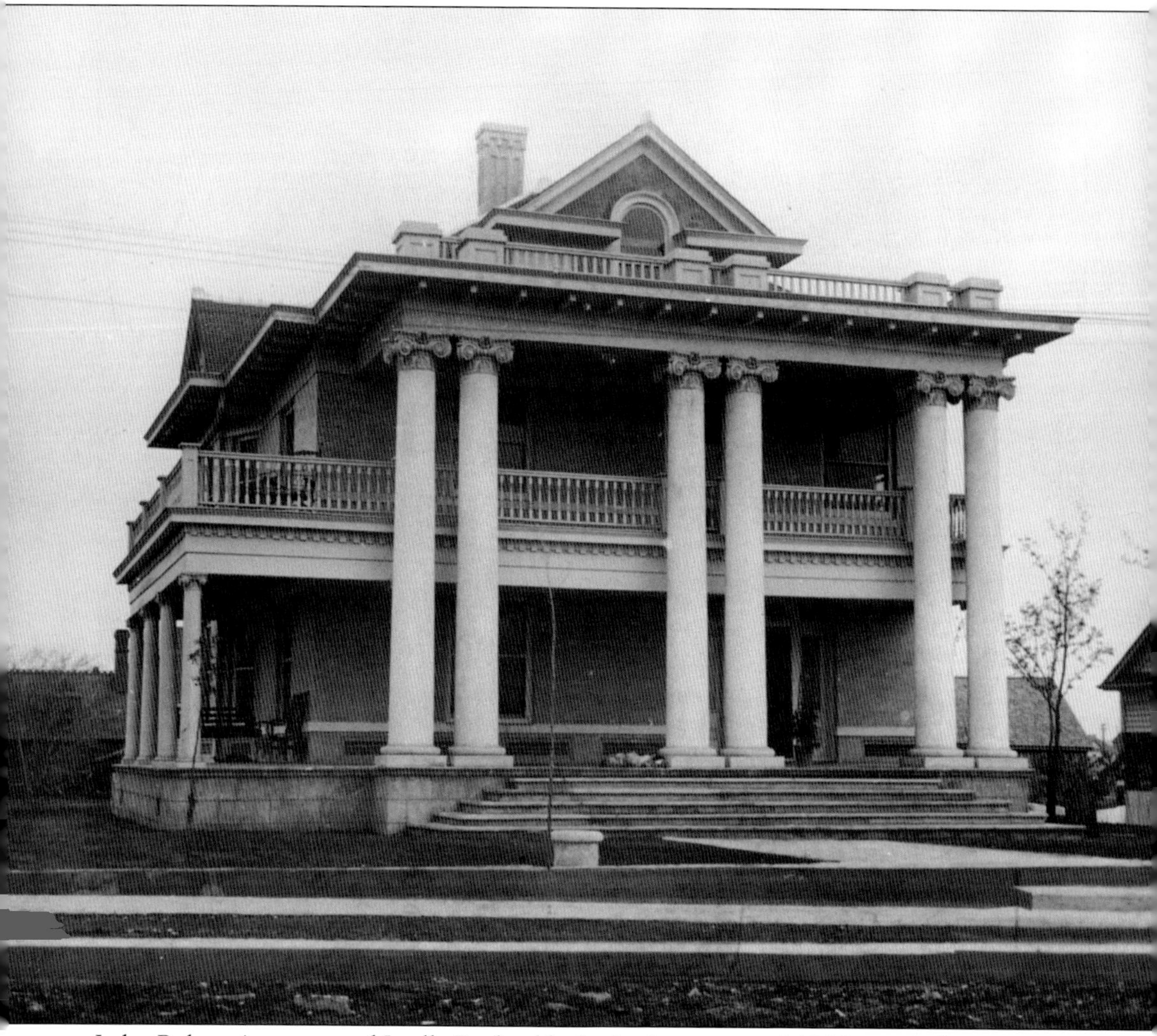

Judge Robert Augustus and Luella Ragland built this home around 1906; pictured in 1916, it is located at the corner of Third and Ragland Streets. The house is colonial style and atypical of homes at this time as it was built with indoor plumbing and electricity. The Ragland family lived in the house from 1906 until the judge's death in 1938. In 1941, the Earl G. Whitaker family bought the home and sold it to Mr. and Mrs. Aubrey O. Patterson in 1946. The Patterson family used this stately home for both a residence and a mortuary. In 1961, a chapel was added to the rear of the house, and beginning in 1970, the Melvin McCoy family took over the funeral business. In 1974, Mrs. Patterson placed the home for sale, and Robert A. "Bobby" Ragland bought it and donated it to the city and county for the express purpose of housing the Pioneer City County Museum.

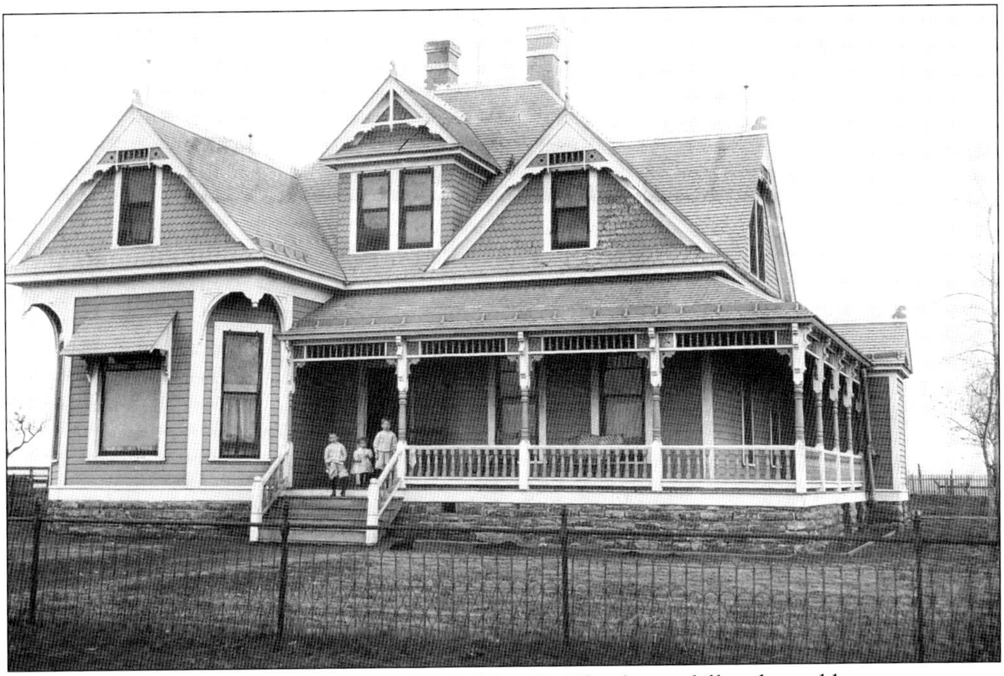

Here is the home of A.T. "Cap" Newman and family. This beautifully adorned home represents Newman's passion for building; he constructed the bank his family owned in Sylvester, J.F. Newman and Sons. Cap was helpful in forming the Chuck Wagon Association with his brothers and had an interest in feed lot operations for cattle. Newman was a longtime Mason and died in 1934 at the family home.

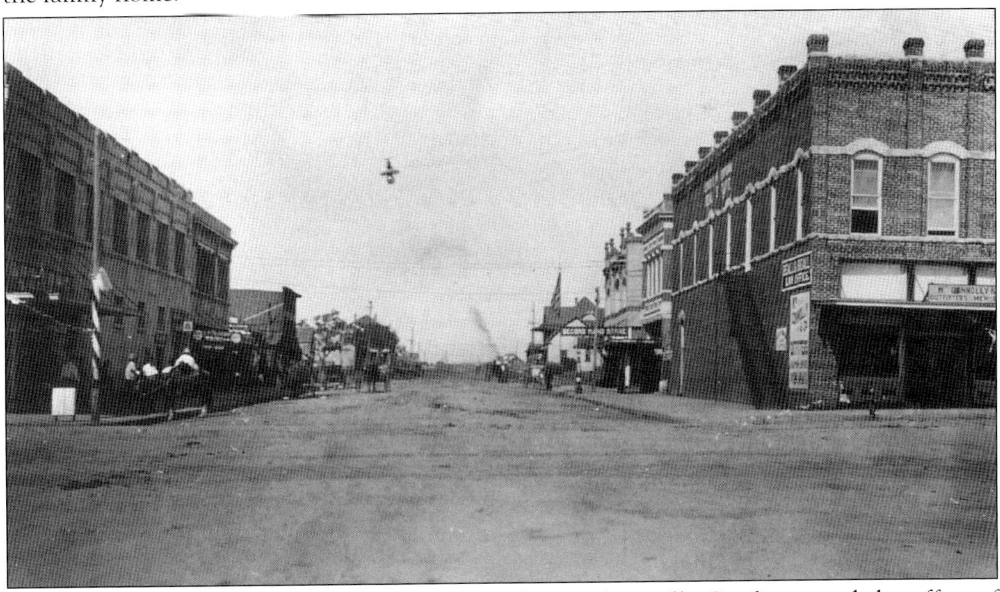

Looking west on Broadway Avenue from Oak Street, Connolly Outfitters and the office of Judge J.H. Beall and brother Warren are visible. At the time of Judge Beall's death, he was the oldest practicing attorney with offices in Sweetwater. To the left of this building stood Al's Café, which is no longer in business but is fondly remembered for its bigger-than-plate-sized pancakes and omelets.

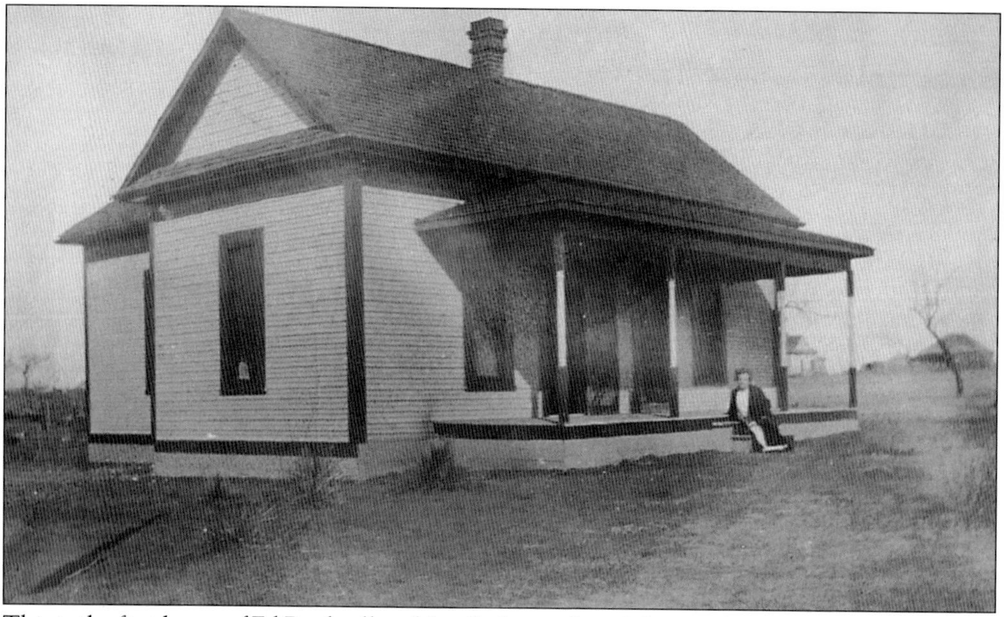

This is the first home of Ed Bardwell and family, located on Arkansas Street, as it looked in 1912. Ed Bardwell came to Sweetwater with his parents in 1885 at the age of four. He served as sheriff of Nolan County for two terms from 1918 to 1922. While sheriff, his duties included serving as jailer, so he and his family lived on the first floor of the jail building while prisoners were kept on the second.

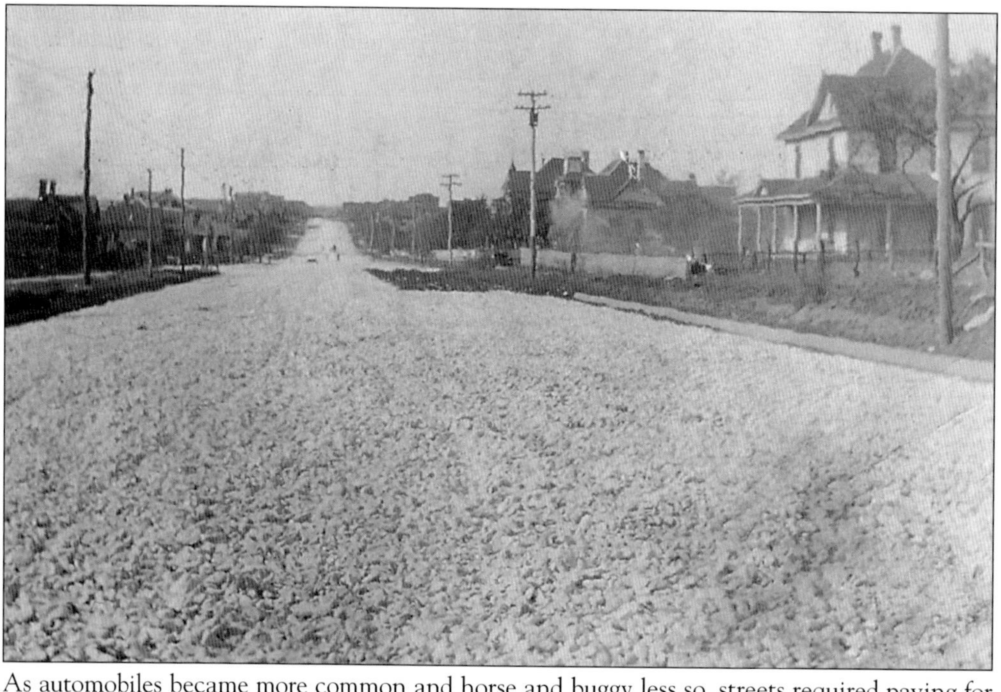

As automobiles became more common and horse and buggy less so, streets required paving for smoother travel. Here paving is underway on Broadway Avenue, which gained its name, like many Broadway Avenues in towns across the country, from Highway 80 being known as the "Broadway of America."

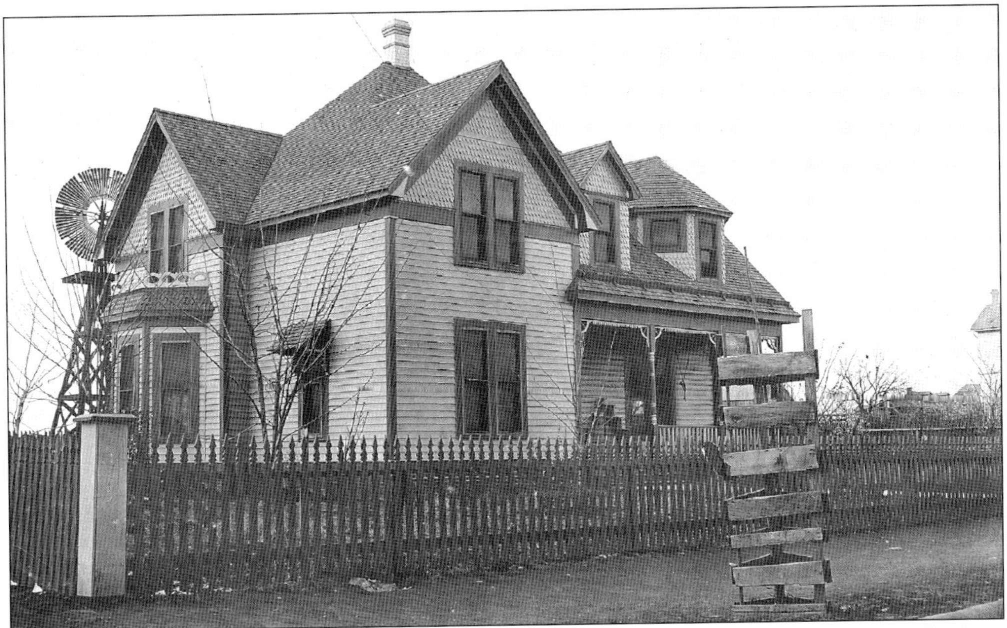

This is the home of Royston Campbell Crane Sr. and his wife, Mamie Douthit Crane, built in the early spring of 1902. Judge Crane was the founder and president of the West Texas Historical Association, served two terms as mayor of Sweetwater, wrote pamphlets for the West Texas Jubilee Celebration, and led efforts to procure a college for West Texas. In 1930, Judge Crane acquired $200,000 from the Texas Centennial Historical Advisory to mark historic spots in West Texas.

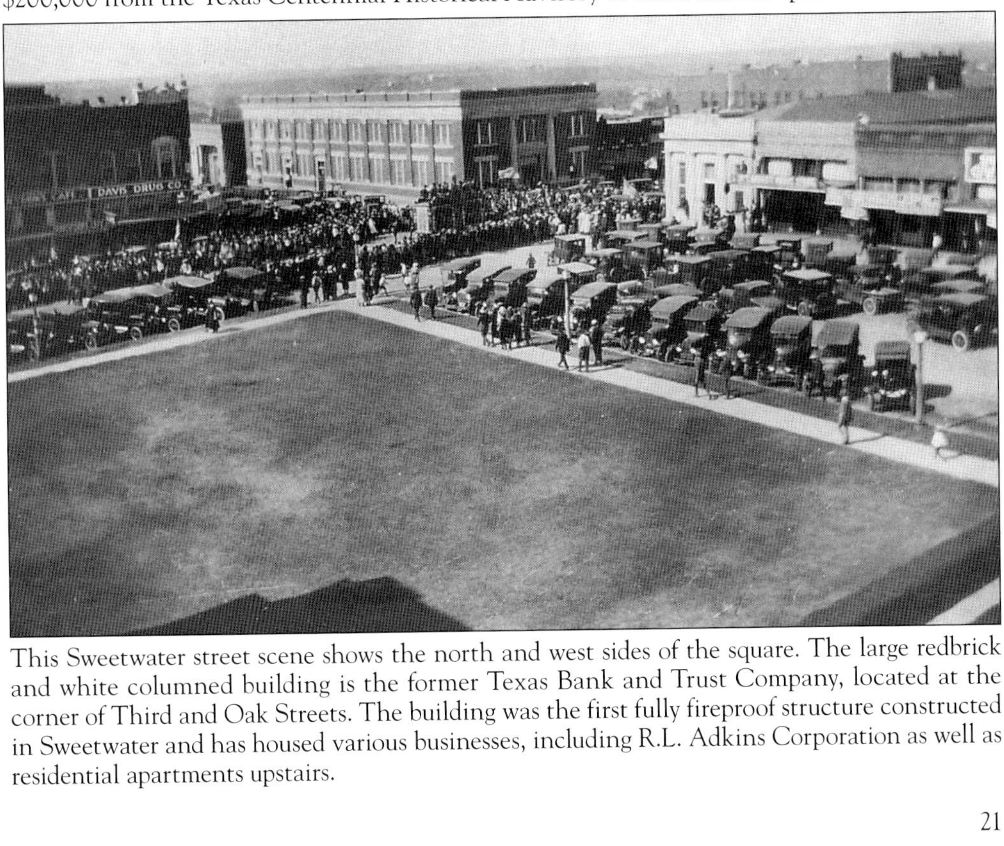

This Sweetwater street scene shows the north and west sides of the square. The large redbrick and white columned building is the former Texas Bank and Trust Company, located at the corner of Third and Oak Streets. The building was the first fully fireproof structure constructed in Sweetwater and has housed various businesses, including R.L. Adkins Corporation as well as residential apartments upstairs.

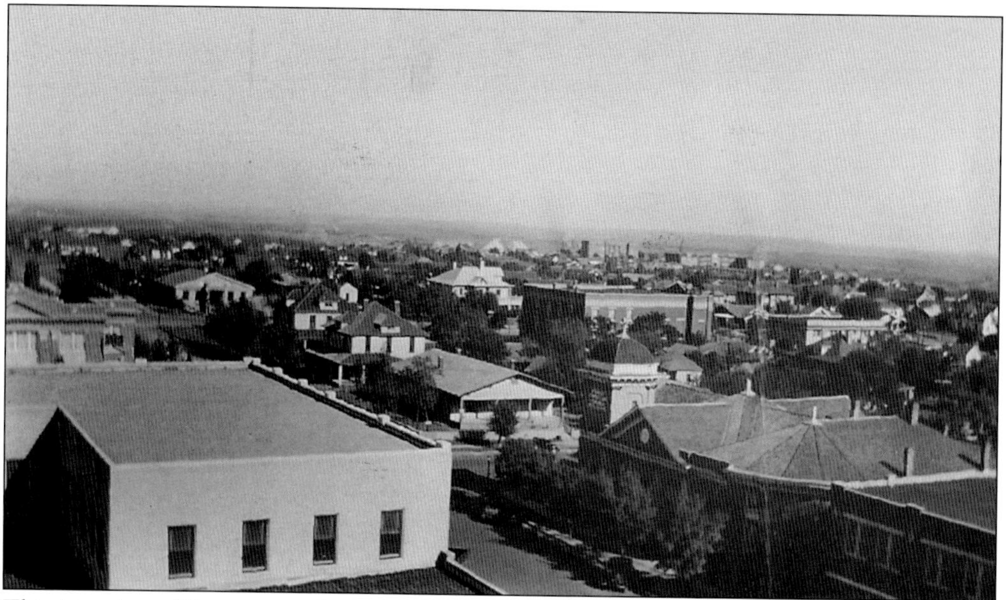

This is a view of Sweetwater from the rooftop of the Bluebonnet Hotel. First Financial Bank, previously known as First National Bank, now occupies this site. The First Christian Church can be seen across the street where the Nolan County Appraisal District is now located.

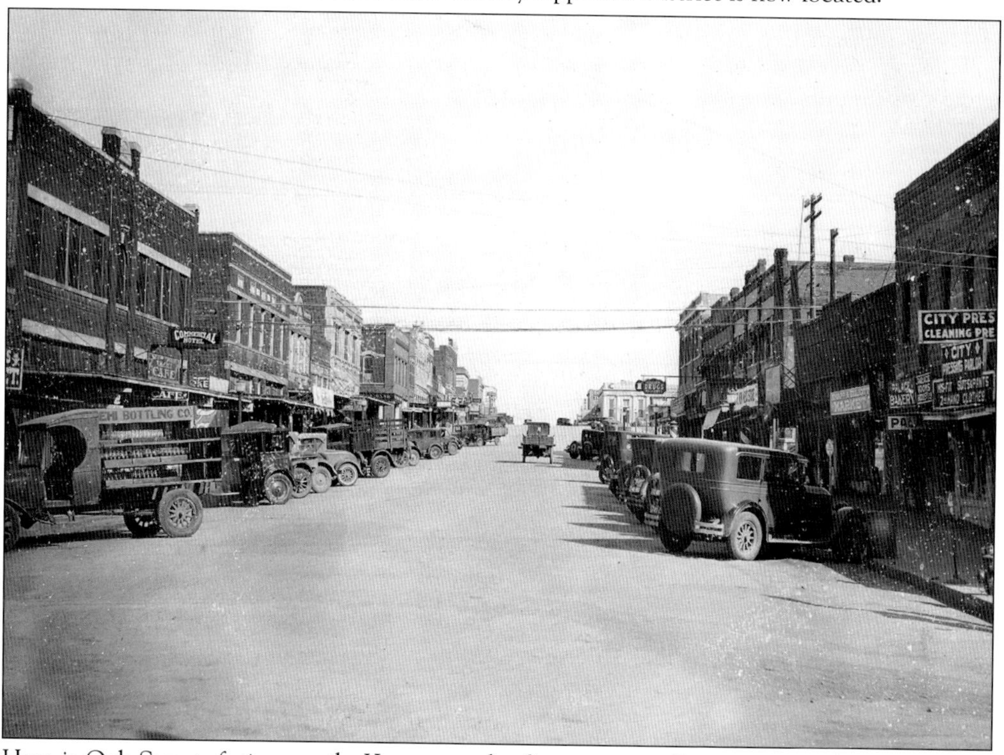

Here is Oak Street, facing north. Known as the first street in Sweetwater and affectionately referred to as Rat Row, Oak Street housed the original businesses in town, those being mostly saloons and hotels. Commercial Hotel was originally City Hotel, and across the street near the drugstore sign now stands Arlene's Book House and Paperback Exchange.

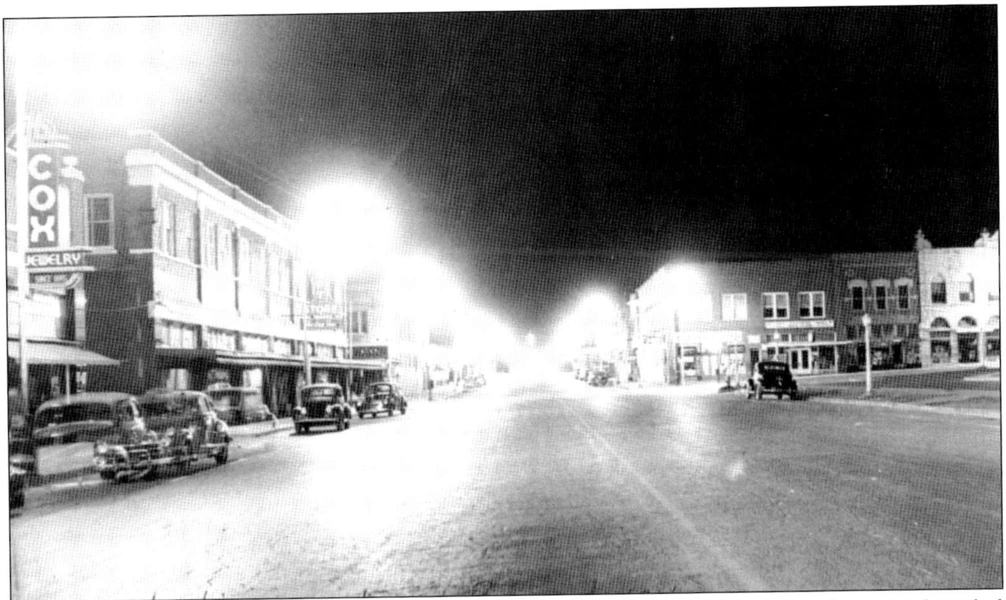

This is Broadway Avenue, facing westward, in the 1950s. To the left is Cox's Jewelry store, founded by John R. Cox on September 15, 1895. Cox had become fascinated with watchmaking when an itinerant watchmaker came through town, fueling his desire to open a jewelry store. This location next to the present-day Texas Theater was the third location of Cox Jewelry. In the rear right can be seen Harris Drugstore in its former glory. The building burned down in December 1987, and the lot, now owned by the Alvarado family, remains empty but cared for and displays a large mural of three of Sweetwater's most important events.

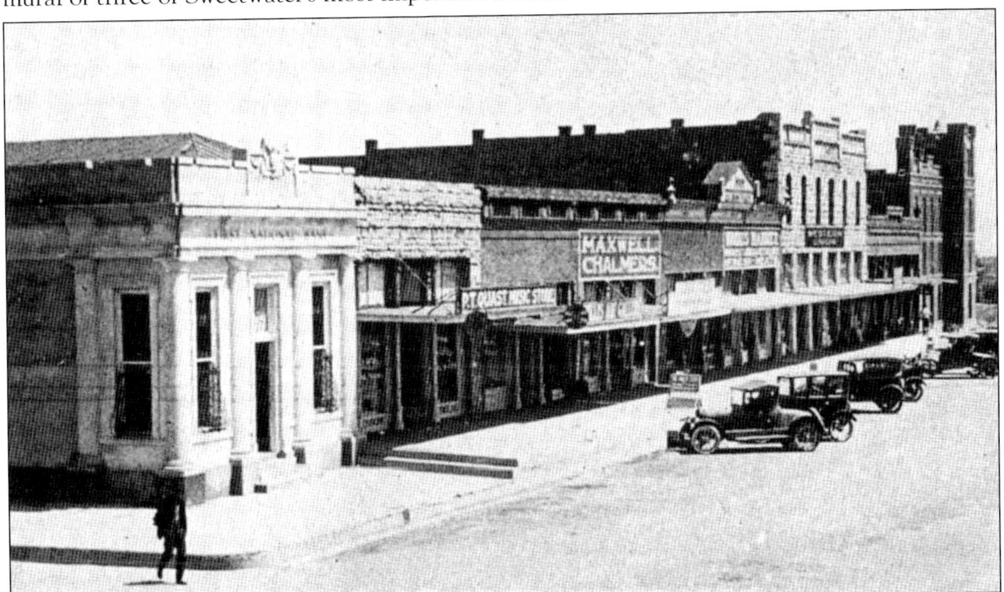

This is a view of the north side of the square in the 1920s. The closest building, First National Bank, now houses the law firm of Zollie C. Steakley and Meghan Cantu. In fact, most of the buildings are now home to law firms, including Rees, Rees, and Fuller; John S. Young; Kenny Maxwell; and Lance and David Hall. Other businesses also reside on this part of Third Street including Sweetwater Title Company and accountant Ricky Bowman.

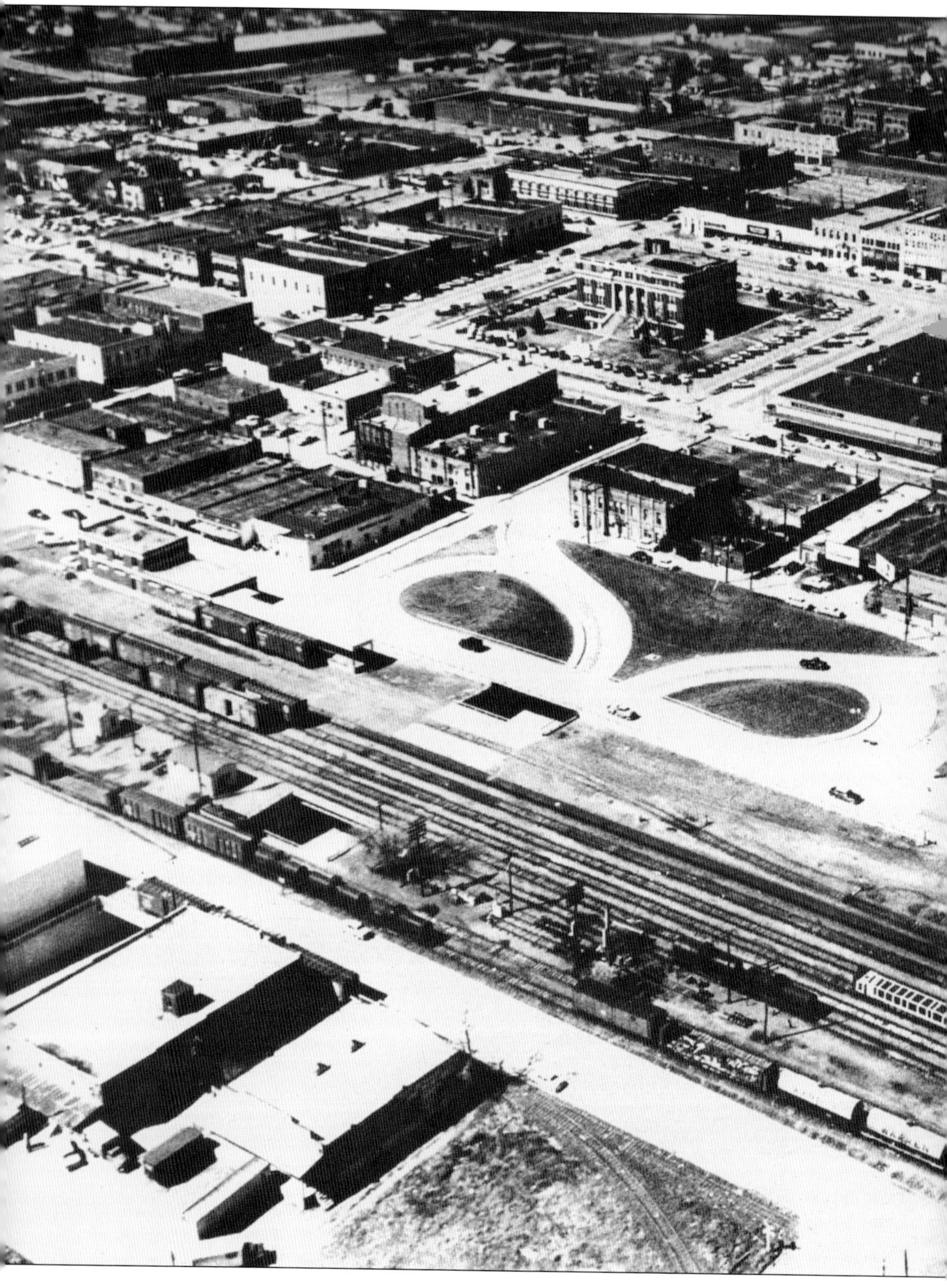

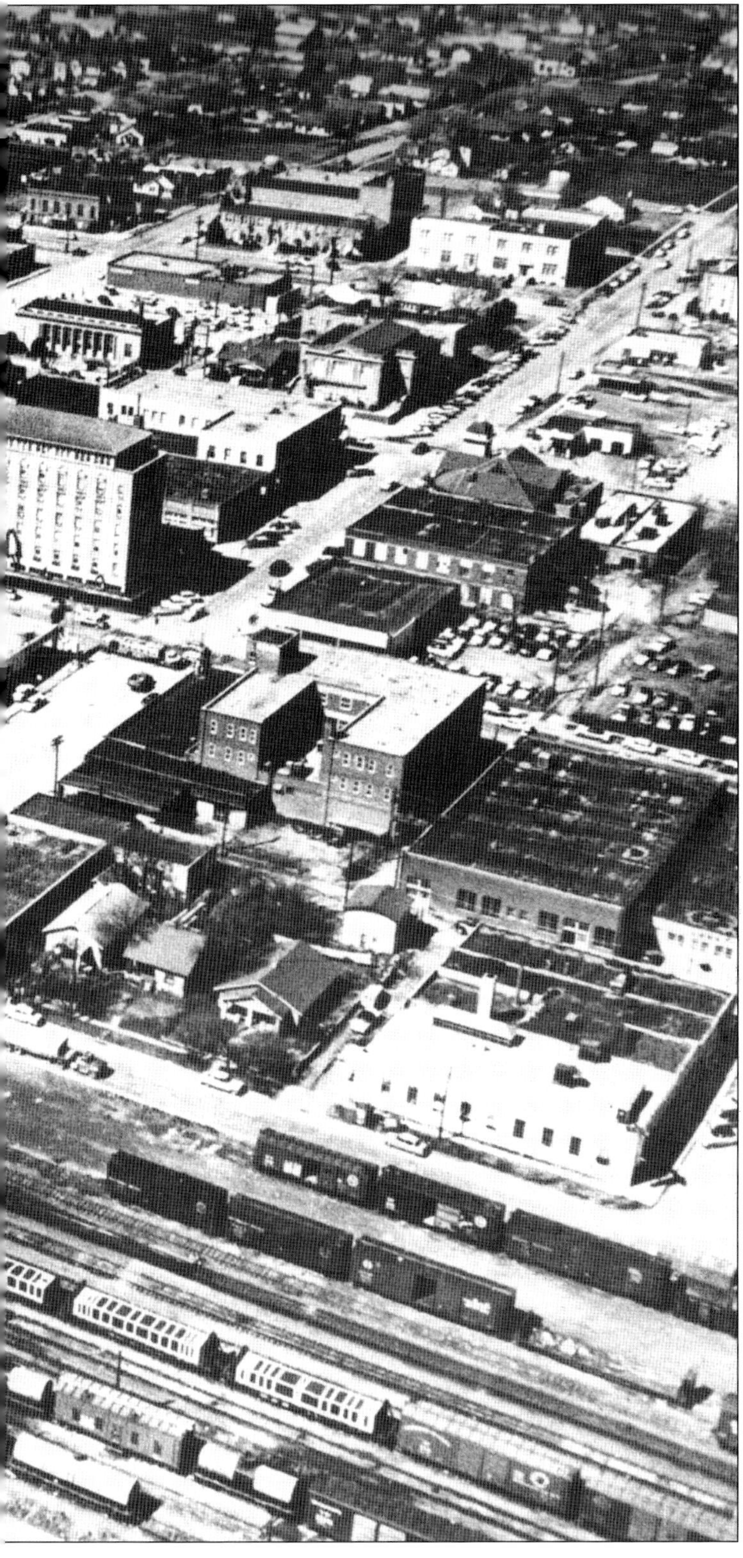

This bird's-eye view of Sweetwater in the 1960s shows the third Nolan County Courthouse and Bluebonnet Hotel still standing. The underpass to Lamar Street was one of the improvements made while Samuel Dale Myres was mayor. The block where the Bluebonnet once stood is now occupied by First Financial Bank and its motor bank. The block to the right of the underpass is now owned and occupied by Texas National Bank and its motor bank. Sweetwater owes much of its current existence to the railroad lines running through the lower center of this photograph. From the Texas & Pacific Railroad, with its crews requiring lodging and spirits, to the passenger trains that brought the likes of Elvis Presley and Fred Astaire here to perform, the railroad has been a lifeline for this community.

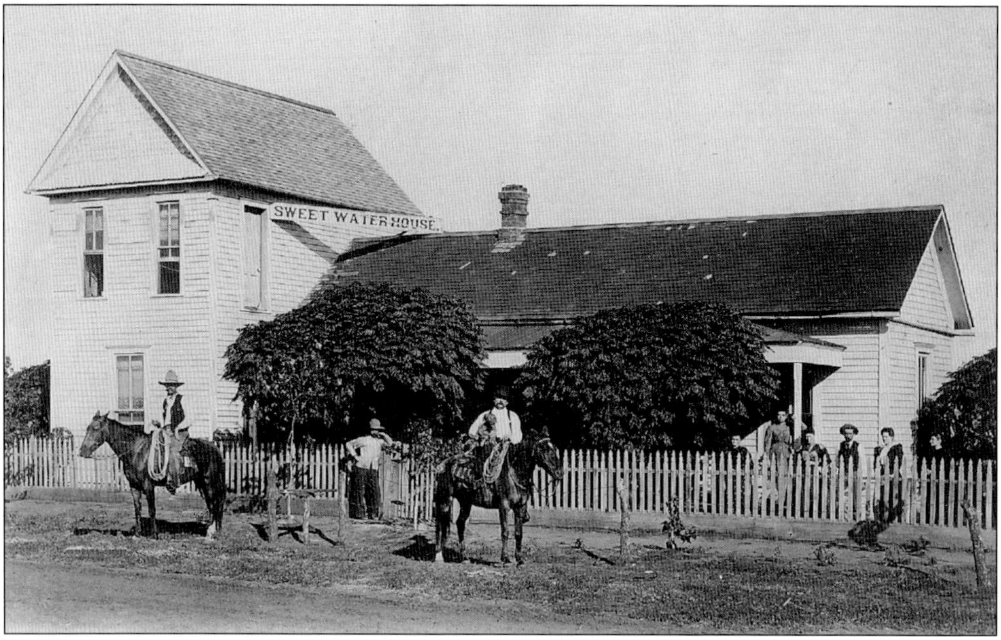

One of Sweetwater's early hotels, Sweetwater House was run by Matilda Wetsel Beula, the grandmother of W.B. Wetsel Sr., who, at the time of his death in 1982, was the oldest native-born resident of Sweetwater, having been born in 1899. Matilda Wetsel Beula began her business by setting up tents to lodge railroad workers and then built this hotel near Broadway and Ash Street. Will Wetsel is standing at the gate, and the gentlemen on the horses are R.T. Burk on the left and Lang Aycock on the right.

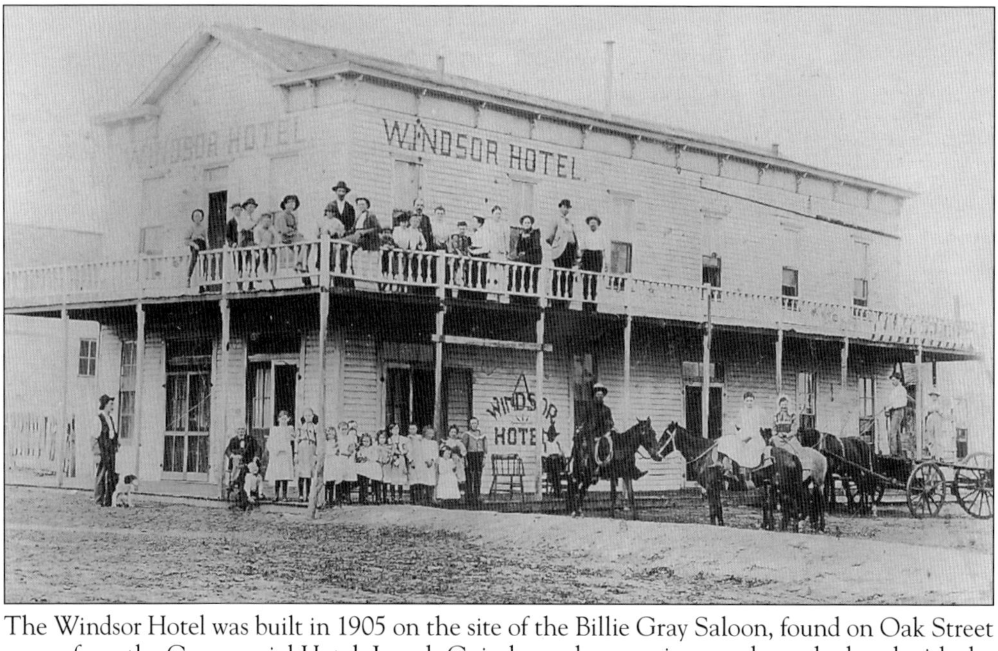

The Windsor Hotel was built in 1905 on the site of the Billie Gray Saloon, found on Oak Street across from the Commercial Hotel. Joseph Guiral was the proprietor and ran the hotel with the help of his nephew Henry Malphette. This site was later occupied by the Texas Hotel and later still by the Day Furniture Company.

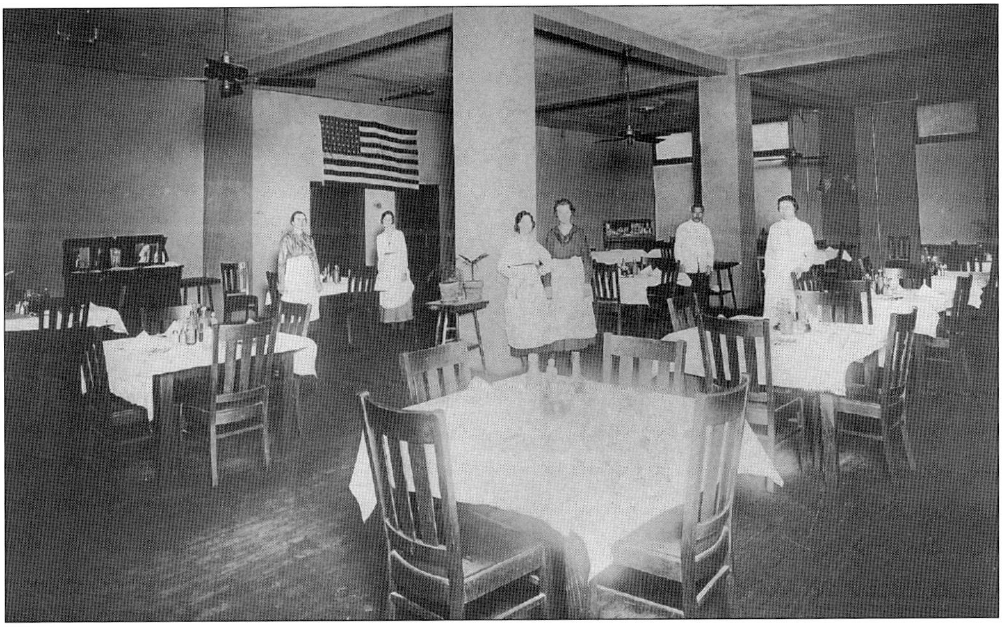

Standing in the dining room of the Wright Hotel are, in unknown order, Mattie Carey, Stacey Curtis, Bess Robertson, Vera Carey, and two unidentified people. The Wright Hotel was one of Sweetwater's more grand hotels and had a ballroom with six glass chandeliers, one of which today hangs in the "living room" of the Pioneer Museum.

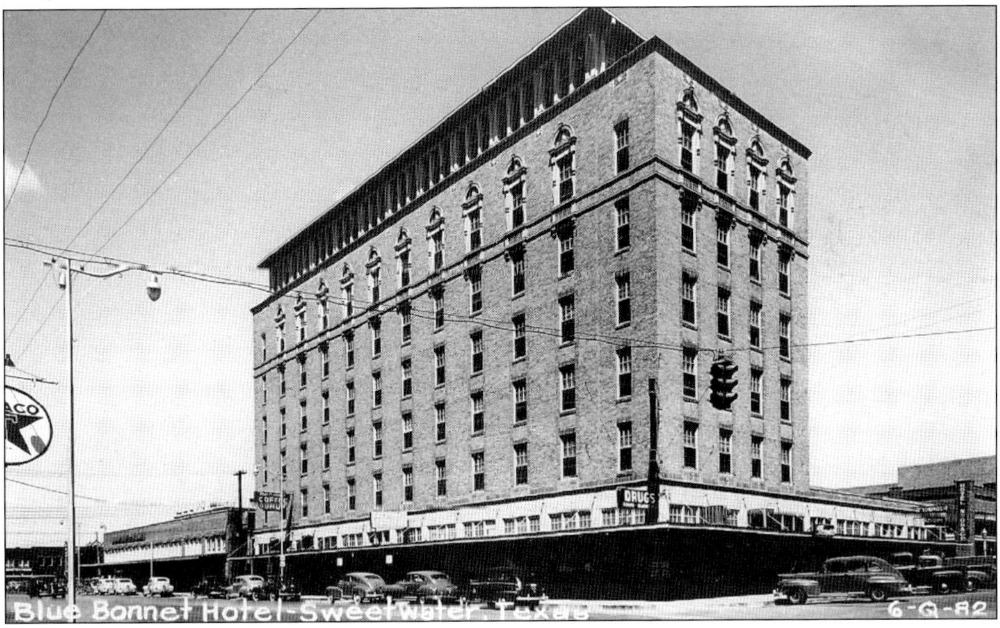

Sweetwater's famous Bluebonnet Hotel was completed and formally opened on May 1, 1928. During the 1930s, the Bluebonnet grew in popularity, and according to Laura Sheridan, "there was not a busier corner in town during the late 20s and 30s." The elegance of the hotel rivaled those in major cities, and its five-course meals included finger bowls, but its West Texas roots showed when rattlesnakes were displayed in the lobby during the Rattlesnake Roundup in the spring. The Bluebonnet succumbed to fire on August 17, 1967, under the name of Baker Hotel.

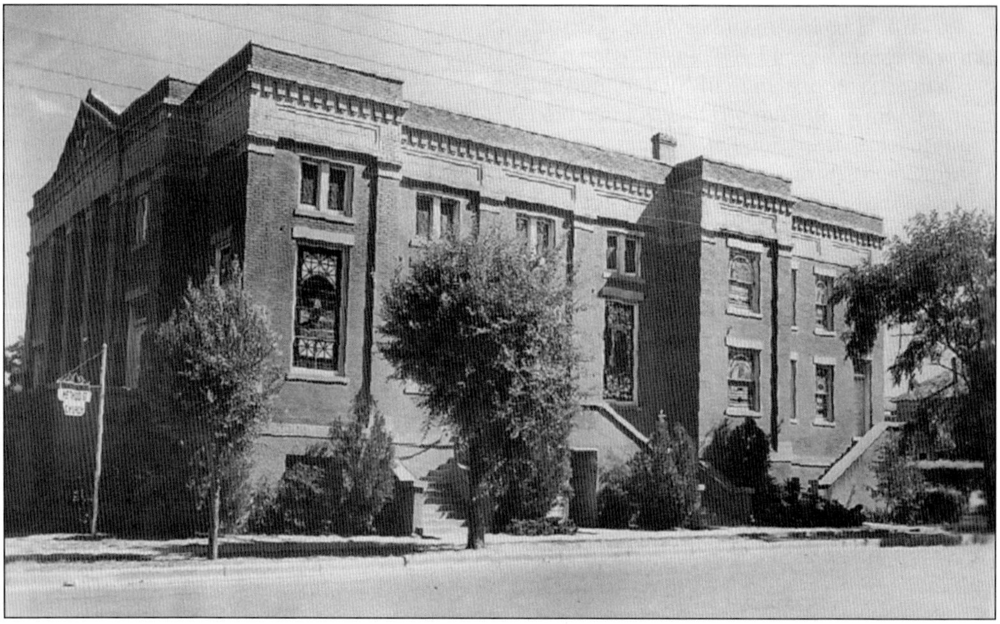

Here is the First Methodist Church of Sweetwater on Third and Elm Streets. There is great debate as to which church organized first in Sweetwater, the Methodists or the Baptists. The Methodists claim that a preacher named Collins came to town in the summer of 1881 from Buffalo Gap and "found seven members of his church there;" however, Rev. R.F. Dunn was the first preacher officially assigned in the fall of 1881, and the Methodist Church was not built until April 8, 1884.

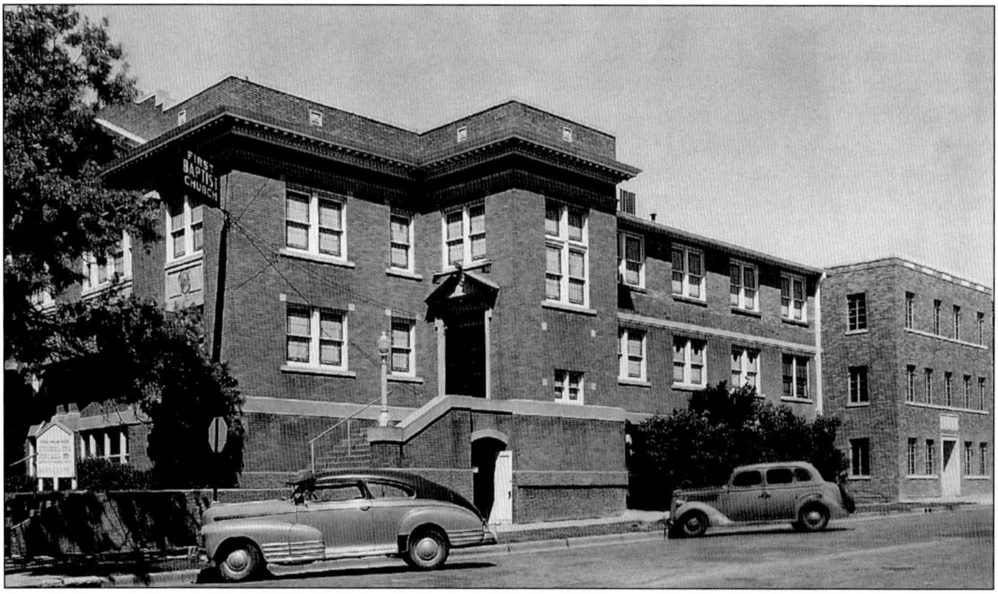

The First Baptist Church was built April 8, 1883, although the paperwork was not filed until August 1883. This church was first organized in December 1881 in the rear room of the Cowan and Posey law office, which was the site of the Texas Bank Building. The first preacher, Rev. Peter Turner, organized this church with his wife and children. The Baptist congregation was said to have a greater number and was able to build its church more quickly than the Methodists, whose membership was about 30 people and included John W. Posey.

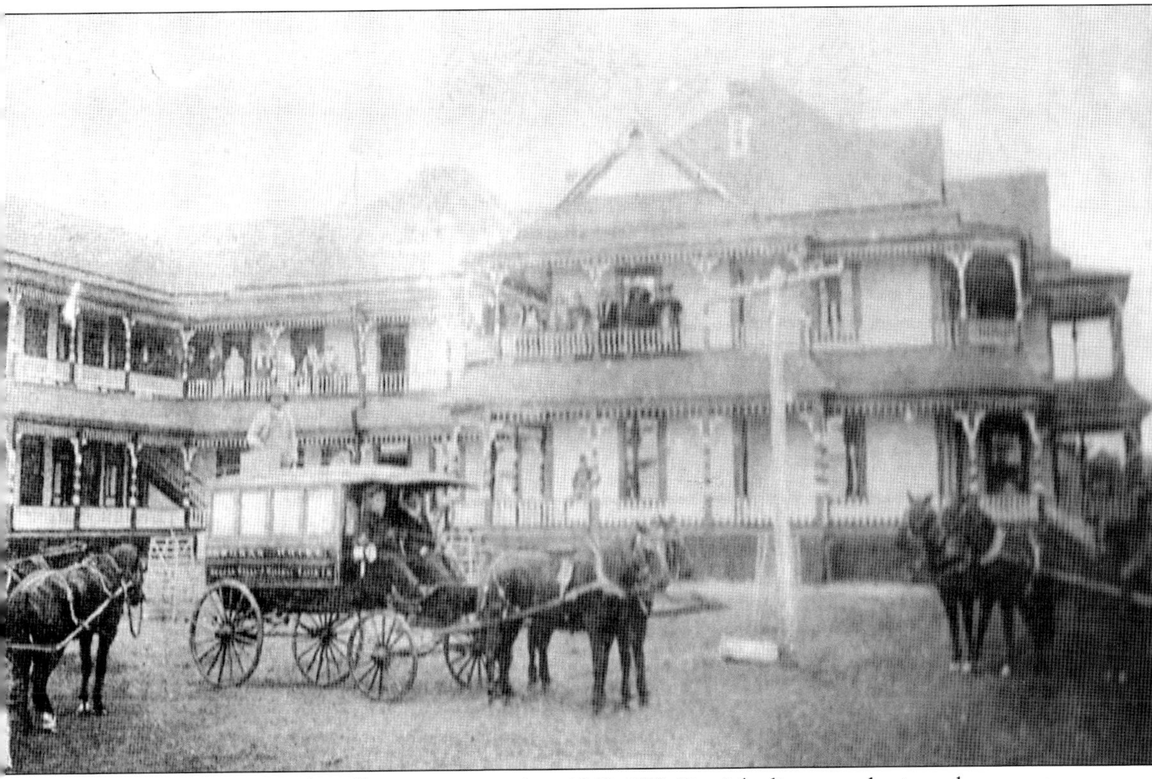

Here is Grogan Mineral Wells as it appeared in 1903. I.W. Daniels discovered mineral water at this site, near where Sweetwater Middle School now stands, in 1897 while he was digging a well to find water for his cattle. After having the water analyzed, he quit the cattle business and hired agents to help him sell the water throughout the United States. John L. Grogan bought the Daniels Mineral Wells in 1905 and erected the hotel to serve as a health resort. The resort operated steam baths and mineral water treatments, and continued to ship water throughout the country. The Sweetwater Municipal Band would play in the large bandstand on the resort grounds, and hotel residents, as well as citizens of Sweetwater, could be found listening to music on the lawn or dancing in the "grand pavilion in the park." With the advent of new medical methods, the mineral water treatments fell out of popularity, and eventually the old building burned and the rest of the hotel was cut into sections and used in various other businesses around town.

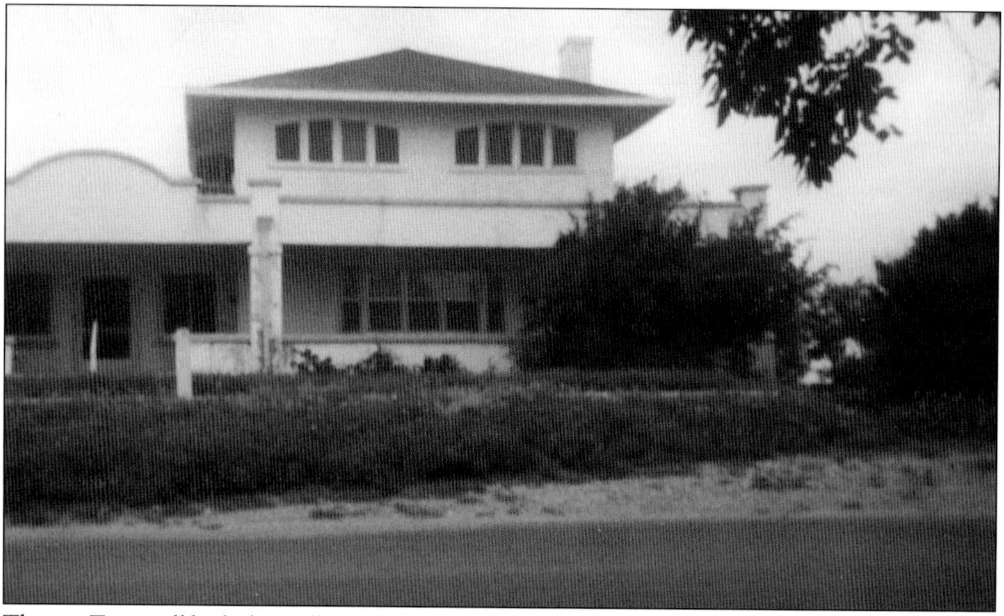

Thomas Trammell built the William S. Chennault home, located on Sam Houston Parkway, between 1912 and 1914. When first constructed, the home had 14 bedrooms and six baths with a total of 29 rooms. Upon the deaths of the Trammells, the home was renovated and used as Sweetwater's first hospital from 1923 until 1932, when the Simmons Memorial Hospital was completed.

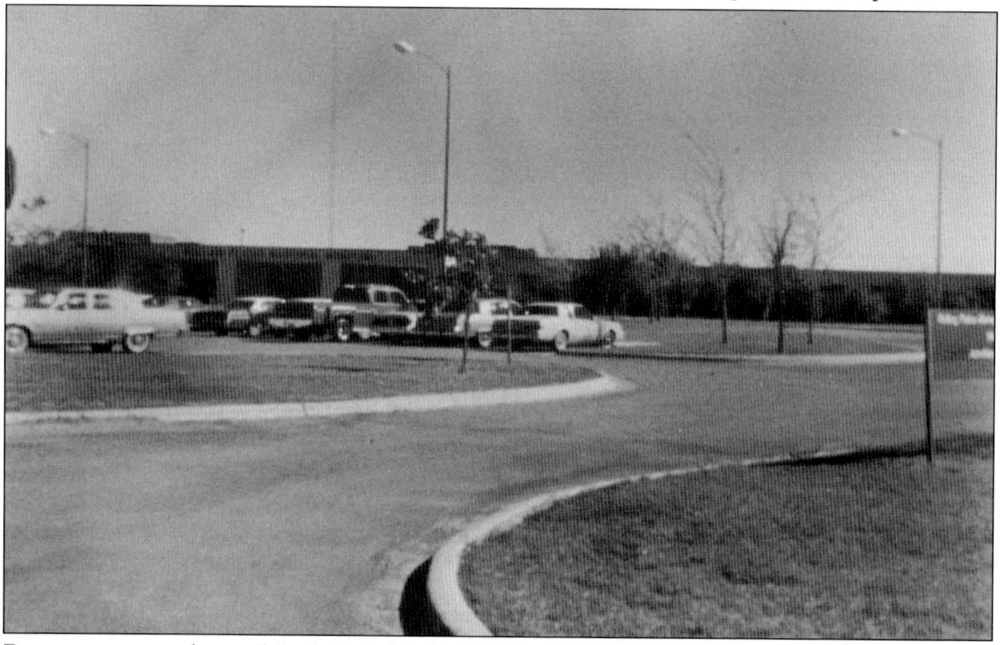

Due to a greater demand for hospital care and new federal regulations, Sweetwater needed a new hospital. Nolan County citizens voted overwhelmingly for a $4.5 million bond issue for the construction of a modern hospital and broke ground on August 20, 1975. Seen here is Rolling Plains Memorial Hospital, completed and opened on August 2, 1976. The hospital has recently undergone a renovation and continues to serve the community with state-of-the-art equipment and a caring, close-knit staff.

Two

EDUCATING SWEETWATER

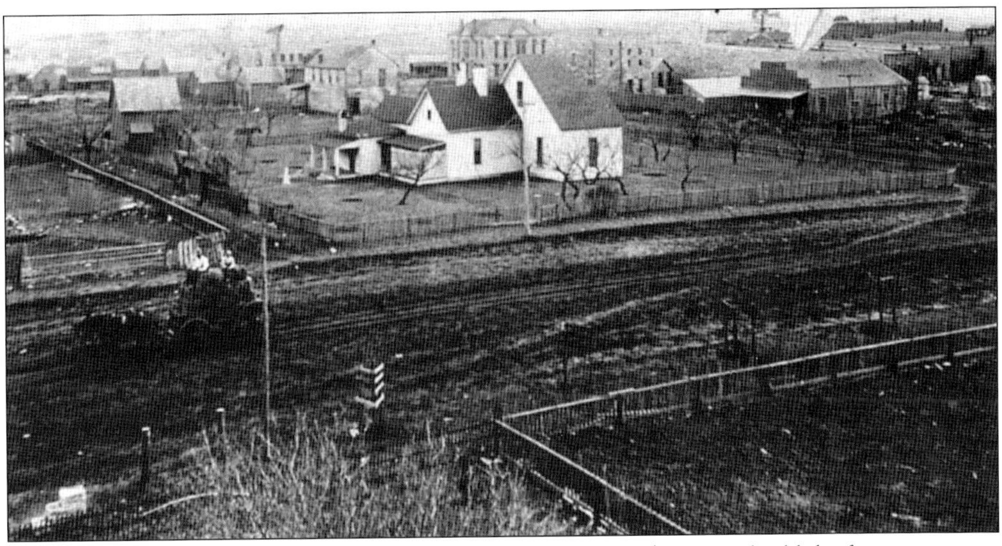

In 1882, citizens organized the first public school and borrowed $2,000 to build the frame structure north of the courthouse on the site of First Baptist Church. J.H. Beauchamp served as principal for the 1882–1883 term; it was sold in 1886 to Jasper Douthit, who moved it to the present post office site. It was torn down in 1914, and the lumber was used in the construction of Willard Sayles's home.

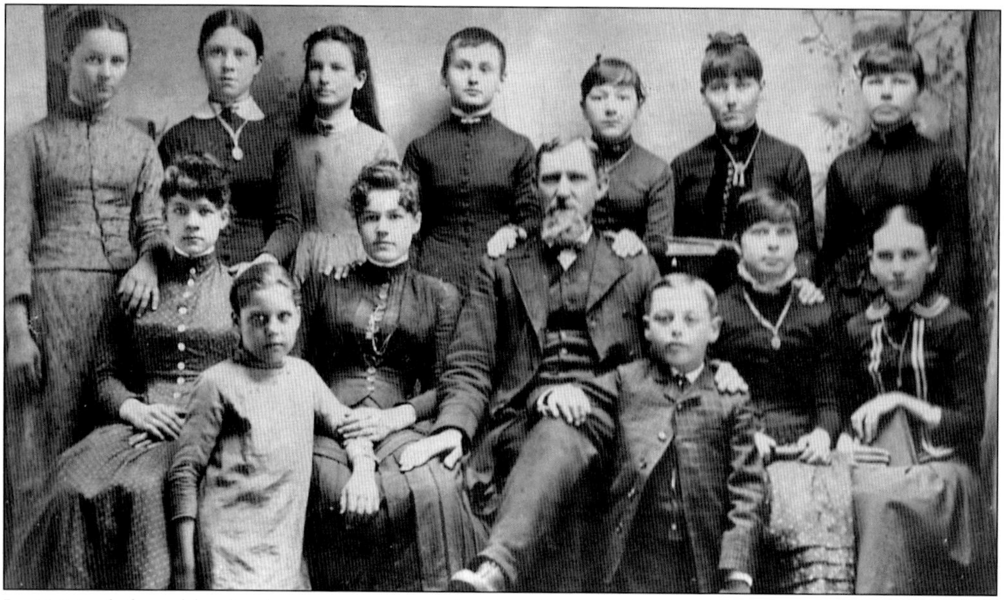

In 1887, while public funds were being saved to build a second schoolhouse of rock, T.E. Douthit and his wife, Louddie (Jackson) Douthit, taught a private school. They are seen here with several students; the young girl and boy in front are W.R. Searcy and A.T. "Cap" Newman, respectively. Cap Newman was the only boy who attended this temporary school.

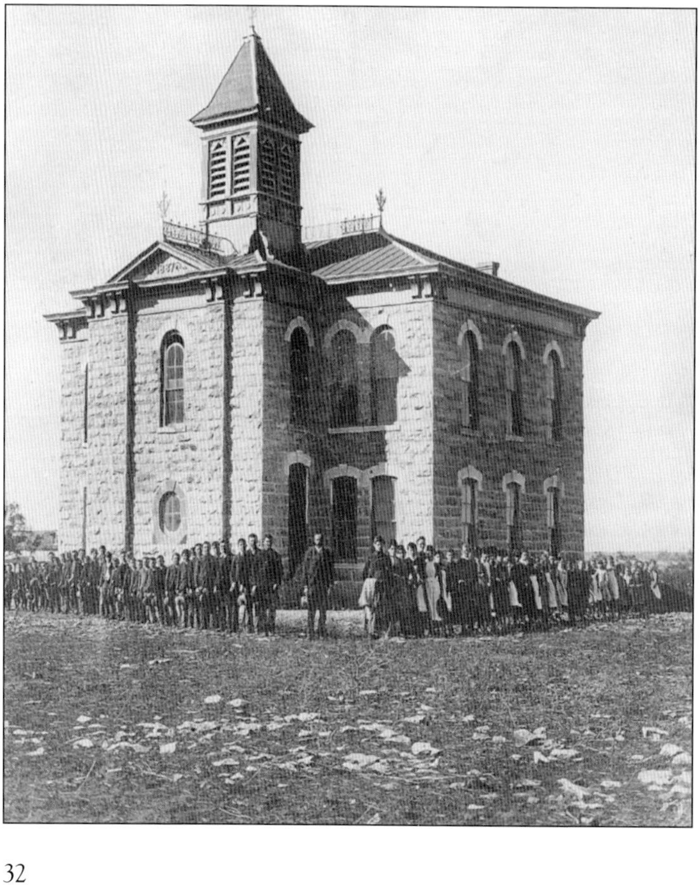

The second school building was erected by the citizens of Sweetwater and was the first made of rock. The people raised $5,600 or $7,500, depending on the source, by private subscription, and in 1887, they erected this schoolhouse, which encompassed all grades on the grounds where Sweetwater Intermediate School now stands. For a time, there was no money to actually operate the school, but by 1889, Supt. W.C. Martin, center, and his students could be found learning.

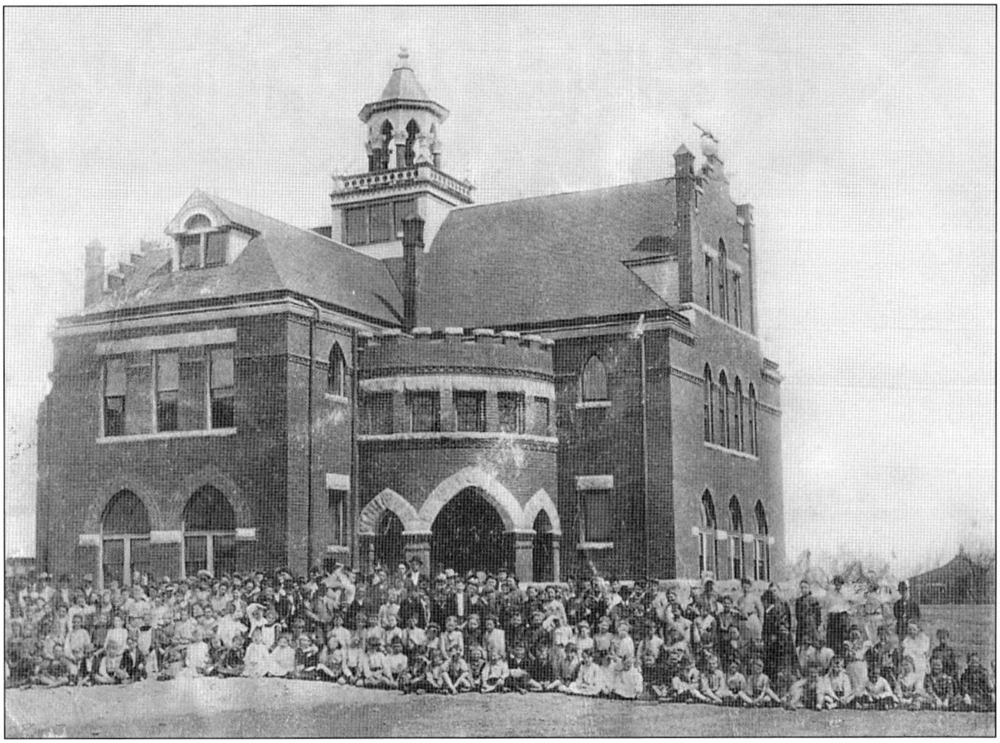

The 1887 school building was poorly constructed and fell down within just a few years, so this third school building was constructed in 1903 on the same site at the cost of $12,000. In 1903, a state law passed allowing school trustees to issue bonds for school construction, so Sweetwater voted to have this three-story structure erected. In 1912, only the first through sixth grades attended here. In the early 1920s, the building caught fire.

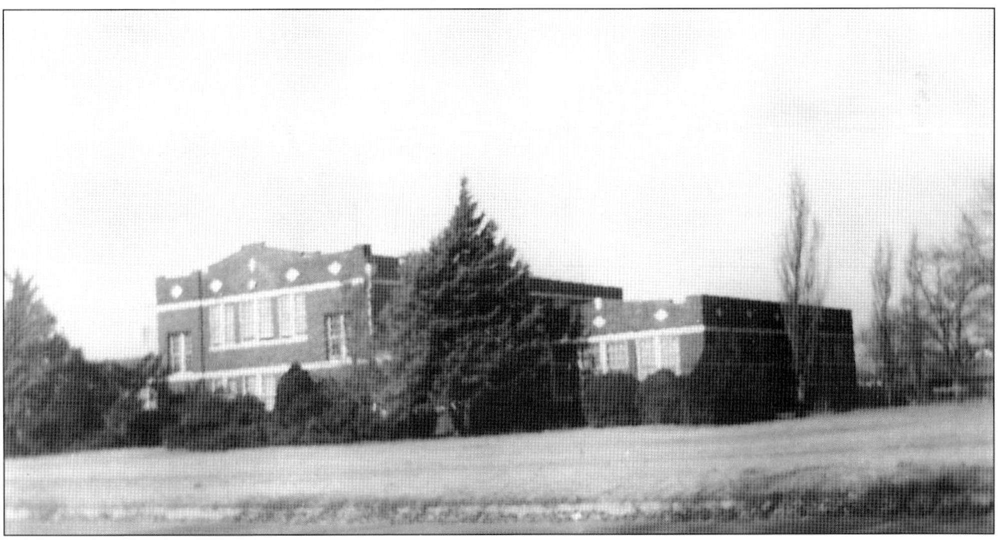

After the 1903 school building burned, a temporary barracks-type building was constructed on the southeast corner of the campus to serve the remainder of the school year. The next year, a $20,000 bond was issued, and this redbrick building was constructed. The school did not provide meals, but there was a designated cafeteria where children ate lunches brought from home.

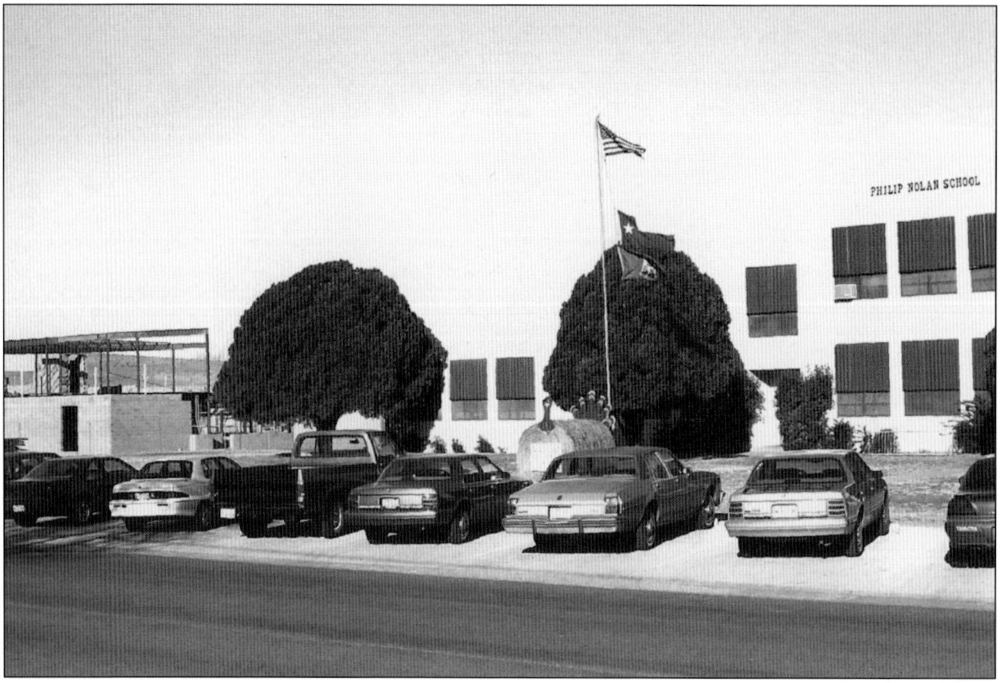

In 1937, fire escapes and sidewalks were added to the redbrick schoolhouse, and planning for additional space began in 1947 and was completed in 1956 at a cost of $350,350, upon which the redbrick East Ward School was transformed to Phillip Nolan School, as seen here. This school was torn down and replaced in about 1996 with Sweetwater Intermediate School, which still stands.

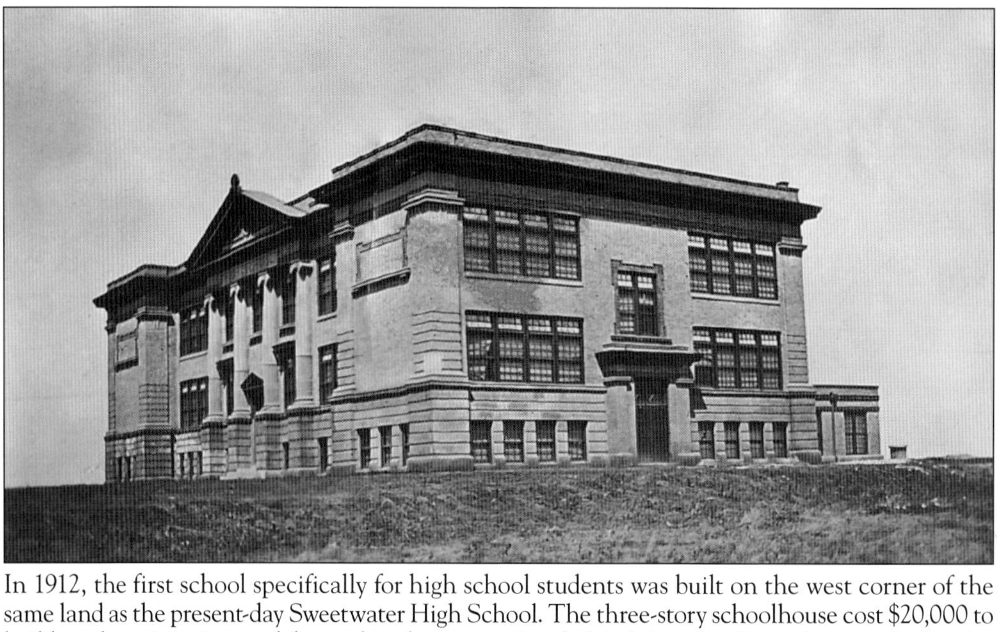

In 1912, the first school specifically for high school students was built on the west corner of the same land as the present-day Sweetwater High School. The three-story schoolhouse cost $20,000 to build, and a swimming pool, housed in the gymnasium behind the school, was its most distinctive feature. In 1921, the building was almost completely destroyed by fire, and classes were conducted in a warehouse near City Park until a new school could be built.

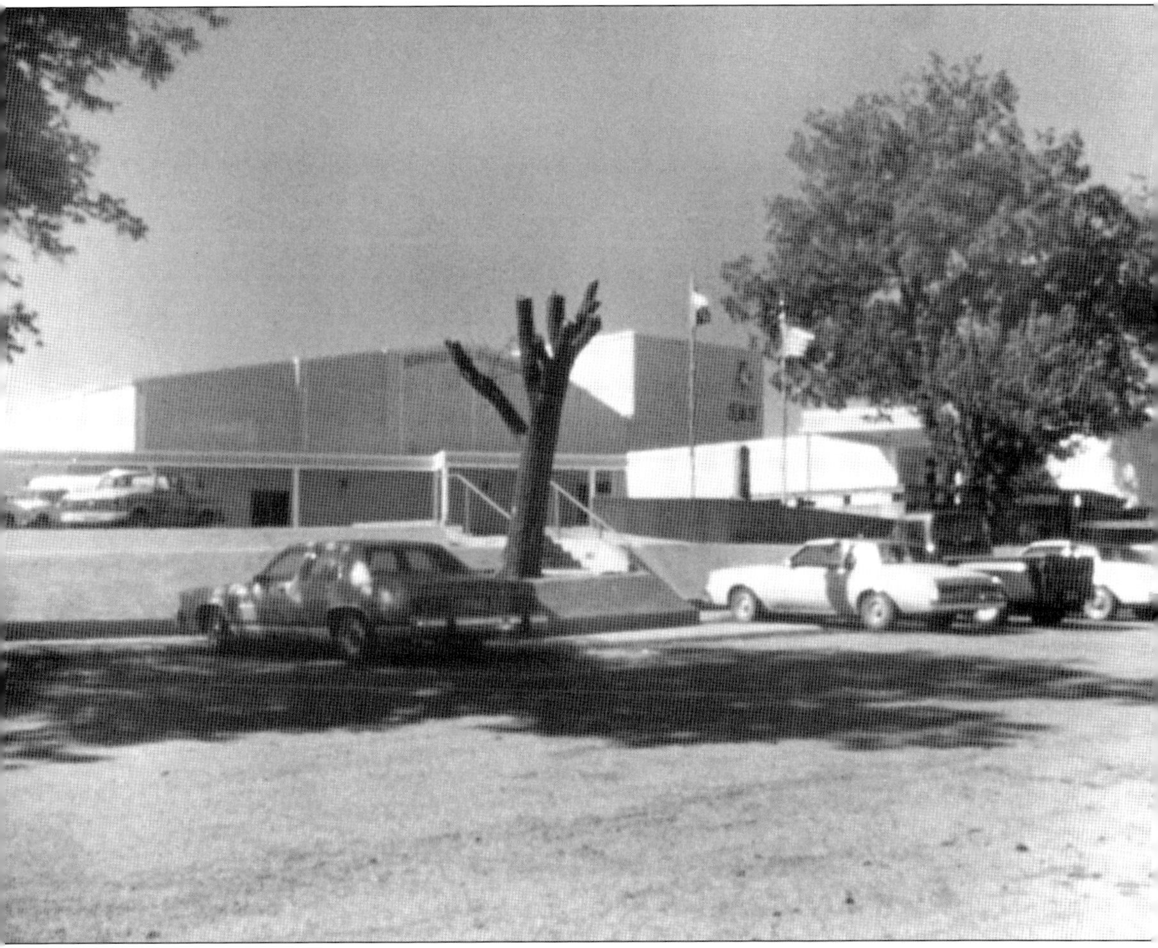

In 1955, a new vocational building was added to Newman High School at the site of the 1912 school. However, the growing community still needed more room, and so bonds were passed, with the new school completed in 1967 at a cost of $1.9 million. The name was changed back to Sweetwater High School at the recommendation of an Interscholastic League representative who said that until Sweetwater had more than one school, there would be less confusion if the town and school shared the same name.

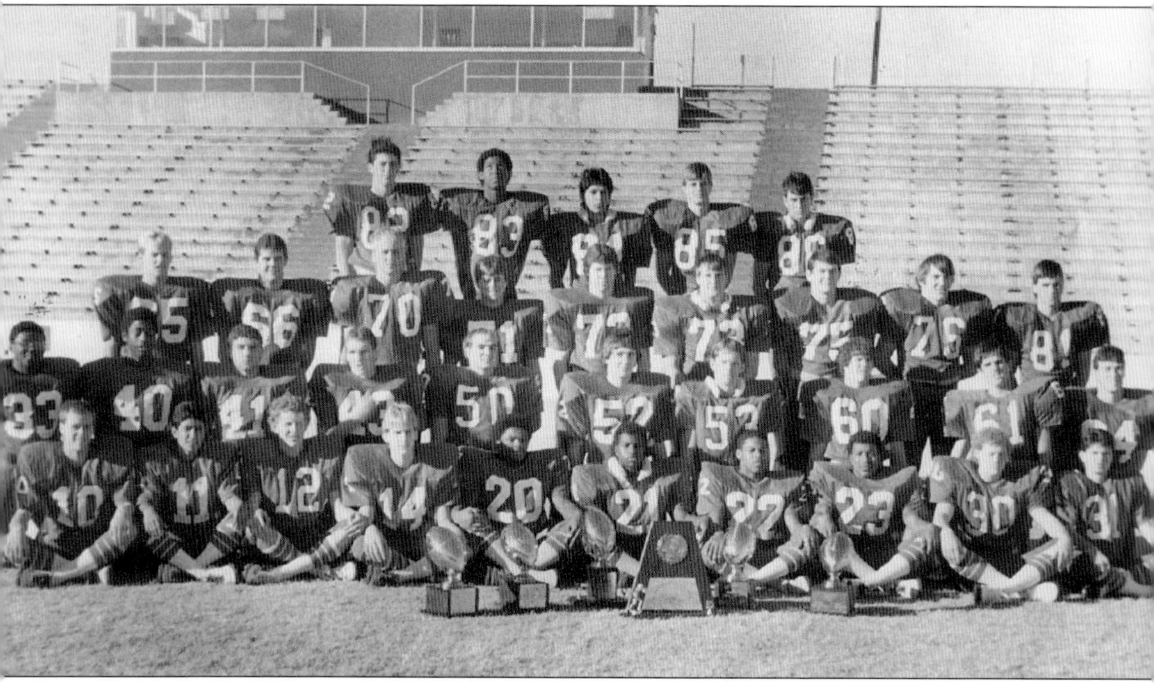

The 1985 Sweetwater High School state 4-A championship football team was coached by legendary W.T. Stapler. When Stapler came to Sweetwater in 1980, the football team had 14 wins over its past seven years and had not been to the playoffs since 1964. The coaching staff included Art Briles, Baylor University's current head coach; Mike Lebby; and Blaine Springston.

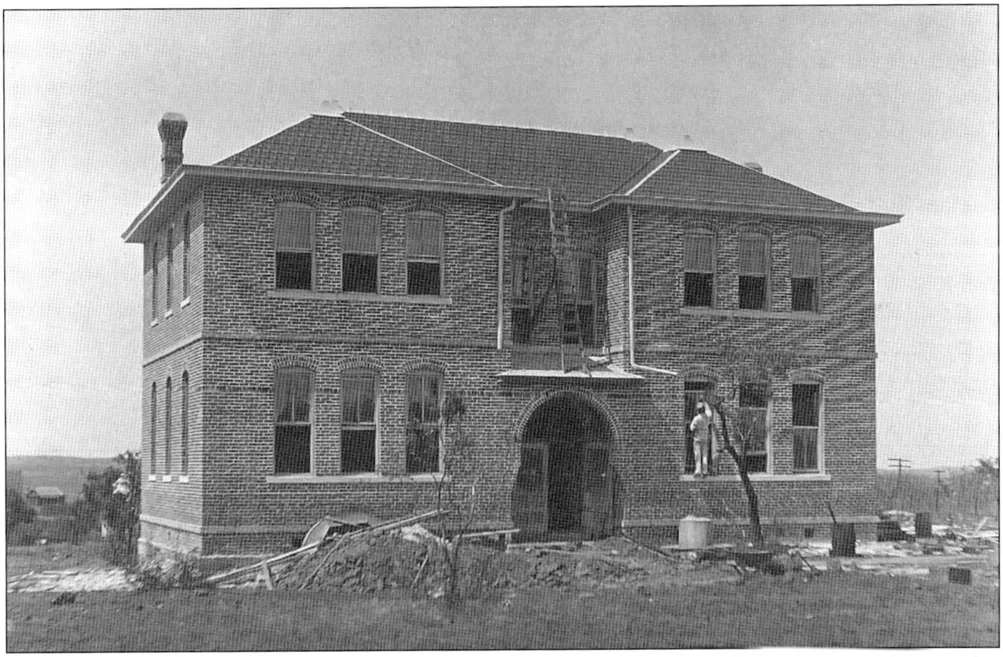

In 1911, a $10,000 bond was issued to build two new elementary schools to accommodate grades one through seven. The next year, the population increased such that the seventh grade was moved to the basement of the high school. This school, West Ward, sat on the current site of J.P. Cowen Elementary and had a large wood-burning stove with a jacket in the center of the room.

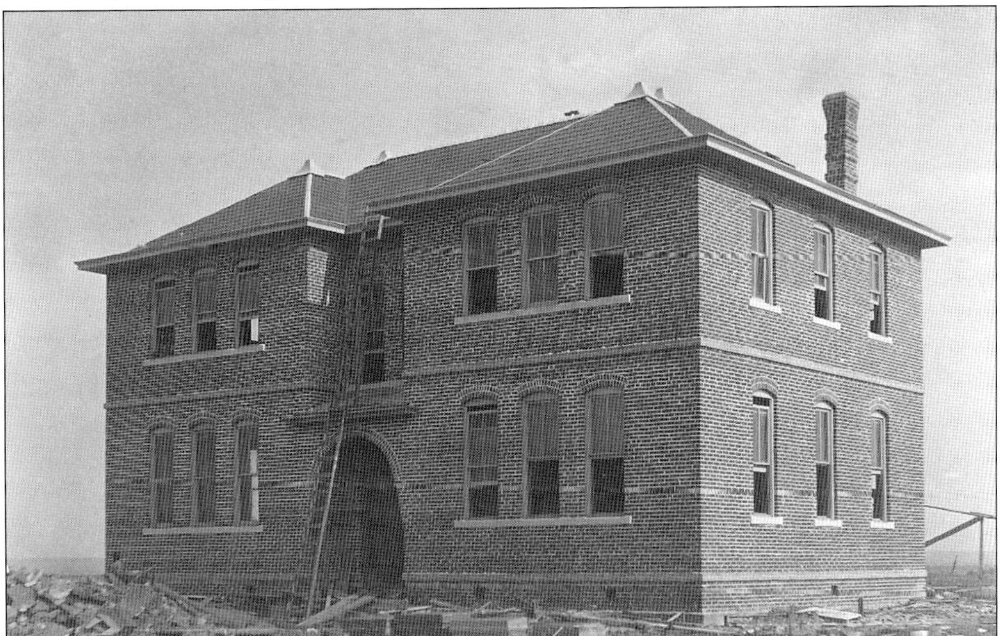

The second of the two wards, this school, South Ward, was located at 301 West Arkansas Avenue. It too had a wood-burning stove and, like the other school, had windows that "fit so poorly that when a sandstorm blew in, the children were sent home." The school name eventually changed to John R. Lewis; both ward schools were torn down in 1927 to build the structures that stand today.

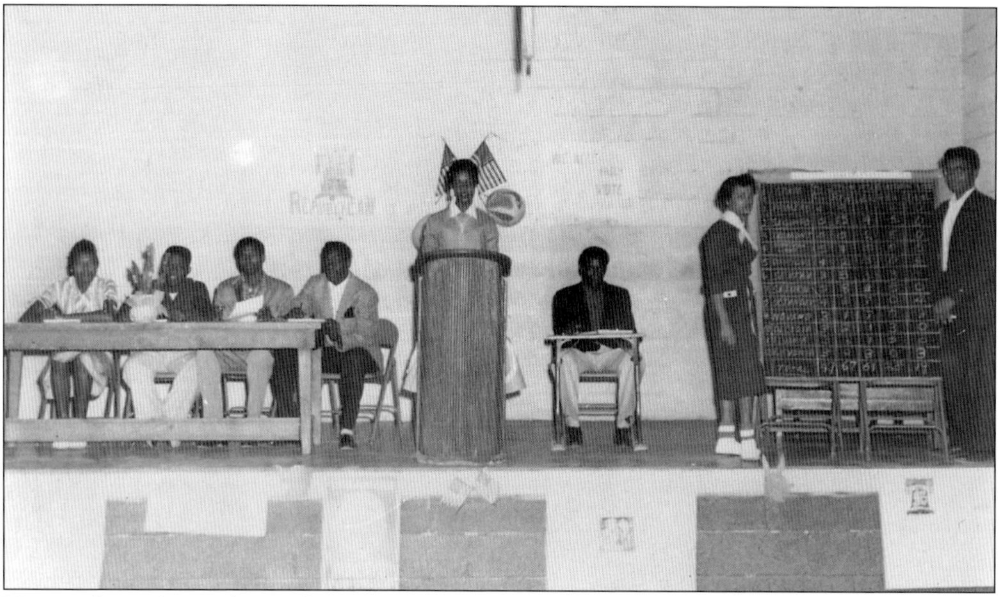

Here is the 1956 mock presidential election at Booker T. Washington School, which operated from 1945 to 1967. Before segregation of schools ended in 1965, African American students from Sweetwater, Merkel, Roby, Roscoe, Trent, and Rotan attended Washington School. During the 1957–1958 school year, all Sweetwater elementary schools participated in a cooperative project sponsored by the Southern Association of Secondary Schools, Colleges, and Universities to promote diversity and fellowship.

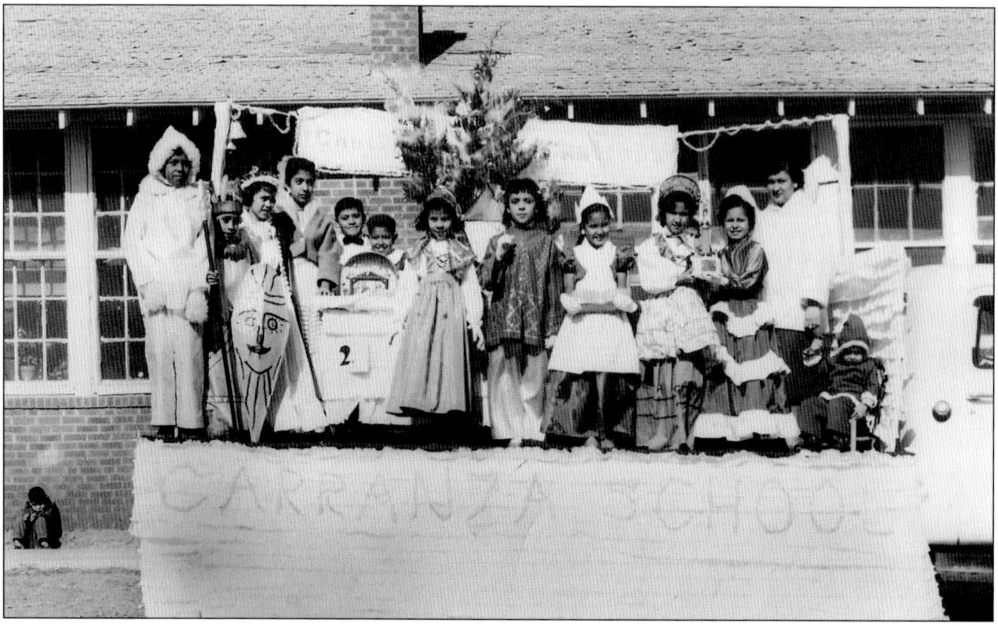

The first Emilio Carranza School was built for Mexican American children in 1917 and was replaced by a larger structure in 1930. In 1936, the school had two new rooms added. The population grew so quickly that, in 1954, those students who could speak English were sent to John R. Lewis or J.P. Cowen schools. Both Carranza and Washington Schools were officially closed in 1964, and the Sweetwater Independent School District became fully integrated.

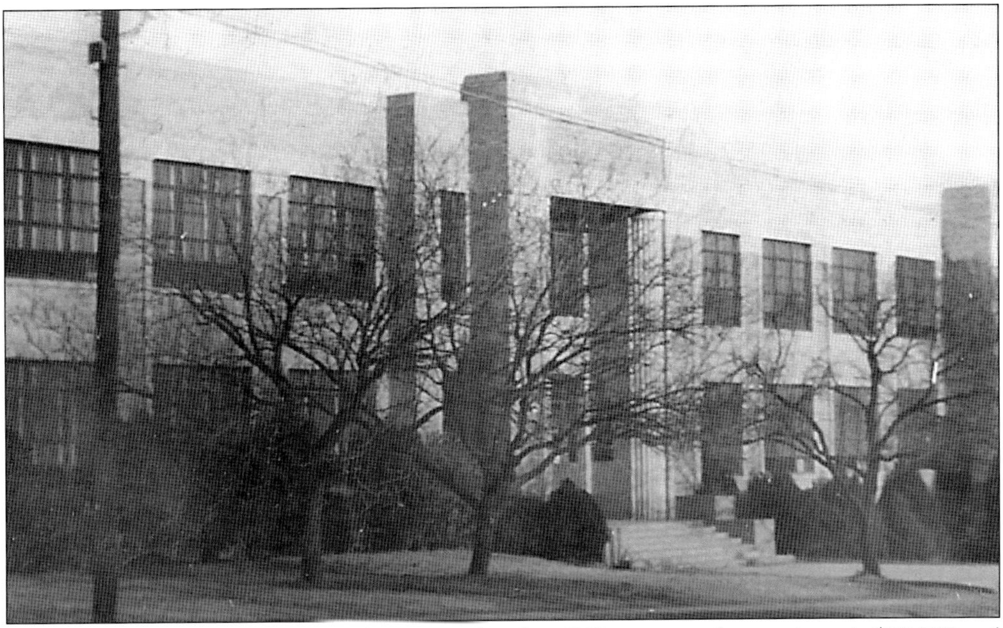

John H. Reagan Junior High School was completed in 1930 at a cost of approximately $83,000 and housed the seventh, eighth, and ninth grades. The end of the 1940 school year marked a notable change as the district moved to the 12-grade system, which led eventually to the ninth-grade students being moved to the high school in 1967. Students attended Reagan until the late 1970s, when an increasing population required a new school and a move to a middle school system.

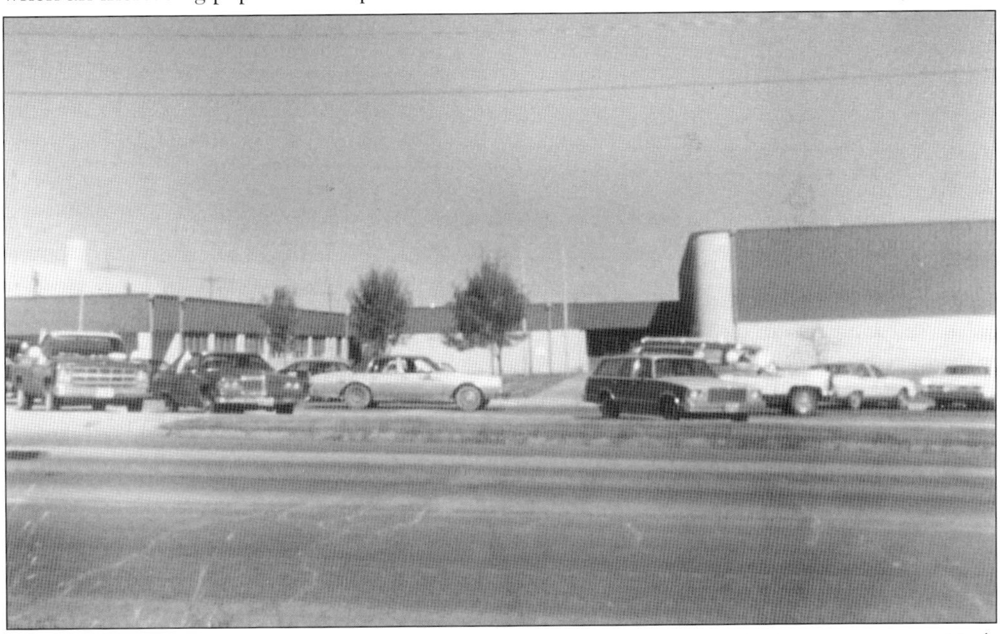

Construction of Sweetwater Middle School began on the playground of Reagan Junior High around 1978. The one-story structure was completed in 1979 and housed grades seven and eight in the spring of that year and accepted sixth-grade students beginning that fall. This school still stands in this same spot on Lamar Street, although it has had a few facelifts including a "new" gym added in the late 1980s.

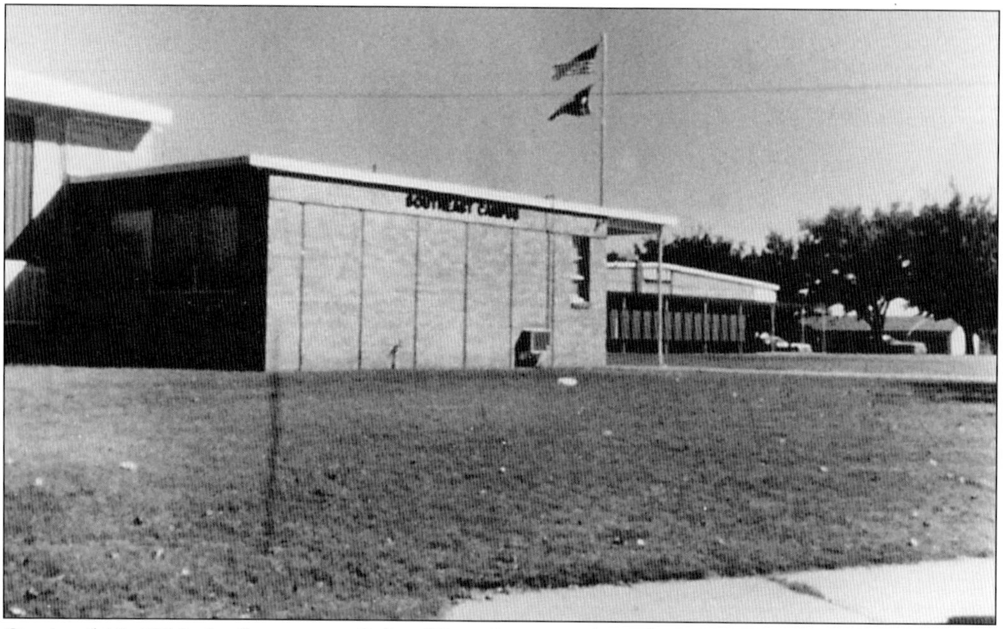

On April 12, 1956, the Sweetwater School Board proposed an elementary school to serve students on the south side of town, and a final site was approved June 14, 1956. Land was bought for the school on August 23, 1956; the school was officially named Southeast Elementary on November 8, 1956, and classes began in August 1957. Although it, along with Eastridge Elementary and J.P. Cowen, was completely remodeled in 1995, the school still stands.

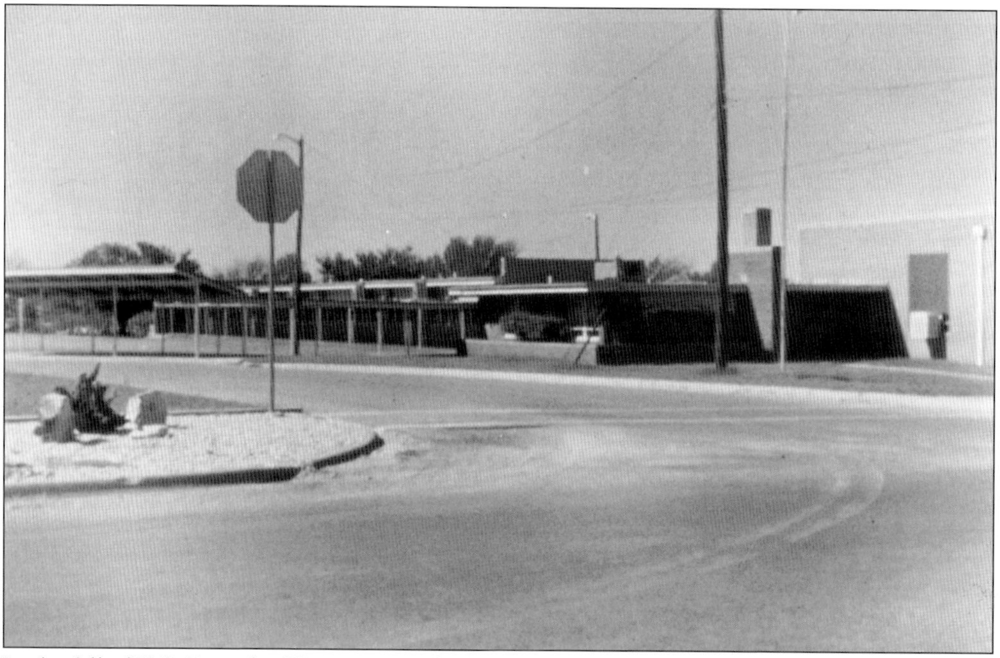

In the fall of 1951 Eastridge Elementary School was built on Hoyt Street and contained 14 rooms, cafeteria, offices, and teacher workroom. In April 1956, the school board voted to add six rooms to the north wing. Ben High was both the second and the fourth principal of this school, which still stands and continues to serve as an elementary school.

Three

Civilizing Sweetwater

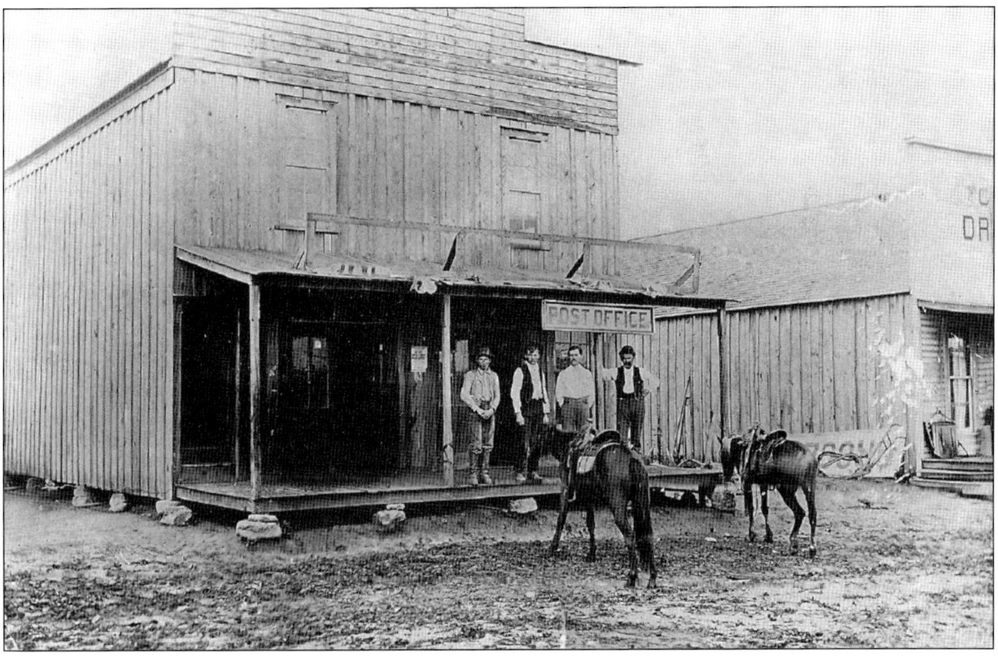

The first post office was established at Manning's store on March 27, 1879, with L.B. Perry serving as postmaster. Seen here is Sweetwater's second post office around 1898 while W.B. Howard of Roscoe was postmaster, with his young son running the office. It was located on the east side of the square where the Nolan Theater operated.

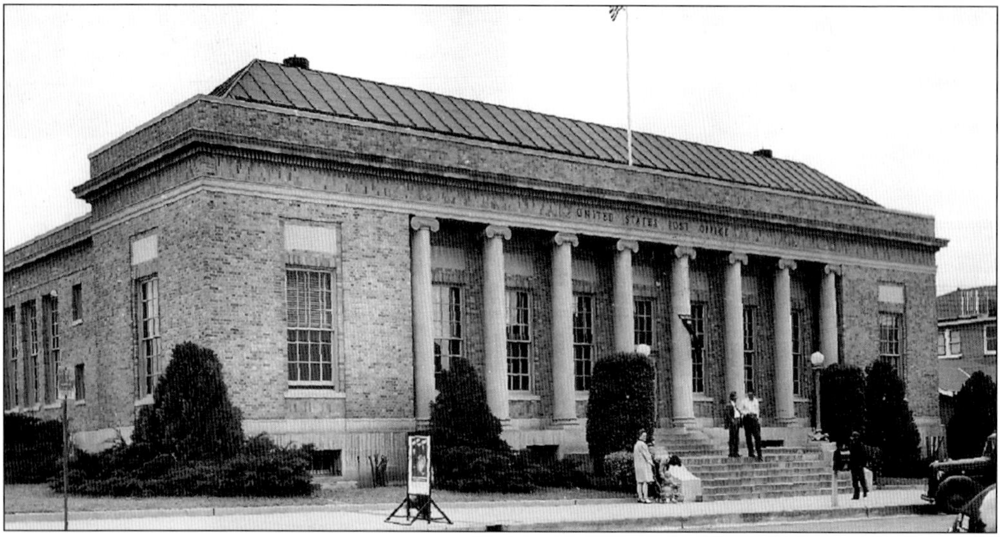

Sweetwater's third post office, as it currently looks, is situated on Third Street between Locust and Elm Streets. Construction was started in 1931 and completed in 1932 at a cost of $130,000. The new building was the result of many years of concerted efforts by the citizens of Sweetwater. At one point, this site housed the remains of Sweetwater's first schoolhouse, which served as a drugstore while on this lot.

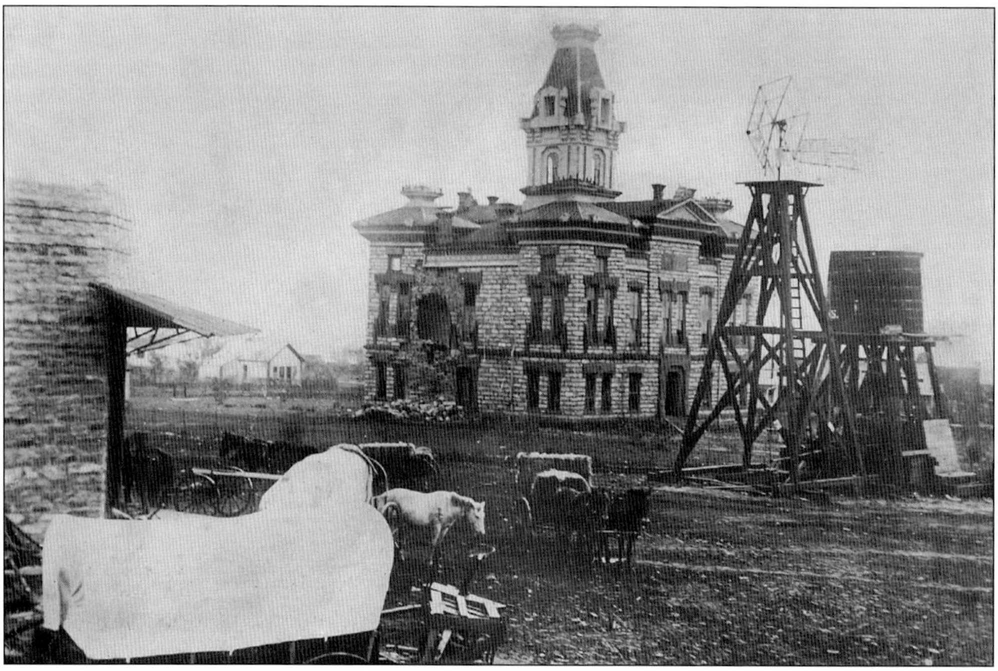

The first Nolan County Courthouse, built in 1883, sat on the same site as the current courthouse and served as the center of the town square. The county opened bids for a courthouse to be built under $20,000 and hired J.E. Flanders as architect. Gypsum plaster was used as the mortar for heavy fieldstones, and the north wall fell in 1885, requiring a new courthouse to be built.

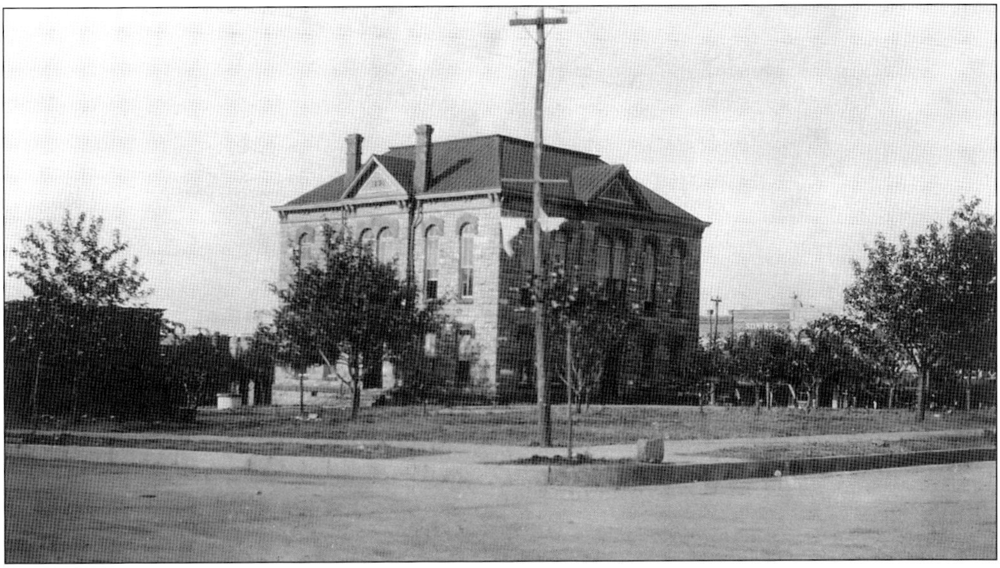

The second courthouse was completed in 1891 and had a windmill and water well on the northeast side, which supplied water for livestock. When the first waterworks was put in in 1909, the well was abandoned, and troughs on the east and north sides were maintained by the water company. This courthouse also featured a bandstand built around 1905 while R.C. Crane was mayor. The stones from this courthouse, torn down in 1917, were used to build a warehouse that still stands today across the railroad tracks.

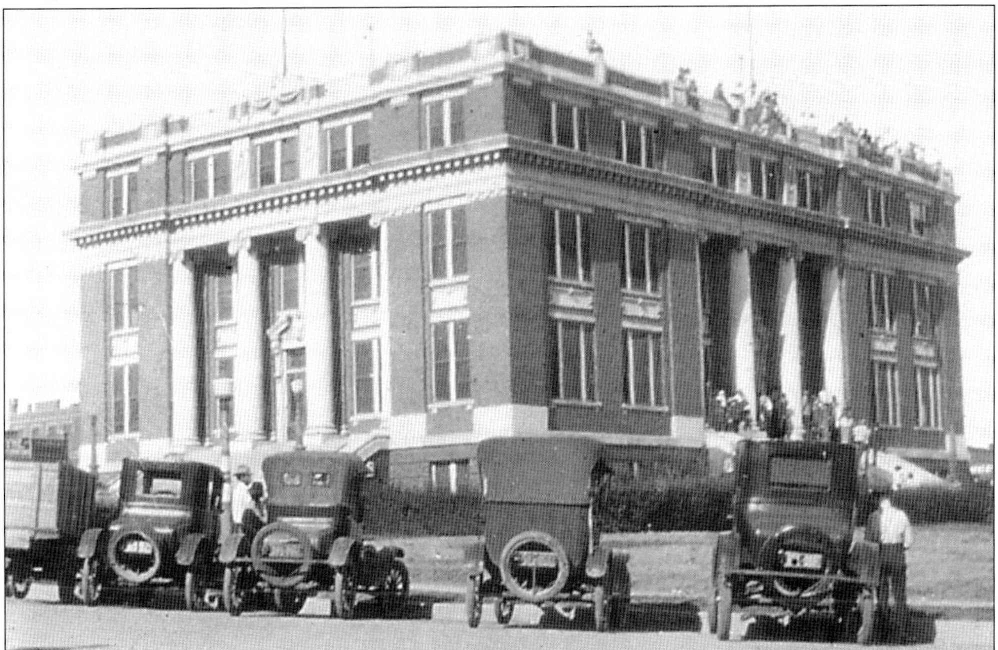

The third courthouse of Nolan County was built in 1918 at a cost of $200,000 and was made of redbrick with cast cement on the outside and slabs of Vermont marble in the interior. This was the most beloved of all Nolan County's courthouses, but a growing jail population, record storage issues, and a lack of women's facilities prompted a fourth courthouse to be built in its place.

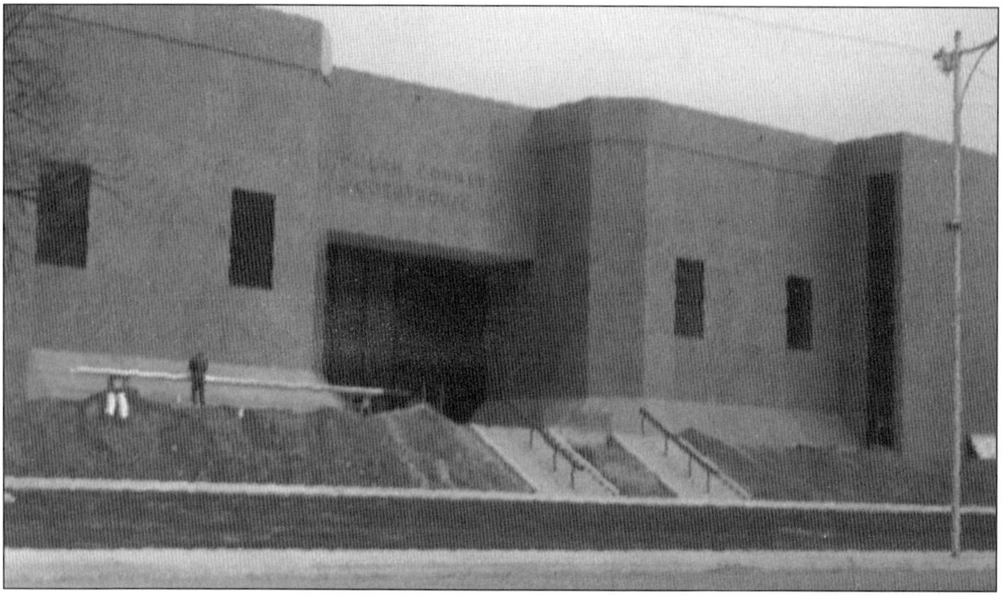

Nolan County's fourth courthouse was completed in 1977 at a cost of $1.5 million. The three-story structure was made of Texas red granite and concrete block exterior walls. The courthouse resembled a fortress, and for many, it was an eyesore compared to the Georgian third courthouse. In 2012, the granite slabs on the north side of the structure began to fall, and a restoration project is currently underway. This new fifth courthouse will be faced with Austin stone, and completion is expected in the summer of 2014.

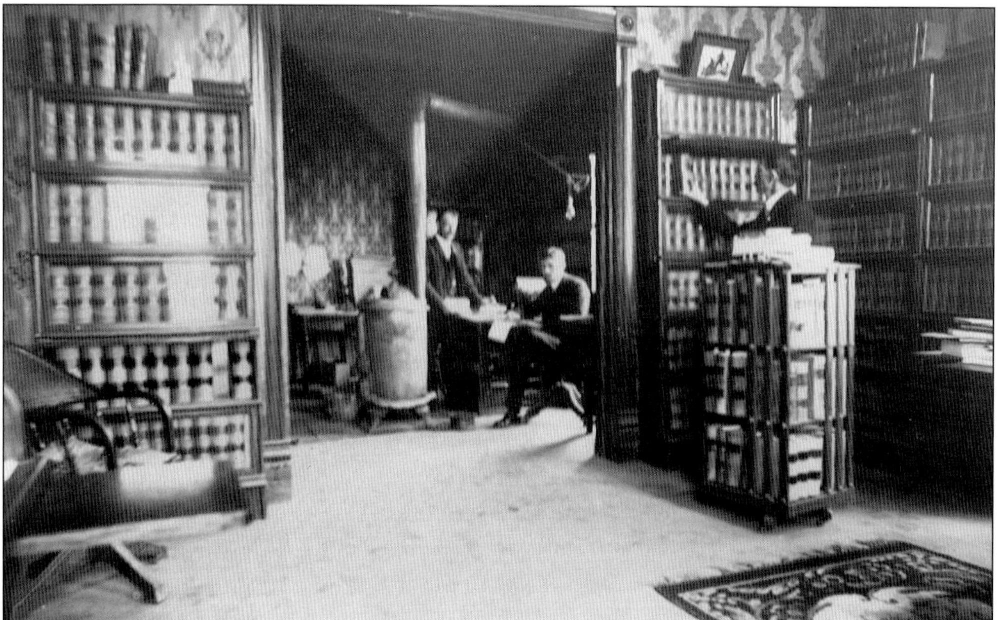

The law office of Judge R.A. Ragland and R.C. Crane was located above the Trammell Bank on Oak Street. Both men were instrumental in the building of early Sweetwater. Crane was a lawyer and real estate agent who became mayor of Sweetwater in 1904. He served as deacon of First Baptist Church and used his personal funds to spur the development of Sweetwater.

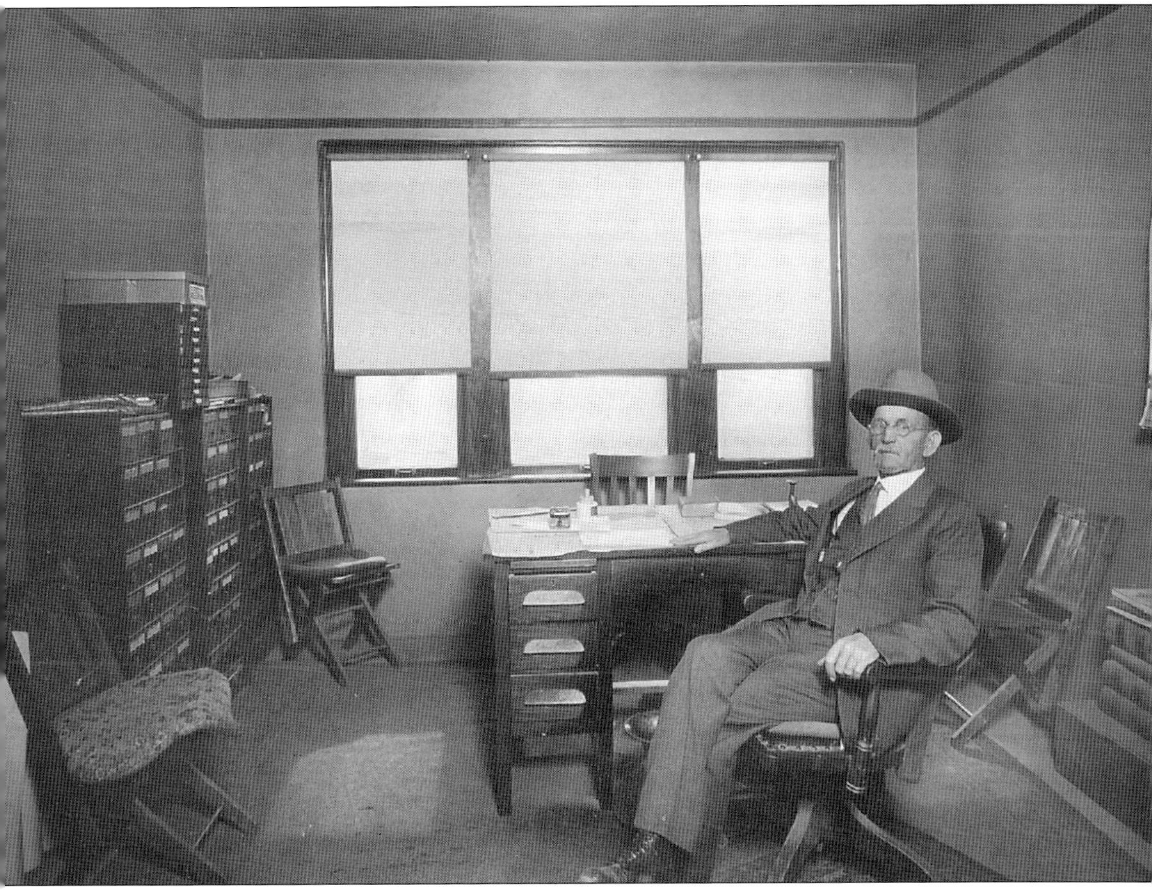

R.A. Ragland served two terms as district judge, was once county attorney, and had extensive land holdings in Nolan County. When the bank he owned failed, he sold all his land to pay the bank's debts; he died a penniless man in 1938. His wife, Luella, who suffered a stroke while putting away canning in their basement, preceded him in death. Their home, at the corner of Ragland and Third Streets, now houses the Pioneer Museum. Before their deaths, they built two structures that still stand on Third and Oak Streets.

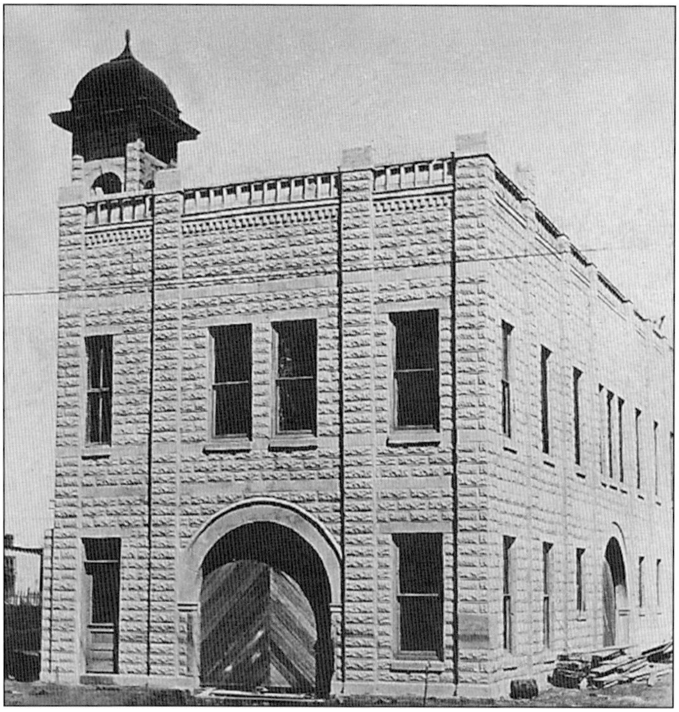

Sweetwater's first fire station, which also housed the city hall, was built sometime between the formation of the fire department in 1884 and 1920, when a picture was taken of this station conjoined with the Mart Hotel. The date of the building is most likely around 1908, when the Sweetwater Volunteer Fire Department was officially organized on May 4.

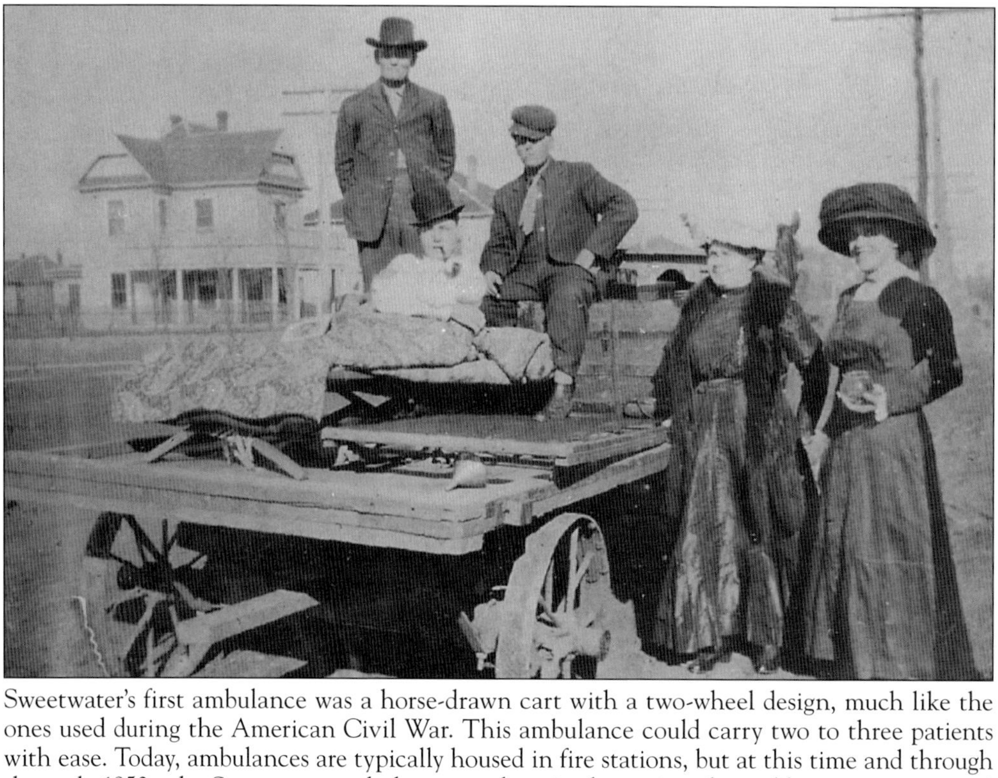

Sweetwater's first ambulance was a horse-drawn cart with a two-wheel design, much like the ones used during the American Civil War. This ambulance could carry two to three patients with ease. Today, ambulances are typically housed in fire stations, but at this time and through the early 1950s, the Sweetwater ambulance was kept in the various funeral homes in town, and morticians would often be first responders.

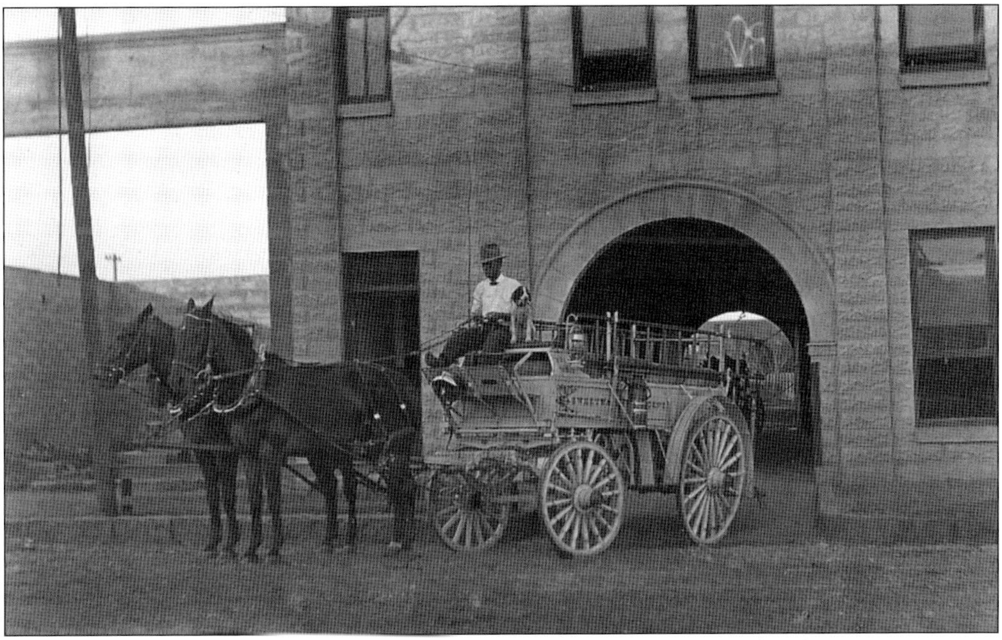

Sweetwater's first fire truck was horse-drawn and replaced the bucket brigade, which had previously been the only way to fight fires. By 1909, this fire wagon was in service as the primary firefighting vehicle. It can be seen in the pictures of the Orient Hotel burning down. A horse-drawn chemical truck was also purchased in 1909; when the fire alarm sounded, every volunteer rushed to the station, as the first one there got the privilege of driving the wagon.

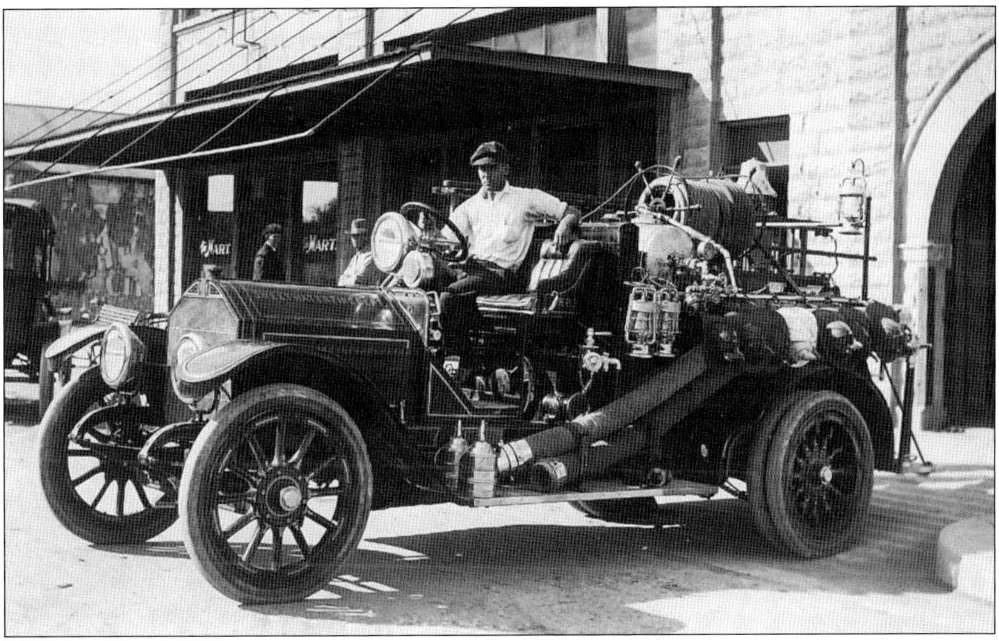

The first motorized fire engine, a 1913 American La France, replaced the horse-drawn fire wagon of the Sweetwater Fire Station, located in the 100 block of Locust Street, pictured in 1910. Jess Robertson is the driver. At this time, the fire department was completely made up of volunteers.

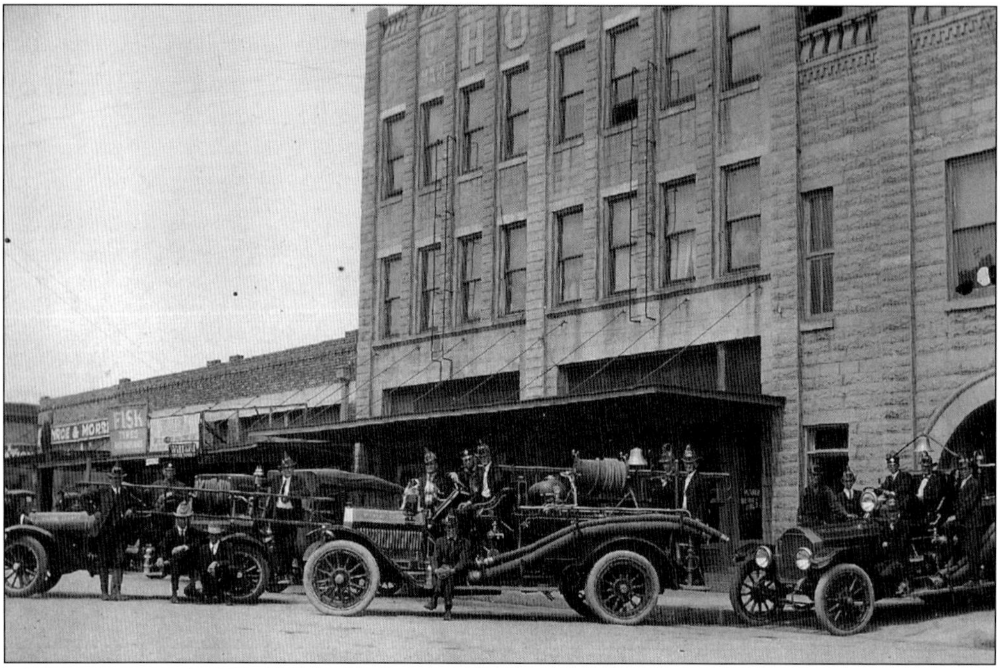

This is a view of the block of Locust Street on which the fire station stood. It was located on the north side of the alley and the east side of Locust Street. On the far left can be seen the tire store owned by Melvin Monroe and Guy E. Morris. This firehouse served the department until 1926, when a new central station and substation were built.

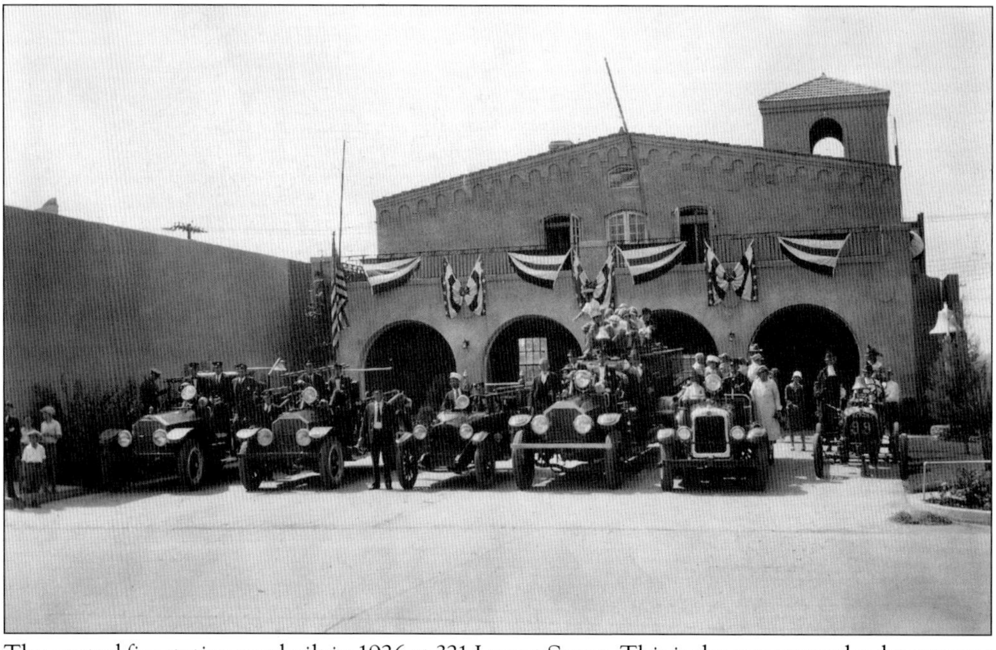

The central fire station was built in 1926 at 321 Locust Street. This is the same year the department received the 1926 American La France ladder truck. This station was remodeled over the years; the arched entries were taken out, and big square doors put in to allow for the larger new motorized fire engines. The balcony was later walled in to create more indoor space.

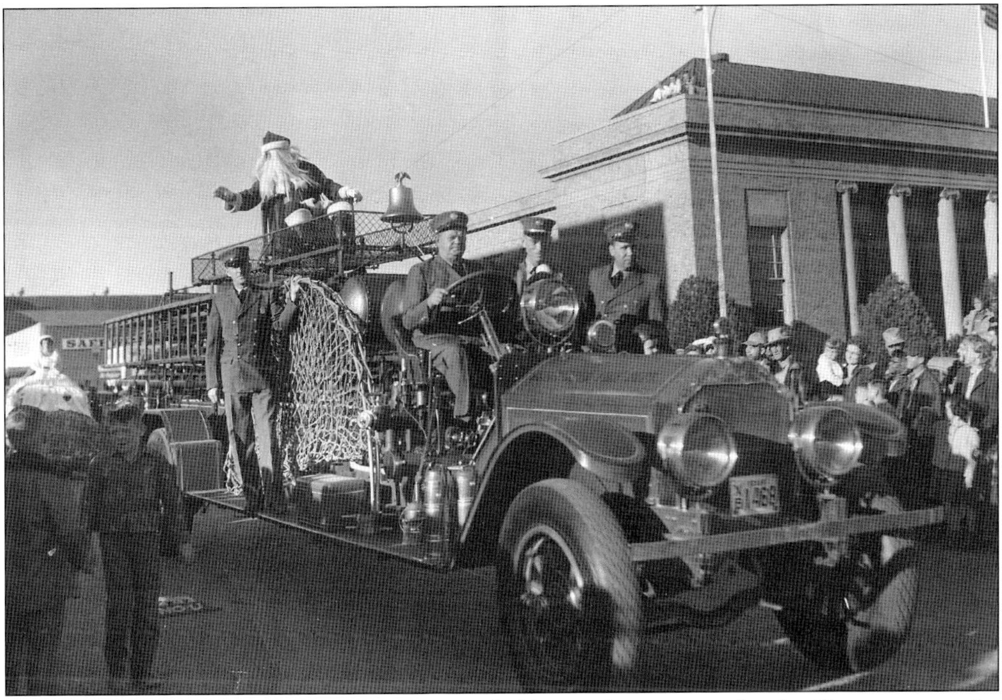

Santa Claus used the 1926 America La France ladder truck every year for the Christmas parade. Martha Taylor fondly remembers riding on the truck with her father as a young girl. It is said the truck was bought for the specific purpose of protecting the Bluebonnet Hotel, Sweetwater's only skyscraper, in case of fire. Today, the truck can be viewed at the Pioneer Museum.

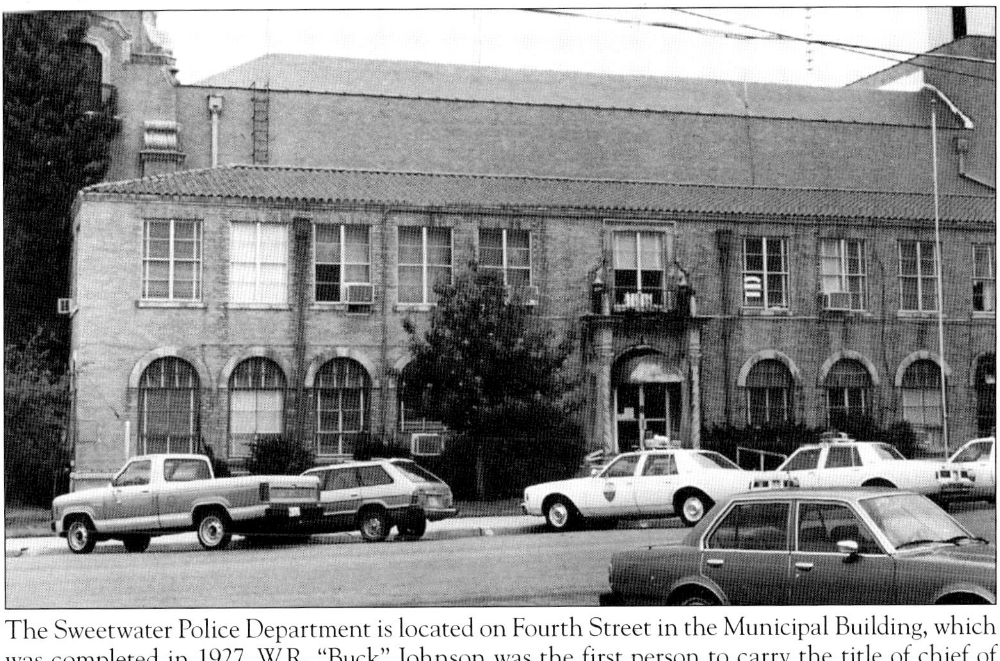

The Sweetwater Police Department is located on Fourth Street in the Municipal Building, which was completed in 1927. W.R. "Buck" Johnson was the first person to carry the title of chief of police due to a charter election in 1913. This position was preceded by the office of city marshal, whose duties included keeping the courthouse windmill "greased and in operation."

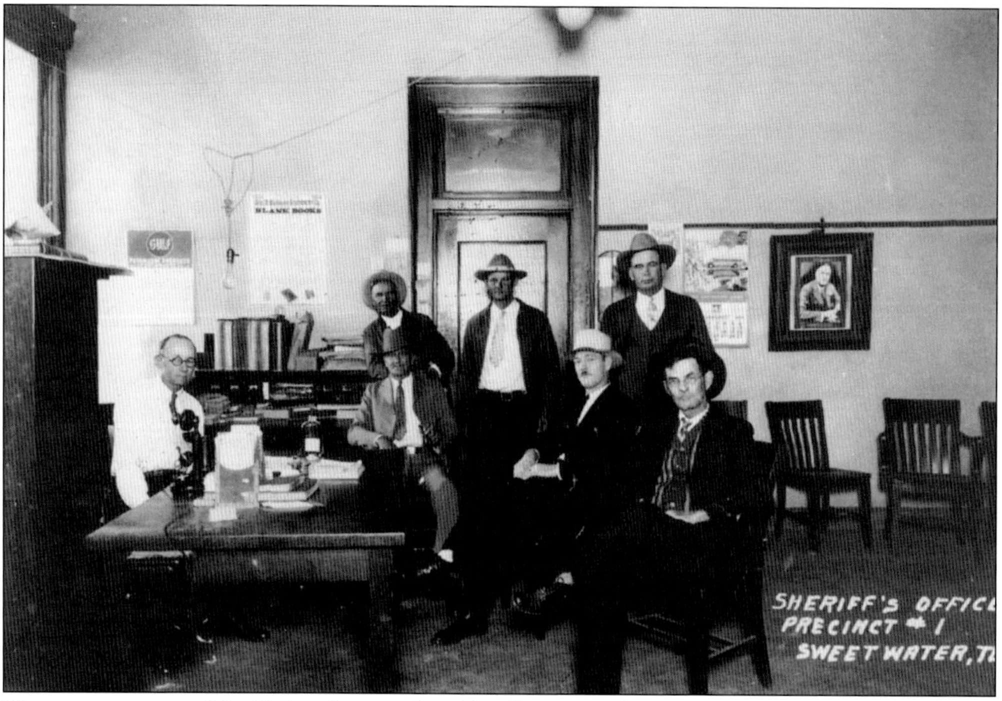

This interior view of the Nolan County sheriff's office around 1935 includes Tom Crutcher, Sheriff Jess Lambert, "Red" Pool, Tom Withers, and Deputy Sheriff Bland. John Calvin Montgomery was the first sheriff of Nolan County and is called the "No Gun Sheriff" as, according to his granddaughter Franzas Cupp, he never carried a firearm and would instead outwit fugitives.

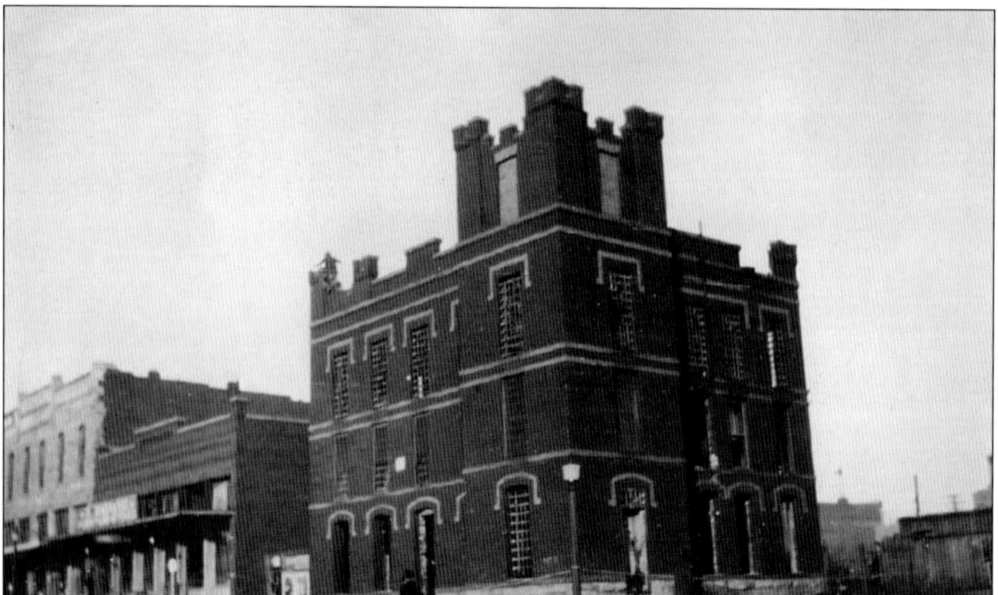

The second Nolan County jailhouse, built in 1912 out of the rocks of the old courthouse, stood on the Doscher Building site. Before the jailhouse was built on April 3, 1882, prisoners were kept by chaining them to mesquite trees; a prisoner could work a 10-hour day, but if he chose not to, he would be returned to the tree and fed bread and water until his sentence was complete.

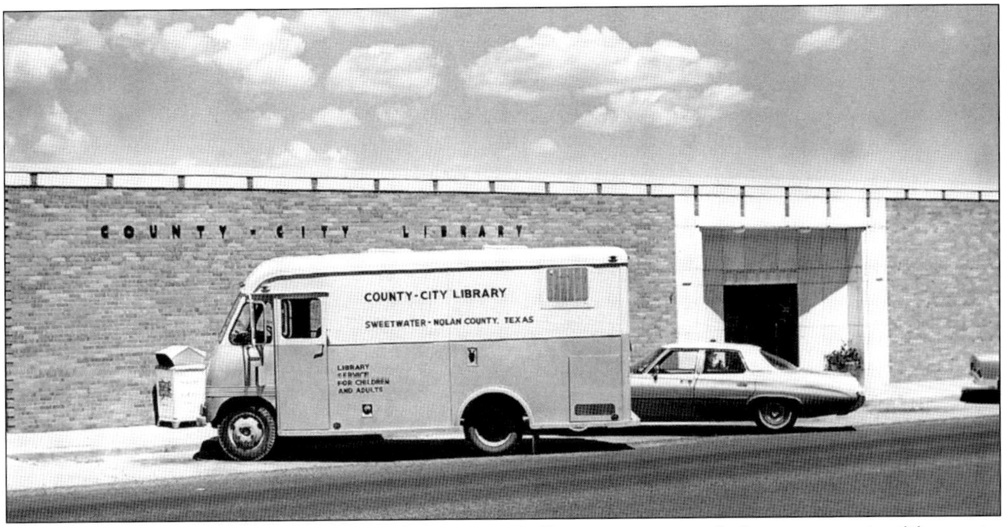

The Saturday Club, now known as The Woman's Forum, organized the county-city library in 1907, and its collection was started by hosting receptions where the cost of admittance was "one good book." The collection was kept in various places, such as the fire station, a candy kitchen, and drugstore, before finally coming to its current home at 206 Elm Street on July 15, 1965.

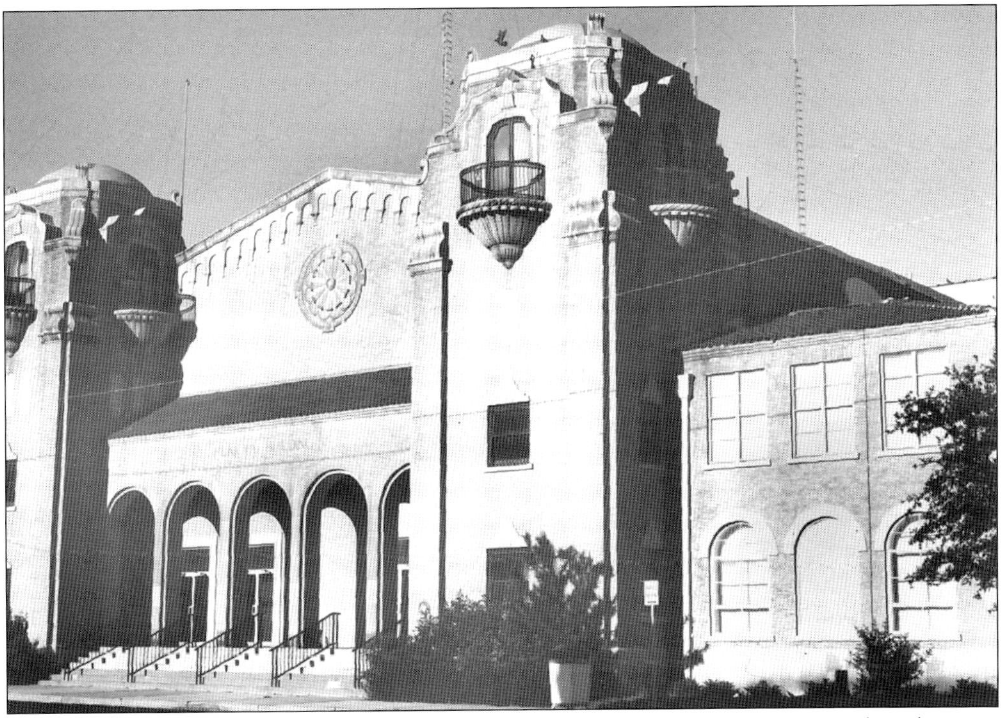

The Page Brothers architectural firm of Austin designed the Sweetwater Municipal Auditorium in 1926. The building is in the Spanish Colonial Revival style and has recently had a facelift due to a renewed interest in this historic landmark. The auditorium has hosted many famous faces over the years, from Fred Astaire and Elvis Presley in the 1930s and 1950s to Dr. Shelley Wachsmann in 2013.

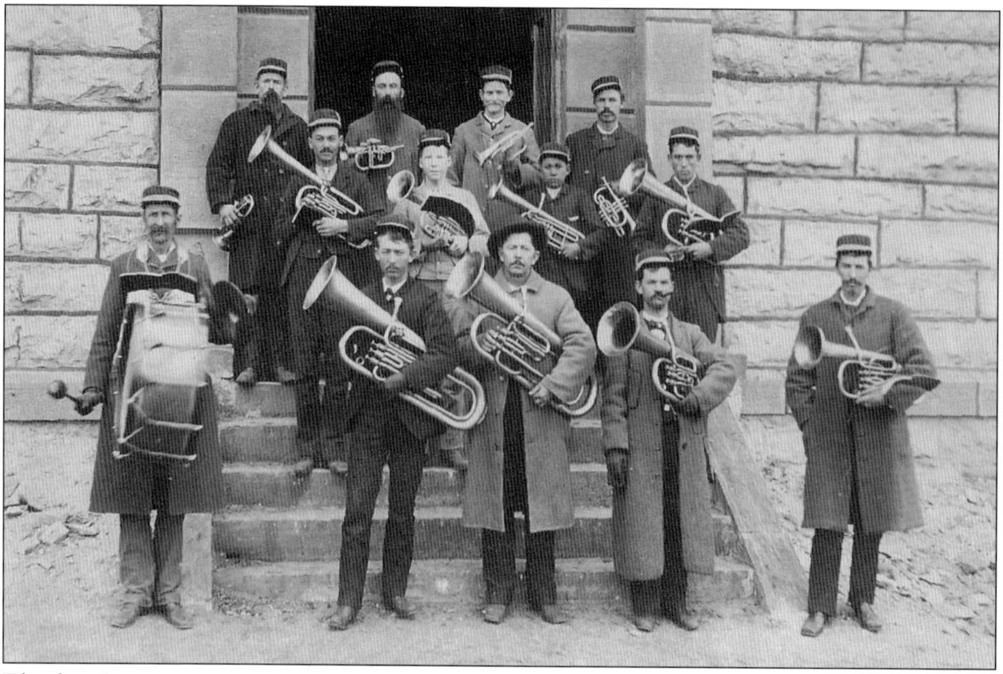

The first Sweetwater Municipal Band, shown here in front of the first courthouse around 1886, played throughout the region, including performances at the courthouse and Grogan Wells gazebos. Over the years, the Sweetwater Municipal Band has performed at the Municipal Auditorium alone and as a backup band to performers. Defunct for several decades, the band was started up again in the late 1980s and has been going strong since then.

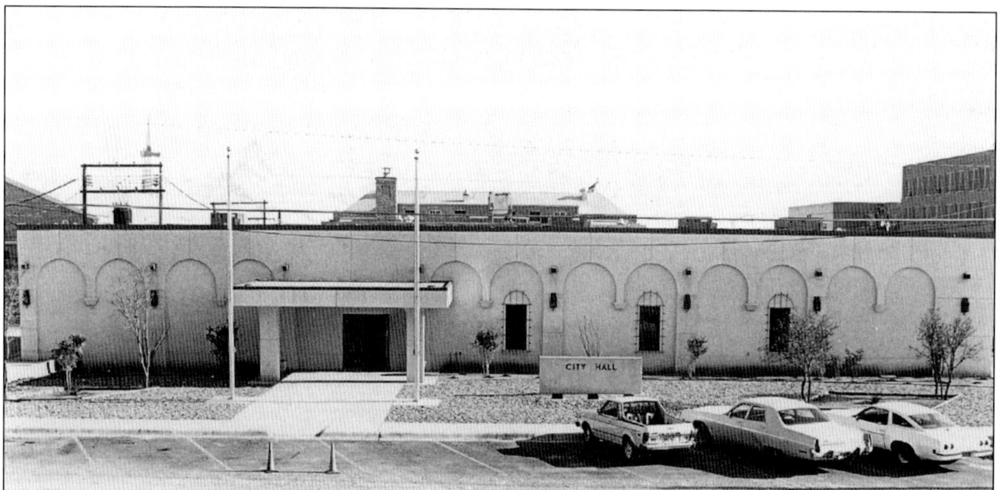

Sweetwater's city hall is located just across the street from the police department on Fourth Street in the old Safeway Building. This building was once home to the Pioneer Museum until it moved into the Ragland House. After the museum vacated it in 1976, the building was expanded and re-faced and became home to the city's offices.

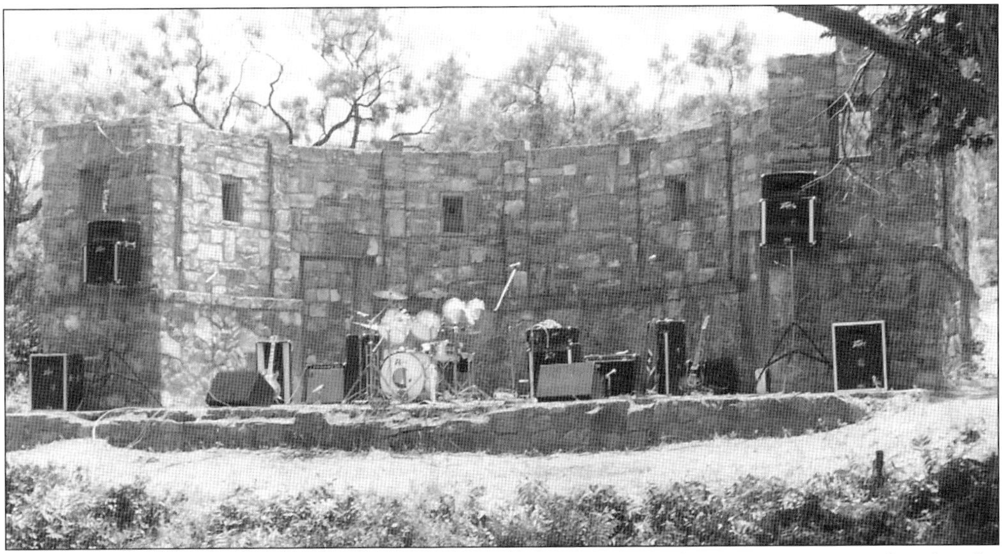

Sweetwater Amphitheater, located at Lake Sweetwater, was one of the many projects undertaken by the Civilian Conservation Corps under Pres. Franklin D. Roosevelt's New Deal. The amphitheater has been the performance home for many local bands over the years and was once a regular hangout spot for the high school students of Sweetwater.

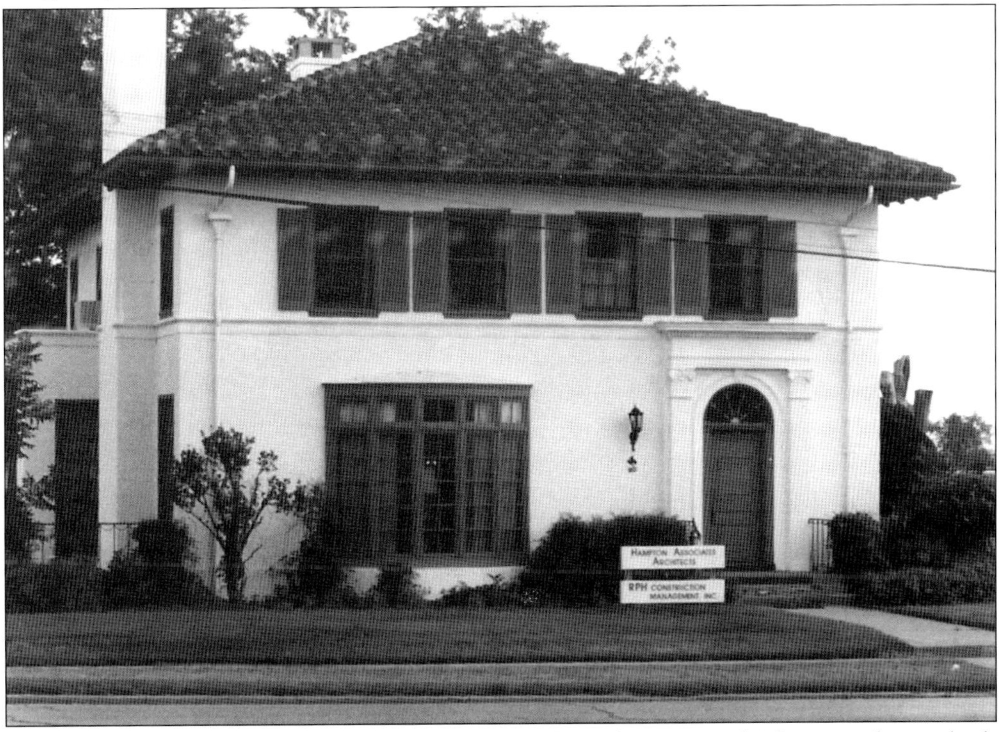

The Sweetwater Chamber of Commerce resides in the Robert M. "Bob" Simmons house, built in 1920. The building features a barrel tile roof and multipaned bay window. Originally, the home was one story but was remodeled in 1934 into the two-story home it is now. Sweetwater Enterprise for Economic Development offices are on the second floor; previous tenants include Hampton Associates Architects.

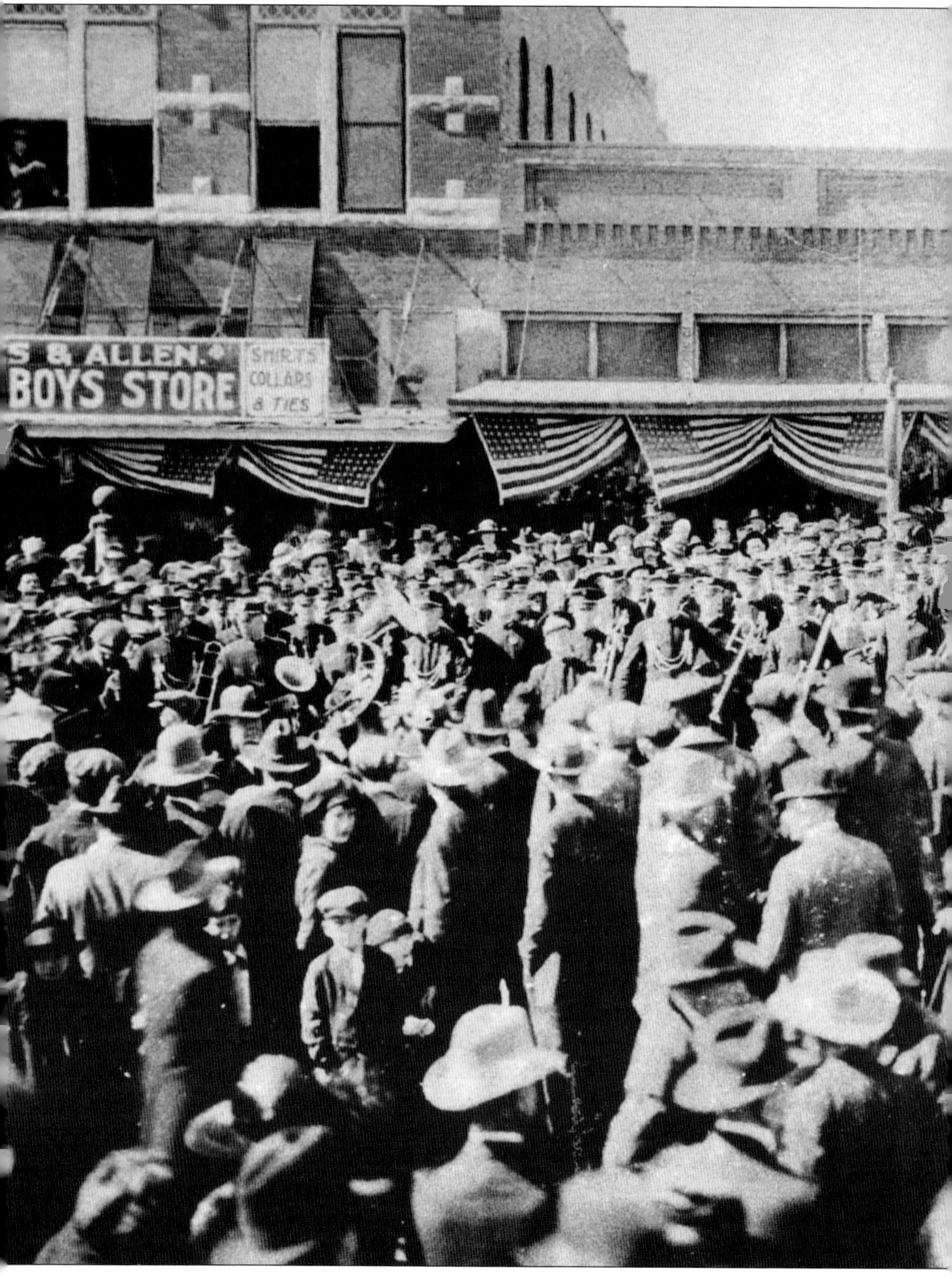
S & ALLEN.
BOYS STORE
SHIRTS
COLLARS
& TIES

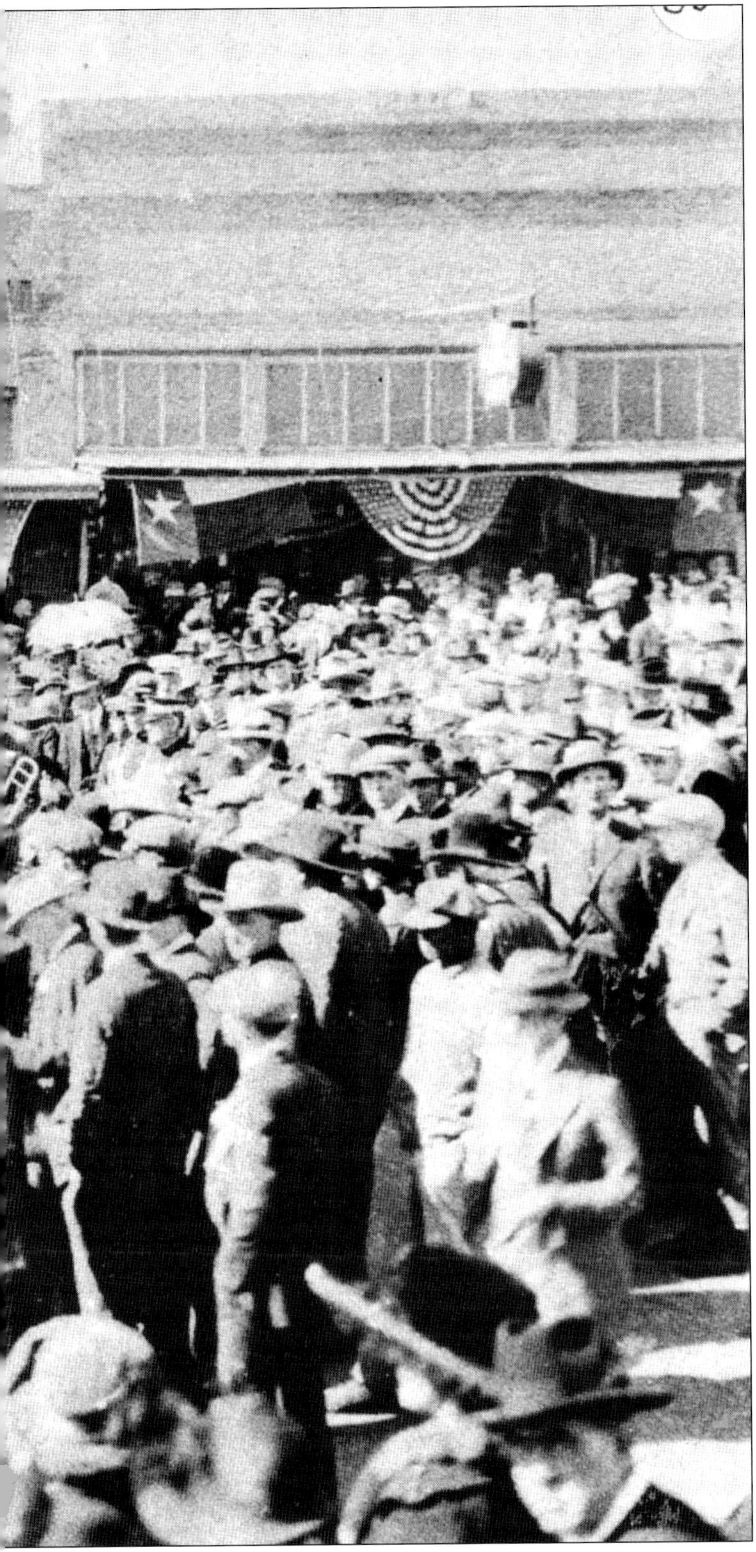

The west side of the square on March 2, 1923, shows the West Texas Jubilee Celebration commemorating the success of the movement for a college in West Texas. The movement was launched in Sweetwater on April 3, 1916, and the West Texas A&M Campaign Association was organized, with Dr. P.C. Coleman as president, Porter A. Whaley as vice president, and Thomas F. Hodge as secretary-treasurer. On July 6, 1917, the first bill to locate the college miscarried; in April 1921, a second bill was vetoed, and a meeting was held in Sweetwater. When the law finally passed and provided for a larger and better college than originally planned, the West Texas Jubilee Celebration was held in Sweetwater in March 1923. This movement eventually ended in the establishment of Texas Tech University in Lubbock in 1923.

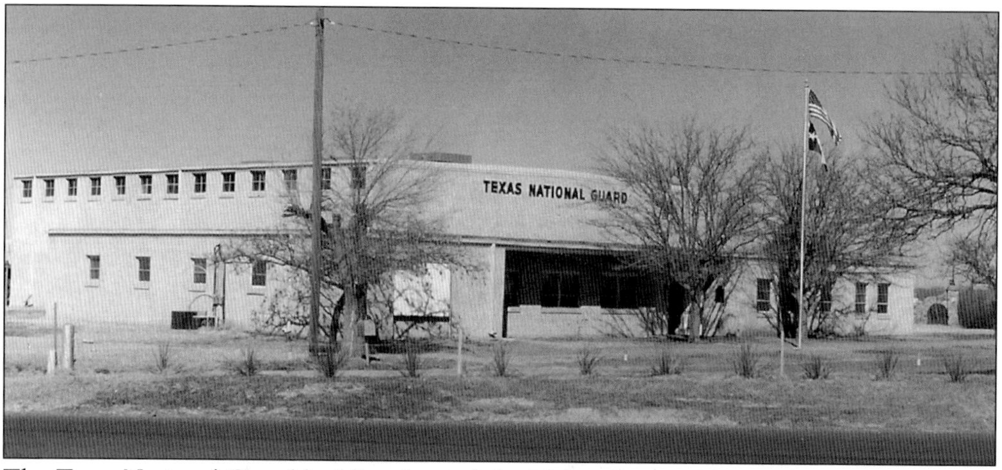

The Texas National Guard building housed the Nolan County National Guard and served as a training facility for the Guard. The Nolan County National Guard was done away with in 1992. The building still stands, but now serves as a 24-hour workout facility for county and city employees.

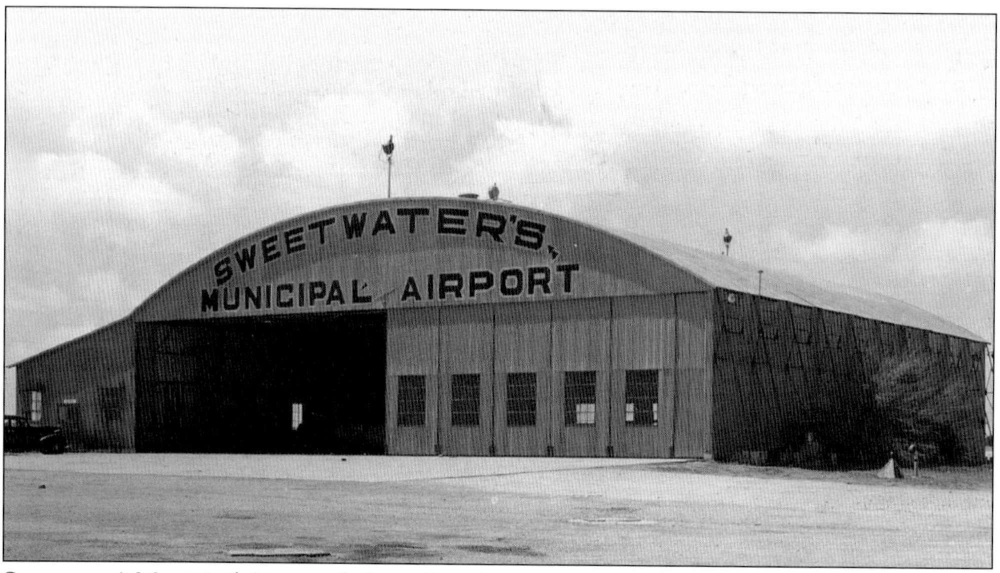

Sweetwater's Municipal Airport, dedicated on August 11, 1929, officially became Avenger Field on May 14, 1942, according to Maj. Bennet Monde. Avenger Field served as the training facility for the Royal Air Force in the summer of 1942 and for the Women Airforce Service Pilots (WASP), beginning in 1943. A WASP memorial museum now stands at Avenger Field near Texas State Technical College.

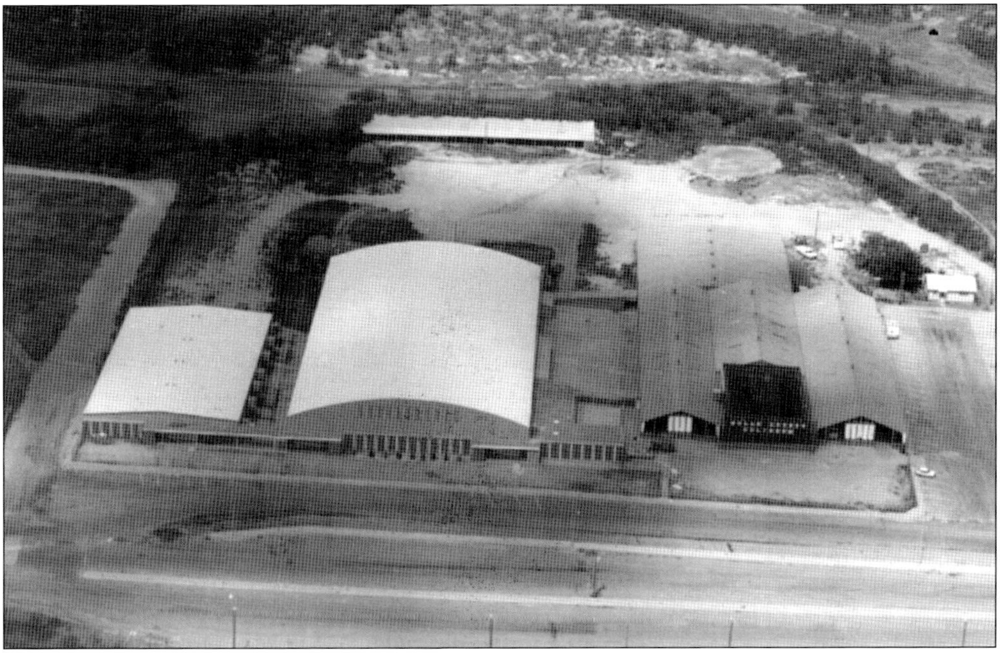

Nolan County Coliseum was built in 1958 and has been the home of many rodeos, stock shows, circuses, and most famously, the Sweetwater Jaycees Rattlesnake Roundup held yearly on the second weekend in March. The coliseum annex is often used for wedding receptions, graduation parties, family reunions, and the end-of-the-year school celebration known as Blow-Out. It is built on the site of H.S. "Auti" Newman's racetrack.

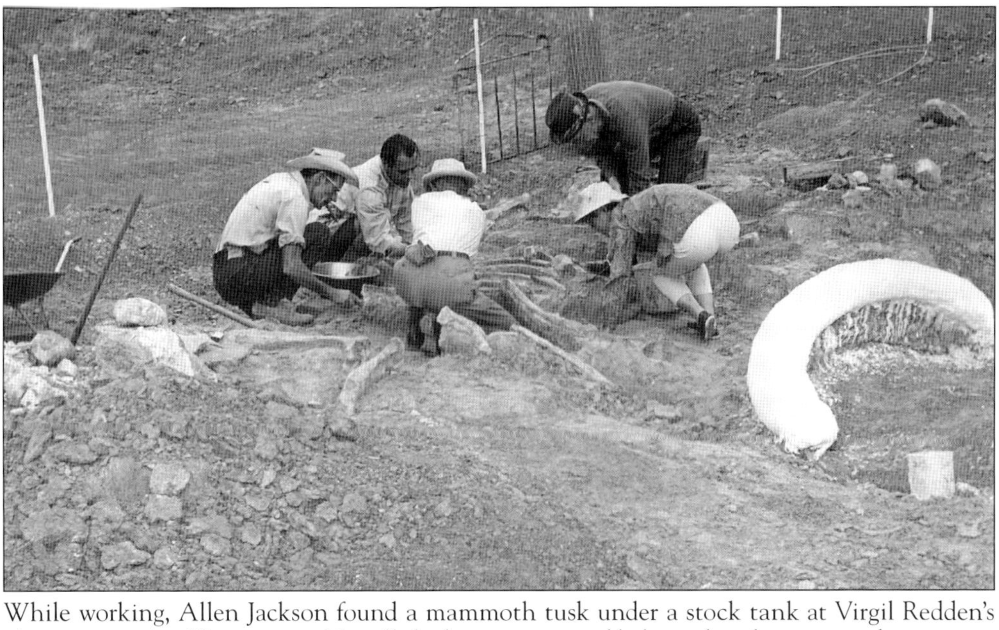

While working, Allen Jackson found a mammoth tusk under a stock tank at Virgil Redden's place just north of Sweetwater. Not all the bones recovered belonged to the mammoth; two were camel bones. The tusk is thought to be between 8,000 and 20,000 years old, and the area it was found in looks to have been an ancient pond. The tusk, a tooth, and camel bones are on display at the Pioneer Museum.

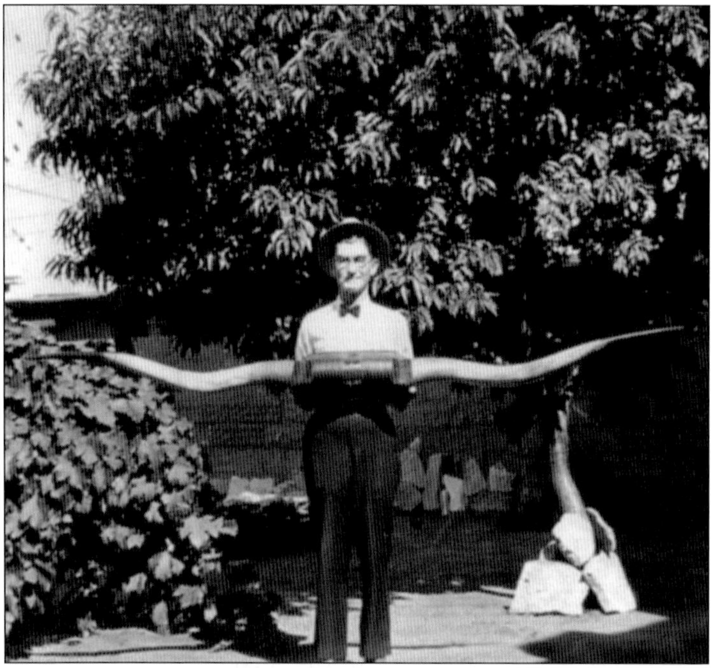

Newt Prince is pictured holding Longhorn horns, which, after his death, were given to Raymond Bishop by Newt's sister. Prince acquired the horns from the saloon owned by Ben Jones in the 1880s. It is said that Ben Jones would often take odd or interesting items from a broke cowboy in exchange for a few drinks.

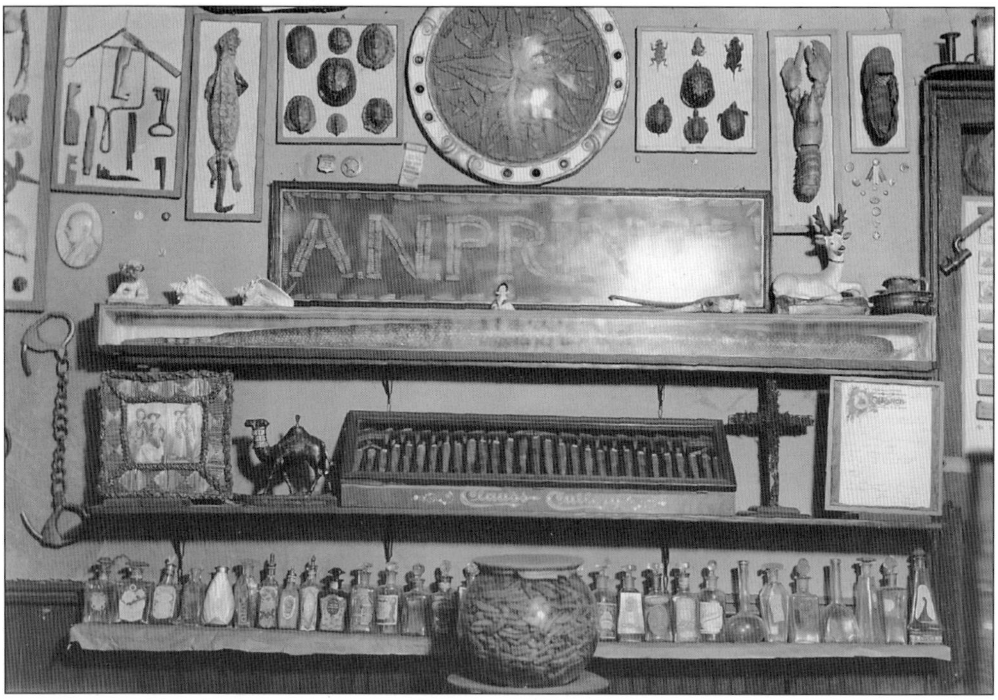

Here is one of the displays in Newt Prince's private museum. Newt Prince had the first museum in Nolan County inside his house; he was said to at one point have the largest private collection in the United States. Among the items found in his collection were a copy of the first newspaper printed in Sweetwater in 1882; a gun owned by Billy the Kid, which was presented to Newt by Tom Trammell; and wood from the Manning store, built at Blue Goose. R.C. Crane advocated for turning Prince's collection into an official museum.

The second home of the Pioneer City County Museum, the old Safeway building, now houses Sweetwater City Hall. The Pioneer Museum was organized in 1967 by the now defunct Nolan County Historical Society and was established through the generosity of Lance and Frances Mae (Mingus) Sears. The Searses created the Pioneer Foundation and, in 1970, authorized the purchase of the Safeway building for the purpose of housing the museum.

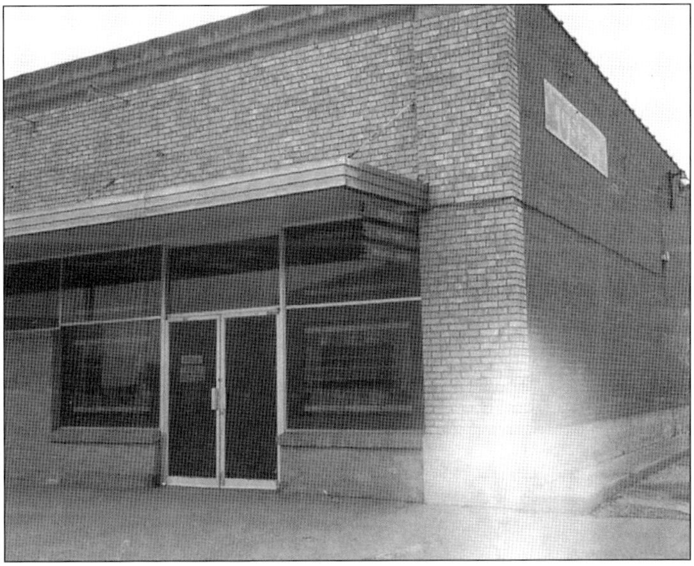

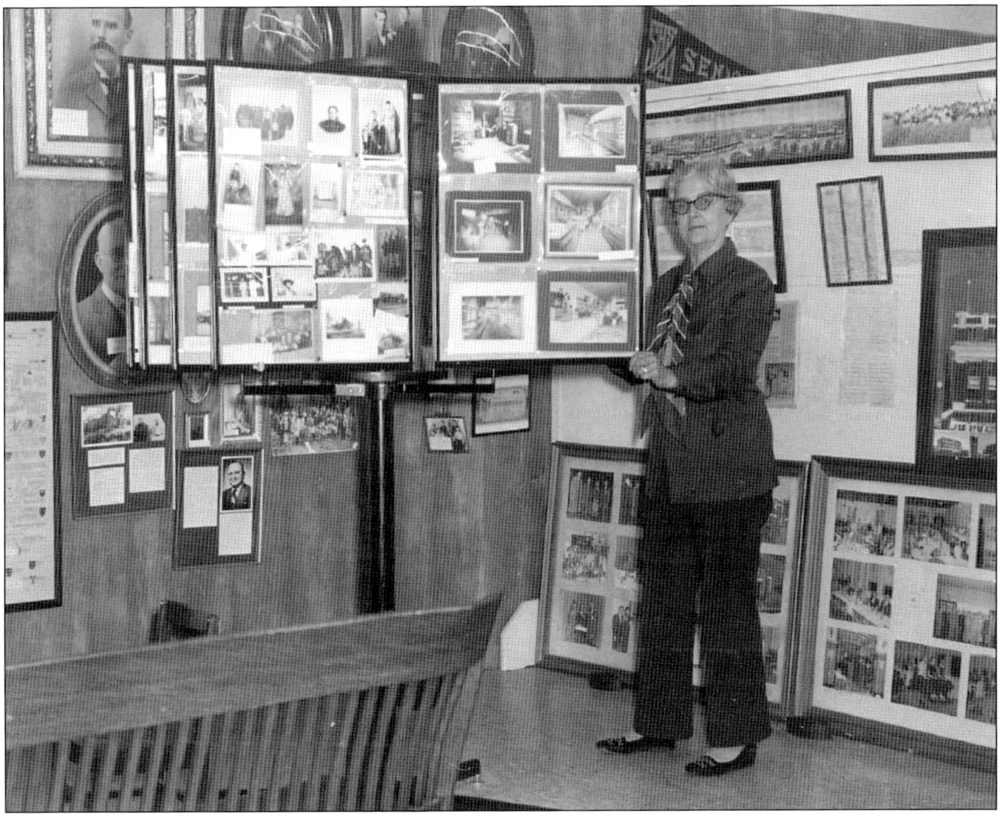

Mr. and Mrs. E.A. Harkins had a dream that Nolan County history would be saved and housed in some way so that future generations would know their history. Gladys Harkins was so interested in Nolan County's history that she had a corner in her classroom set aside to display old relics. The first museum was set up in the old Johnson Funeral Home at the corner of Ash and Third Streets.

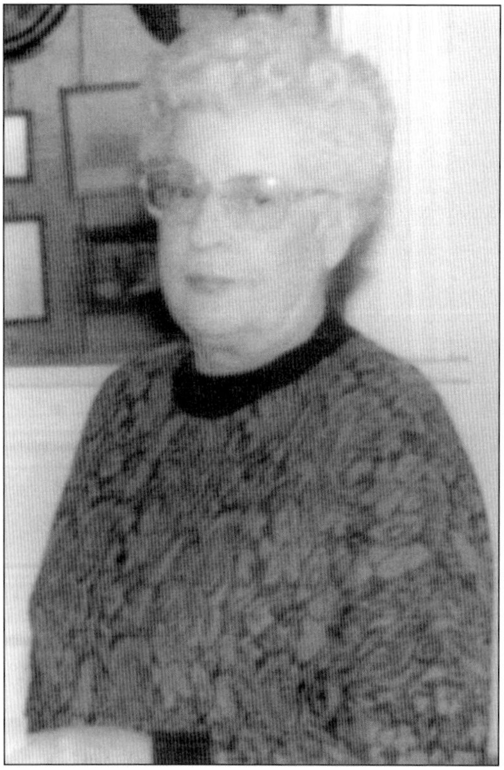

In 1972, Gladys Harkins asked Henri Elizabeth "Hank" Pepper (pictured) to work at the Pioneer Museum; she was the first paid employee of the museum while it was being set up in the Fourth Street location. When she left the museum, Althea Dunn took her place; Hank returned to the museum and was its director after it was moved into the Ragland House until 1992, when Franzas Cupp became the director.

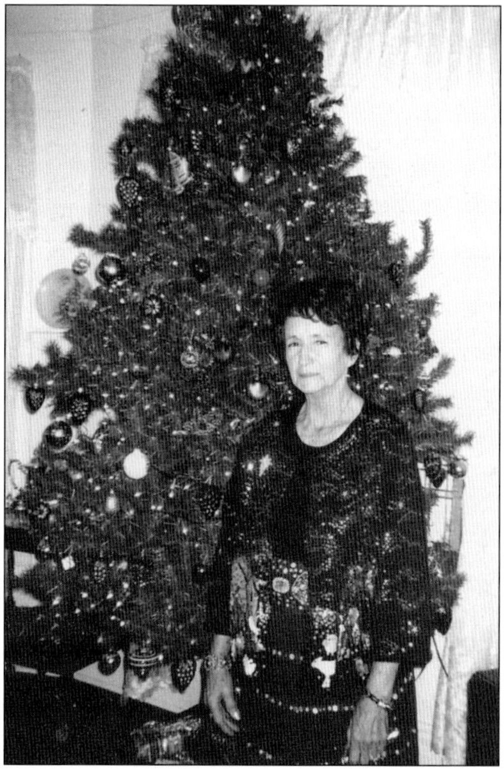

Franzas Cupp became the new museum director in 1992; she served on the Nolan County Historical Survey Committee as well as on the Pioneer Museum Board of Directors. Cupp has used her position at the museum to reach out to the children of Nolan County through school tours that teach about the games children used to play and how to wash clothes on a board, and through pumpkin contests. Cupp retired as director in 2013.

Pictured here is the dress Suzanne Sears wore when she was crowned Miss Wool and Mohair Duchess of West Texas in 1960 at the San Jacinto Fiesta Parade in San Antonio. The Sears family raised sheep just southwest of Sweetwater, and the elaborate train of this dress honors their business.

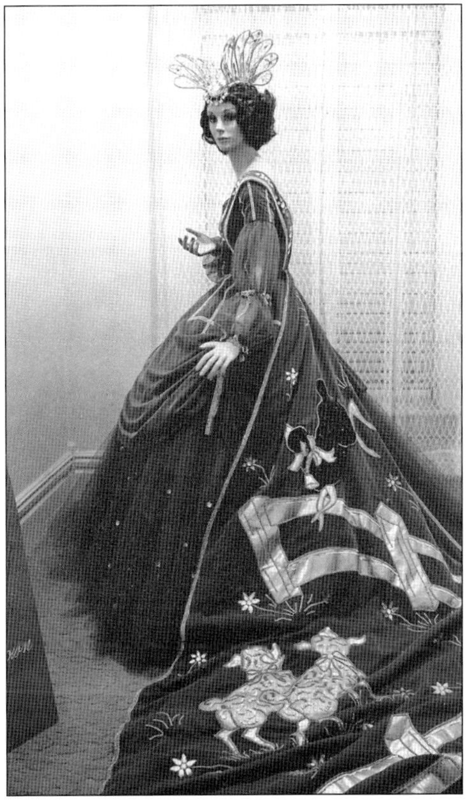

James Paul Turner and his wife, Geraldine, moved to Sweetwater in 1949 and established the Turner Hereford Ranch. They served many years on the museum board, he serving two of those years as president. James Paul was a charter member of the Sweetwater Rifle and Pistol Club, the Blue Goose Skeet Club, and West Texas Knife Club. His extensive gun collection can be found on display in the lobby of the Nolan County Courthouse.

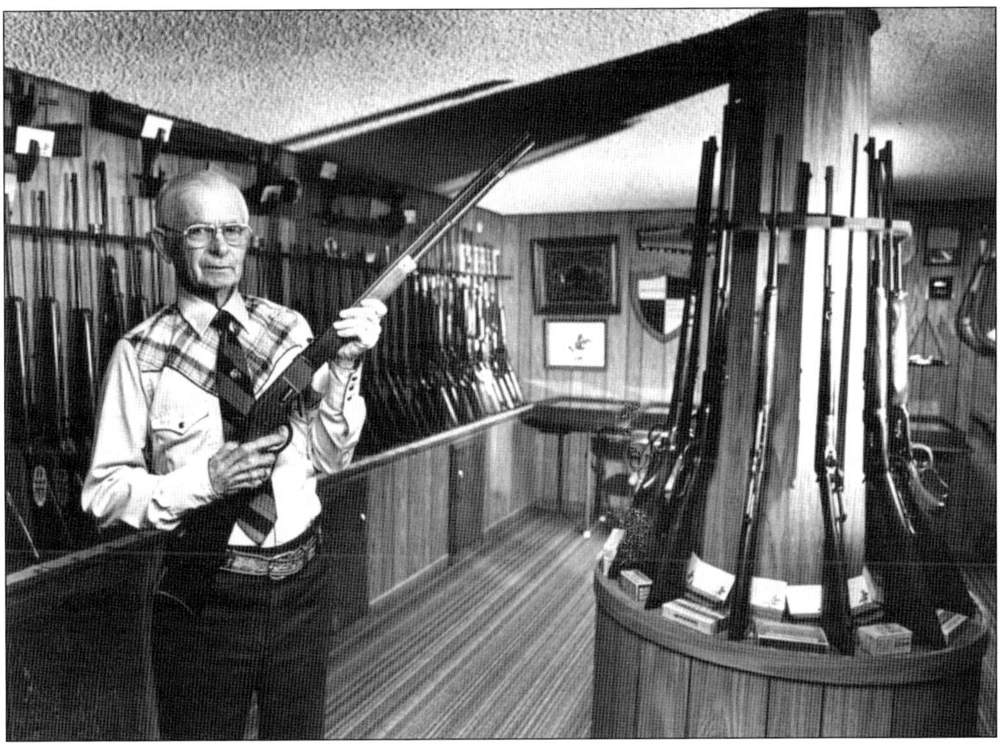

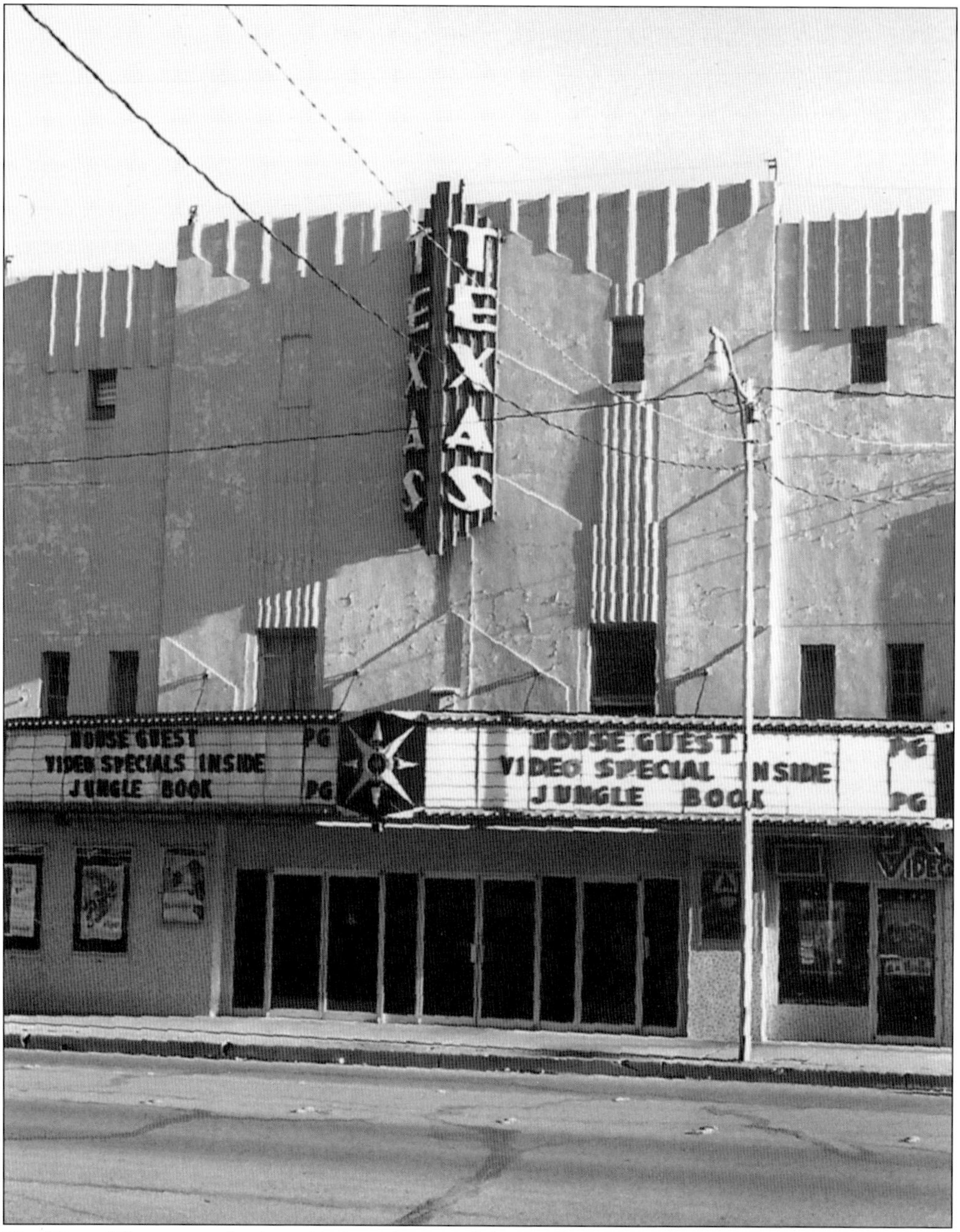

The Texas Theater was built in 1935 on the site of the Archer Building near the corner of Broadway Avenue and Lamar Street. The theater had many managers over its lifetime but was always owned by an out-of-town company until 1998, when Paul W. Hanneman bought it. When the theater opened, it had only one screen and no balcony; the balcony was added as a way to segregate the audience members, with minorities sitting upstairs. The balcony is also where people have sighted the ghost of a boy. Supposedly, when he was about 10 to 13 years old, Oscar, who was often described as a prankster, fell from the balcony during a movie and died. After this incident, the balcony was enclosed, and a second screen was added. Today, the theater is owned by Weston and Vicki Pyburn and offers live music most weekends downstairs and movie screenings upstairs.

Four

Weathering Sweetwater

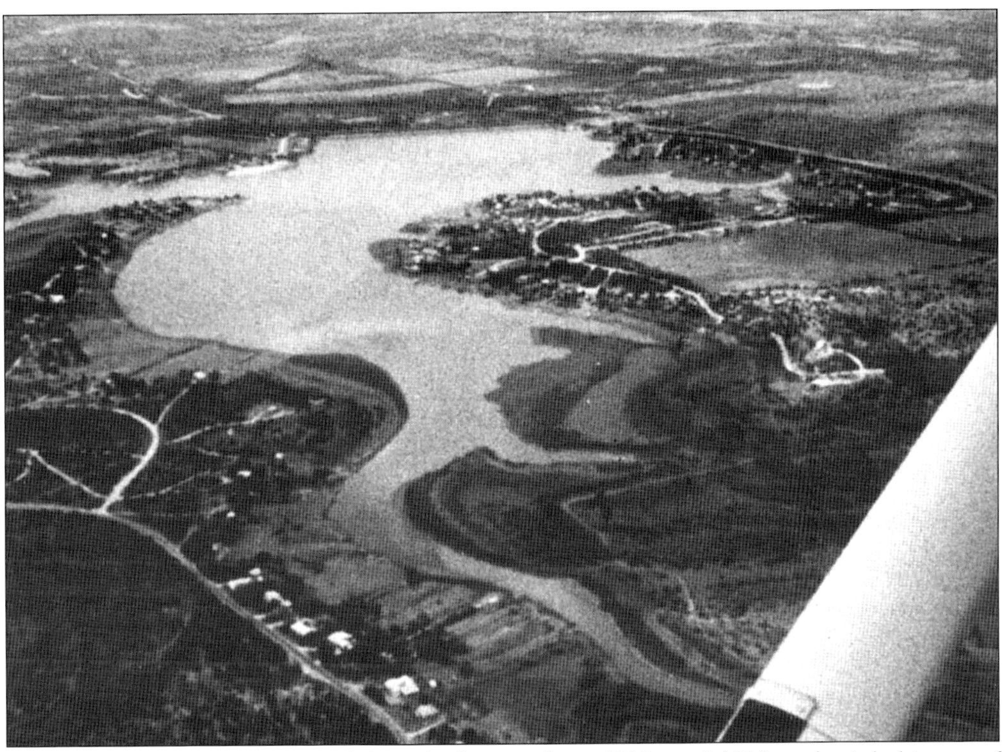

City Lake was built in 1897 and furnished water from 1909 until 1914 to the inhabitants of Sweetwater. In the 1930s, Sweetwater was hit by a terrible drought that worked to dry the lake up. The Civilian Conservation Corps established City Park, now known as Newman Park, at the site of the lake, and some of the buildings they erected still stand.

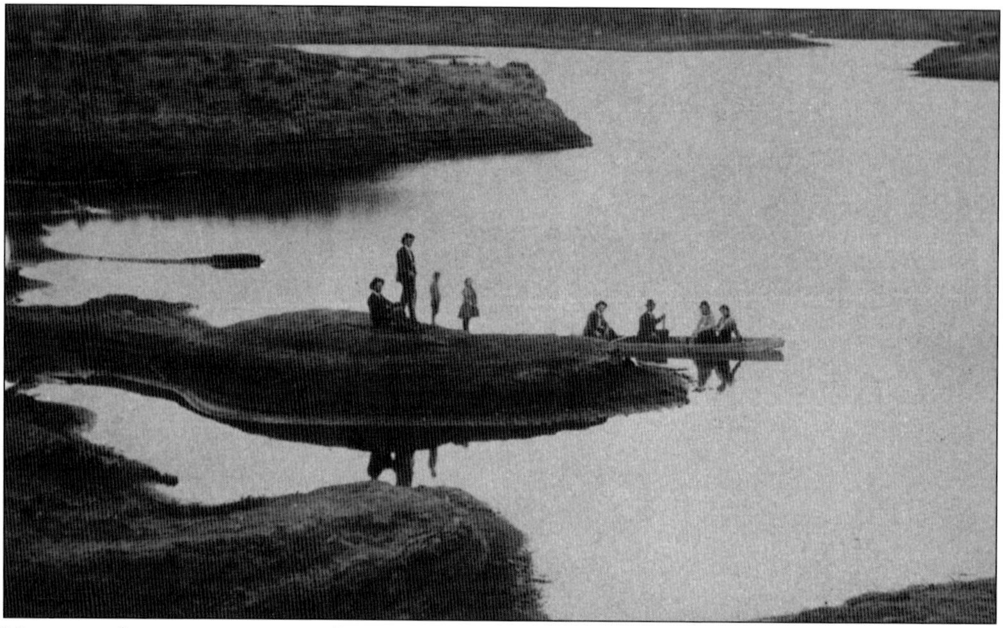

Here, people are enjoying an afternoon at City Lake around 1912; the Sweetwater Municipal Swimming Pool now sits where the lake once sat. When the lake dried up and was replaced by a city park, the Civilian Conservation Corps was put to work in Sweetwater. CCC camps housing 200 men each were put up in every state beginning in 1933. In September 1933, there were 1,468 such camps, and by January 1, 1942, that number was down to just 800.

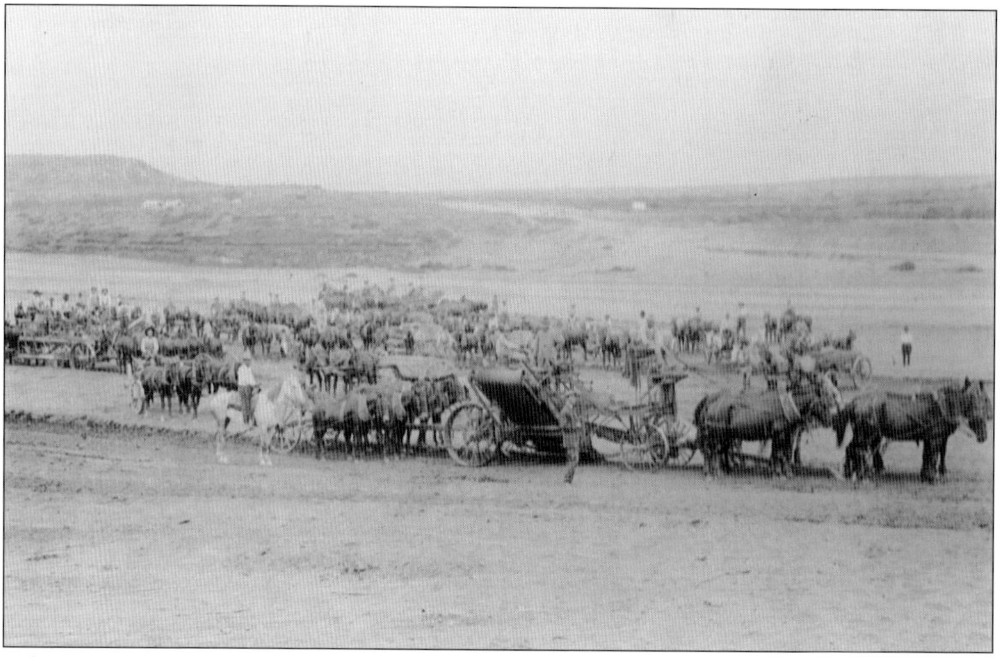

Lake Trammell Dam was completed by Baker Manufacturing Company of Texas in 1915 and is 500 feet long and 61 feet high. Lake Trammell is named after Thomas Trammell and has been used by the city of Sweetwater for municipal, domestic, and recreational purposes. The lake unfortunately has a long history of drownings due to strong undertows.

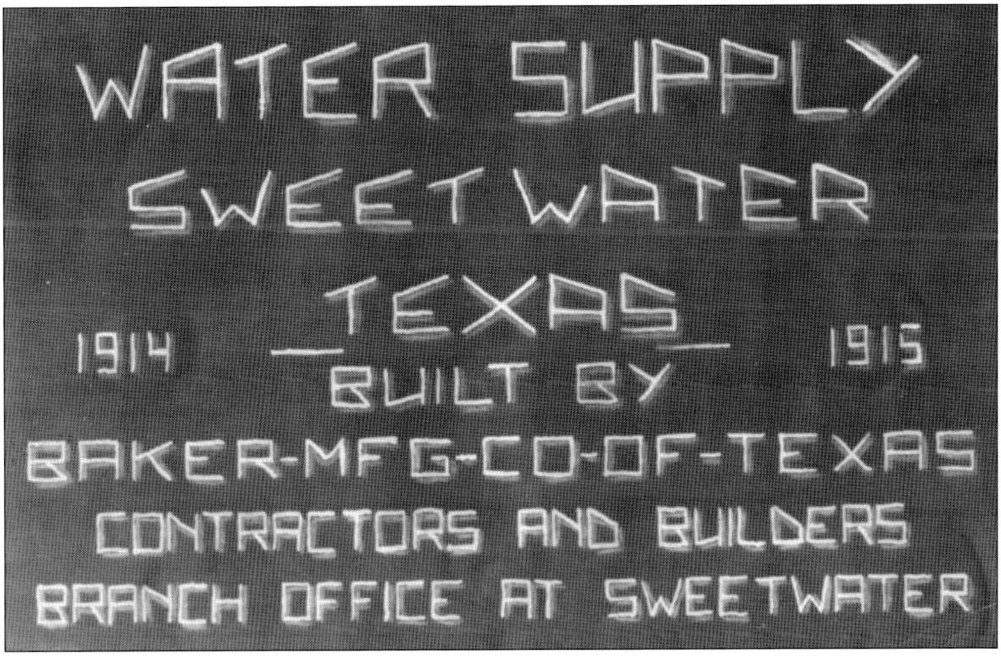

When Lake Trammell was built, the city thought it had solved its water woes, but a drought in 1927 and 1928 left the lake virtually dry, and Sweetwater began using Santa Fe Lake as an emergency source. This prompted the citizens of Sweetwater to look for a new source of water, which they found by damming Bitter Creek and forming Lake Sweetwater.

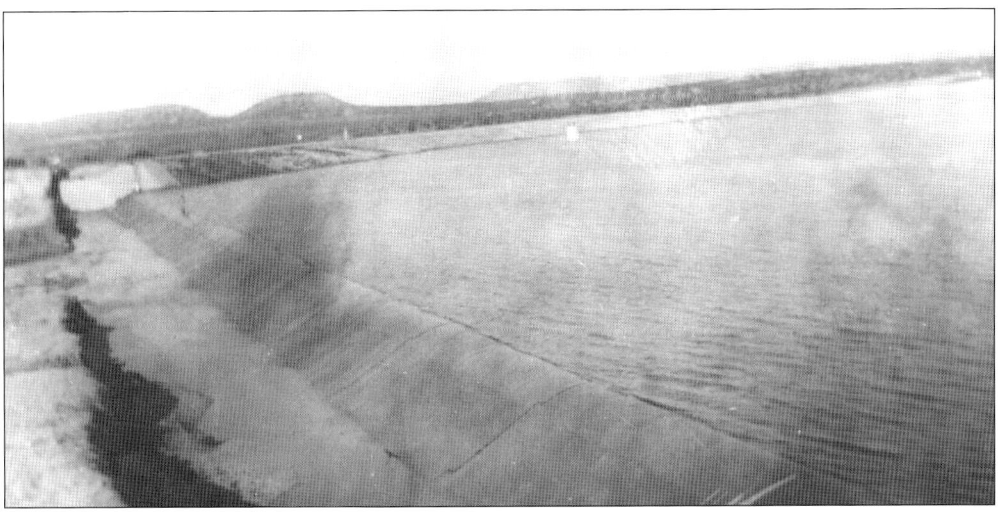

Lake Sweetwater was constructed by damming Bitter Creek in 1929 at a cost of about $450,000; it ran over its spillway for the first time in 1932. In 1934, city officials claimed that the lake, with a 4.5-billion-gallon capacity, could withstand a five-year drought. In 2012, the lake was, for all intents and purposes, empty due to the drought Texas has suffered the last 10 years.

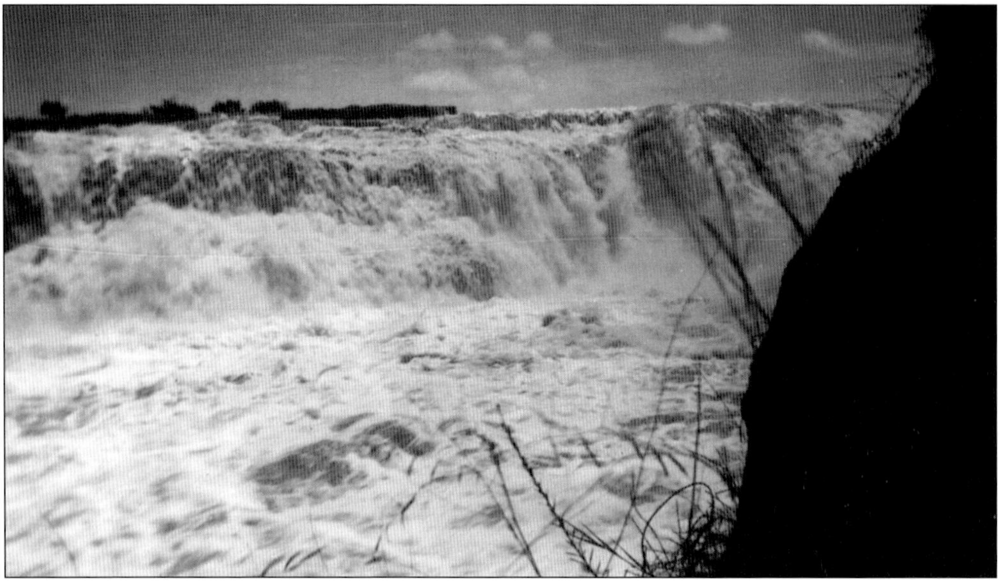

When Lake Sweetwater is at capacity, it has beautiful waterfalls that keep the man-made lake from becoming stagnant. The first drowning occurred on August 20, 1930, when 18-year-old Rudolph Avila, one of the men constructing the dam, was swimming with coworkers.

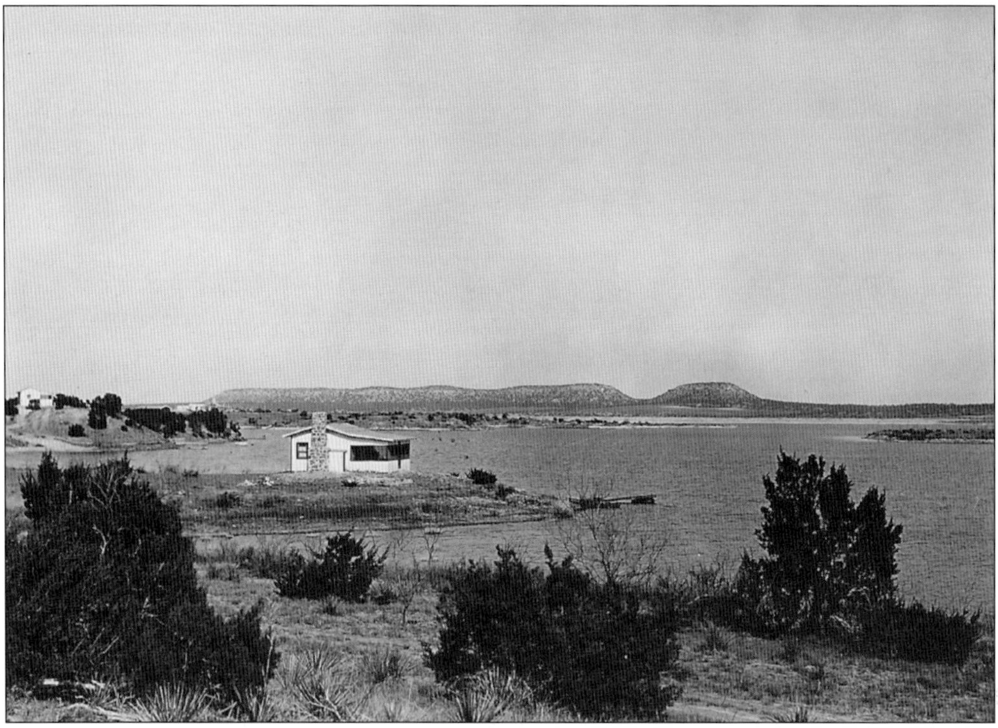

This house on Lake Sweetwater is one of many built by the Works Progress Administration. The Civilian Conservation Corps built other sites around the lake, such as the amphitheater, rock clubhouse, lookout houses, footbridges, boat pier, and golf course. Work on the lake was completed in 1930, but the construction of the adjacent sites took longer, and the formal dedication was not held until June 14, 1934.

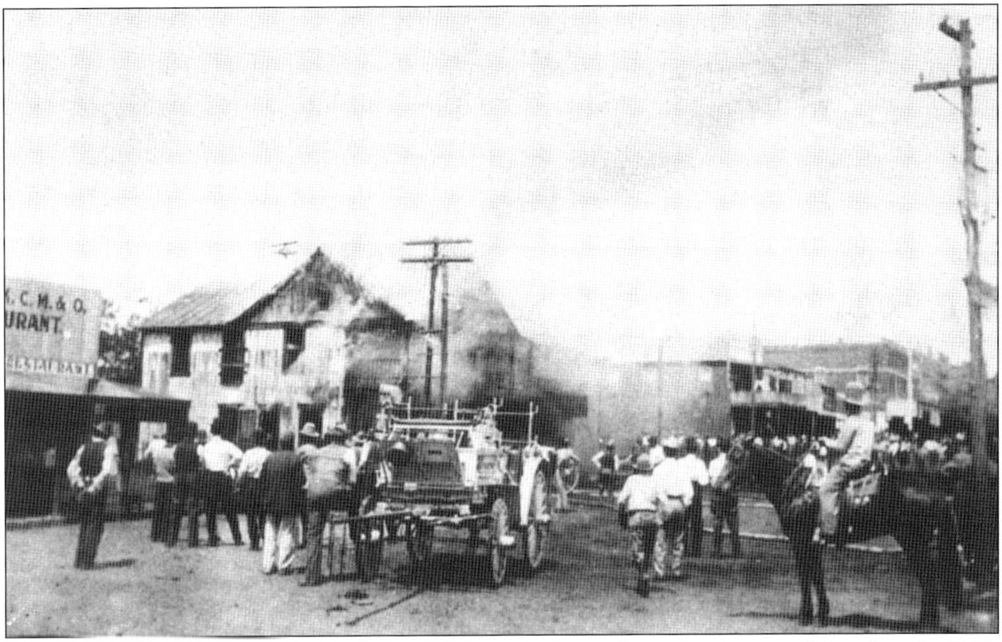

The harsh droughts frequently experienced in West Texas always lead to one thing: fire. In 1909, the Oriental Hotel burned down, as seen here; a horse-drawn wagon was used as the primary firefighting vehicle. The hotel was replaced by the Commercial Hotel and continued as a hotel until the 1960s.

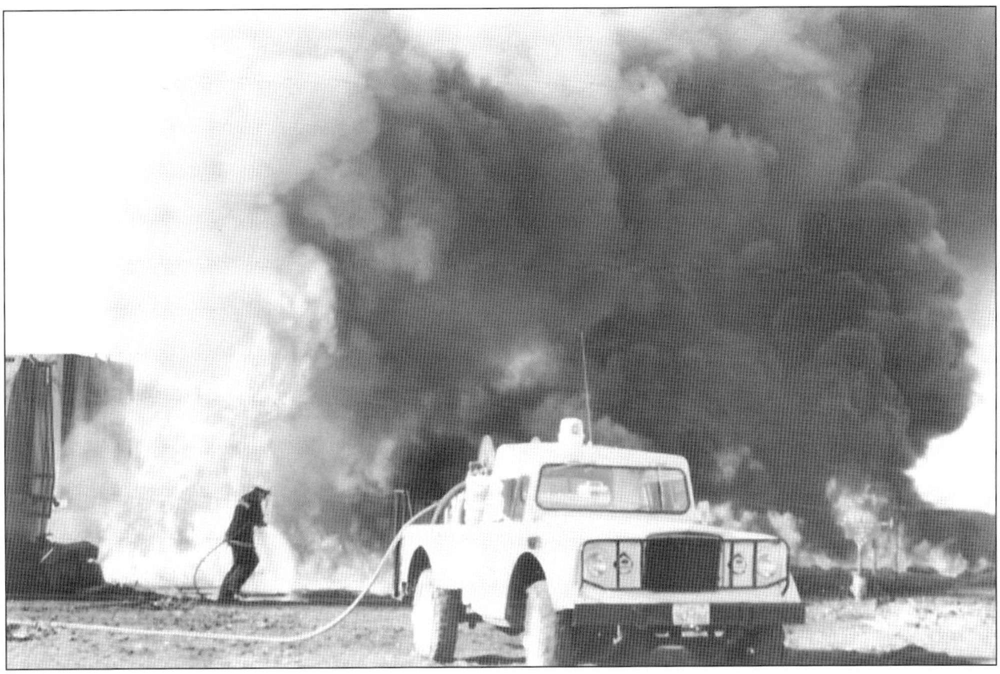

The G.E. Roberts Oil Company fire occurred on June 20, 1953, and is sometimes referred to as the Sheridan Oil Company fire. The fire resulted in the deaths of Virgie Lee Westmoreland (age 38) and Bertha E. McCauley (age 58) when gas flowing under their house ignited from the nearby fire. Judge Jack Aycock took this photograph.

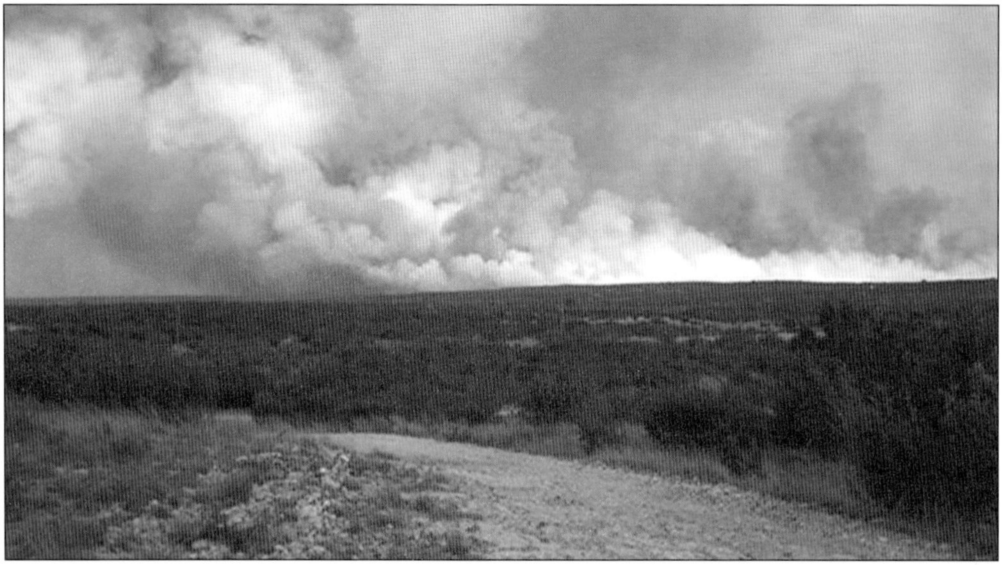

Wildfires are always a concern in the heat of a West Texas summer. This fire, the White Hat fire, broke out in the summer of 2011 and consumed 72,473 acres and 35 homes. Countless livestock were lost when, much like the blizzards of 1885 where 90 percent of sheep and almost half the cattle died, they ran up against fences and became trapped.

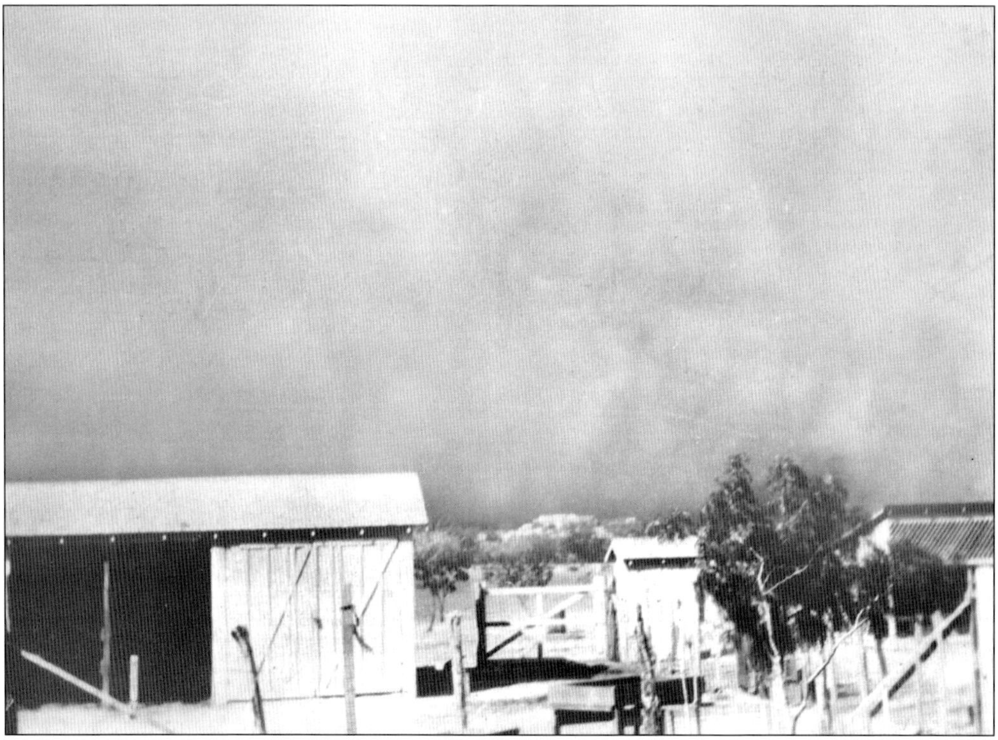

Add drought to the West Texas wind, and a dust storm is inevitable. Storms like this one in 1946 look like a "black wall that reaches from earth to clouds and as far as [one] can see north or south," according to Rayburn Blair. These dust storms can take the paint off buildings and cars and always leave a fine red dust over every person, place, and thing in their path.

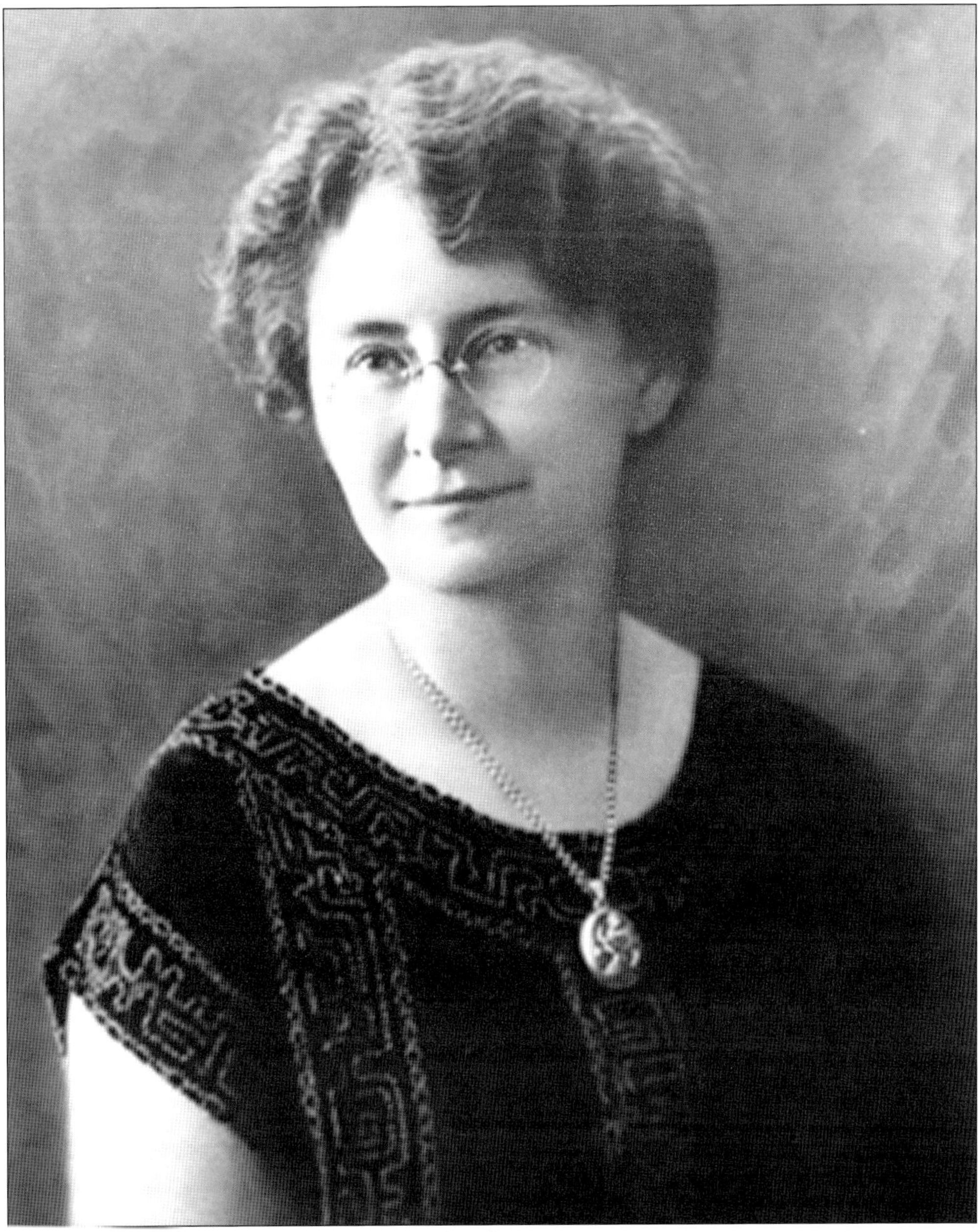

The incessant West Texas winds combined with seemingly endless droughts can drive a person crazy, or at least, that is the plot of the novel *The Wind* by Dorothy Scarborough. Dorothy lived in Sweetwater in the mid-1880s because the dry climate was thought to be good for her mother's health; the family soon moved to Waco so that the children could attend Baylor, and Dorothy eventually found her way to New York. Before writing *The Wind* in 1925, Scarborough was already an accomplished teacher and novelist, but this book, in which the heroine is driven to murder and insanity by the incessant wind, catapulted Dorothy's name to the top of the literate set. Originally published anonymously, whether as a publicity stunt or because of a feared backlash from Texas readers, *The Wind* caused quite a stir that ended with Scarborough traveling to Sweetwater and absolving the town the wind had condemned.

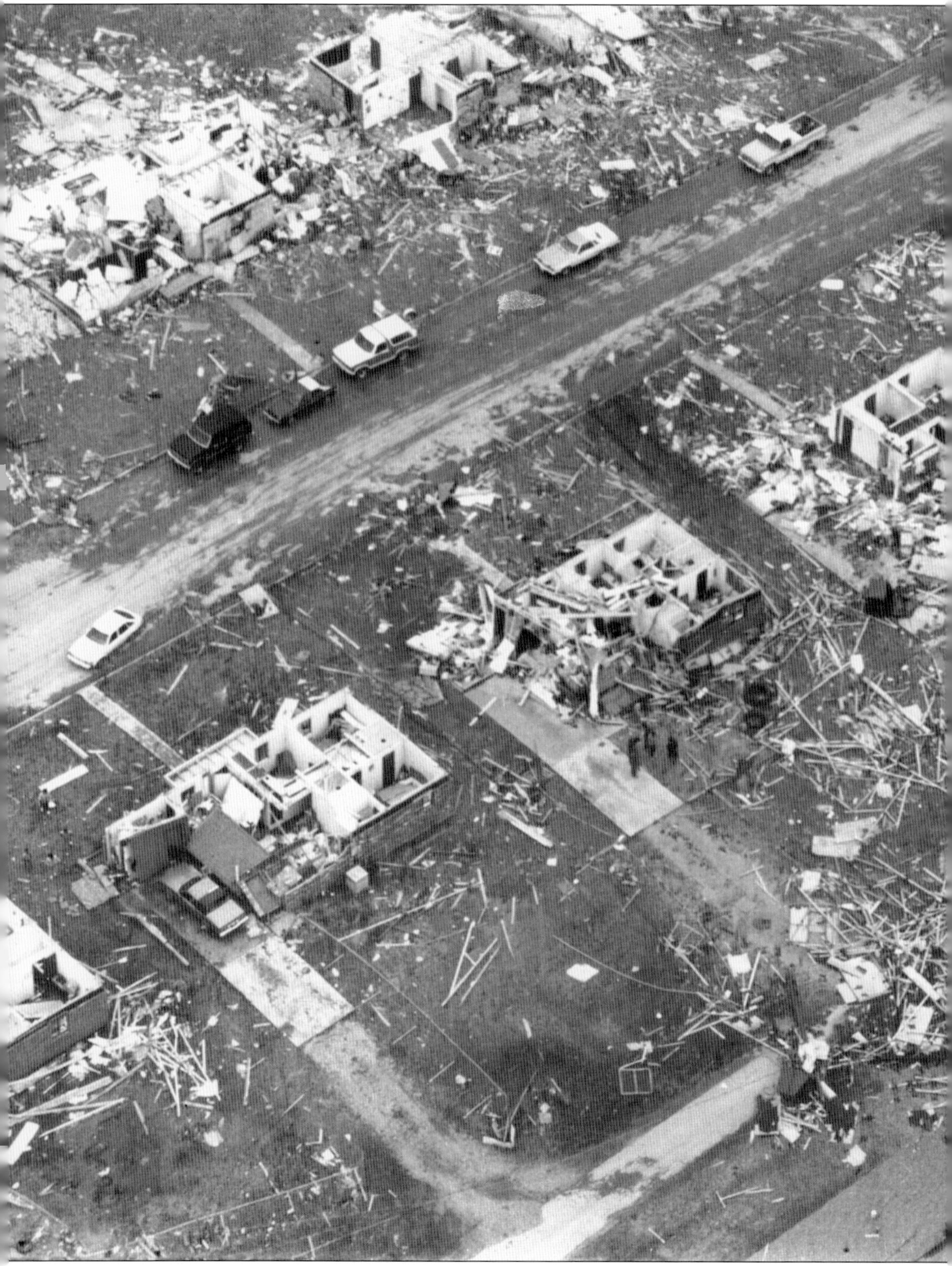

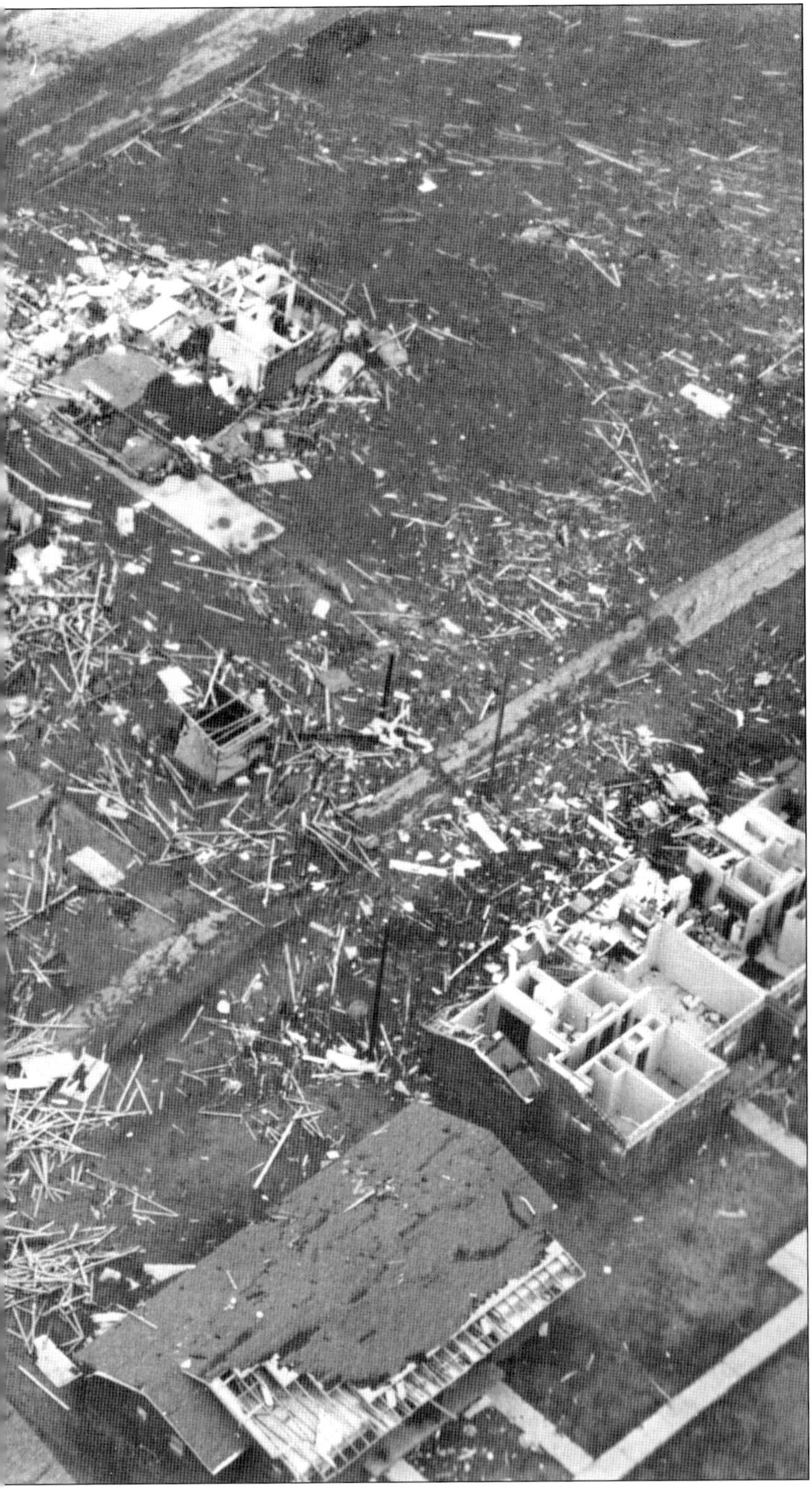

On April 19, 1986, at 7:15 a.m., two tornadoes hit the southeast side of Sweetwater with almost no warning. The day's forecast had called for a 40-percent chance of thunderstorms with no warning of severe weather. Approximately 600 homes were destroyed, and $15 million in damages were sustained. There was one fatality, and one woman was left paralyzed when the winds picked her up from her home and dropped her and her child several blocks away. Parts of the city were without electricity for several days, including the water filtration plant, which prompted residents to boil all water before use. A curfew was imposed after the disaster, but looting was not a problem, as most residents banded together to help each other rebuild.

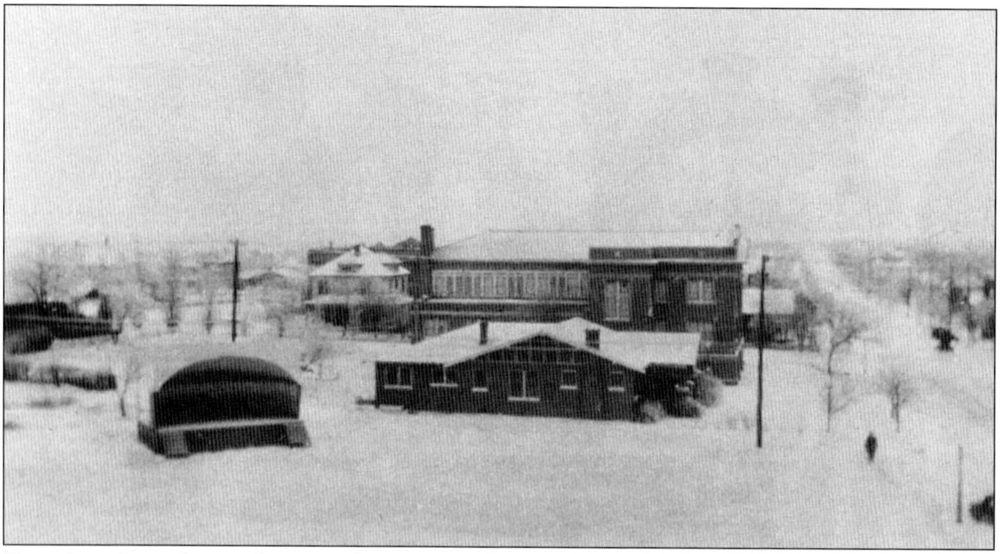

Snow has always been a factor in Sweetwater's history, beginning with the "die-out" in the mid-1880s in which 90 percent of all sheep and almost half of all cattle were killed. Before that year, animals were allowed to roam more freely, and when the snows hit, mostly in the form of blizzards, the animals would travel as far as 100 miles away. To prevent this, fences were built, and that same year, piles of bodies could be found along fence lines. On Easter weekend in 1996, a blizzard dropped 18 inches of snow within just a few hours, leaving hundreds of Interstate 20 travelers stranded and citizens stuck working double and triple shifts to accommodate unexpected visitors. These photographs are from snows in the 1950s (above) and 1980s (below).

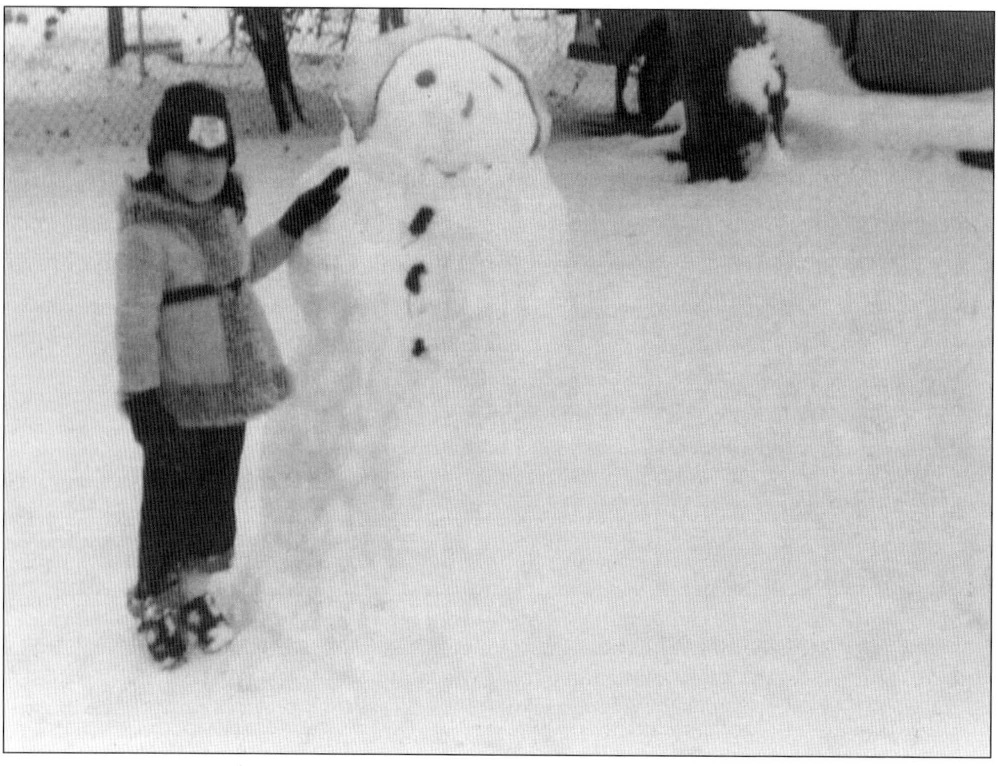

Five

Growing Sweetwater

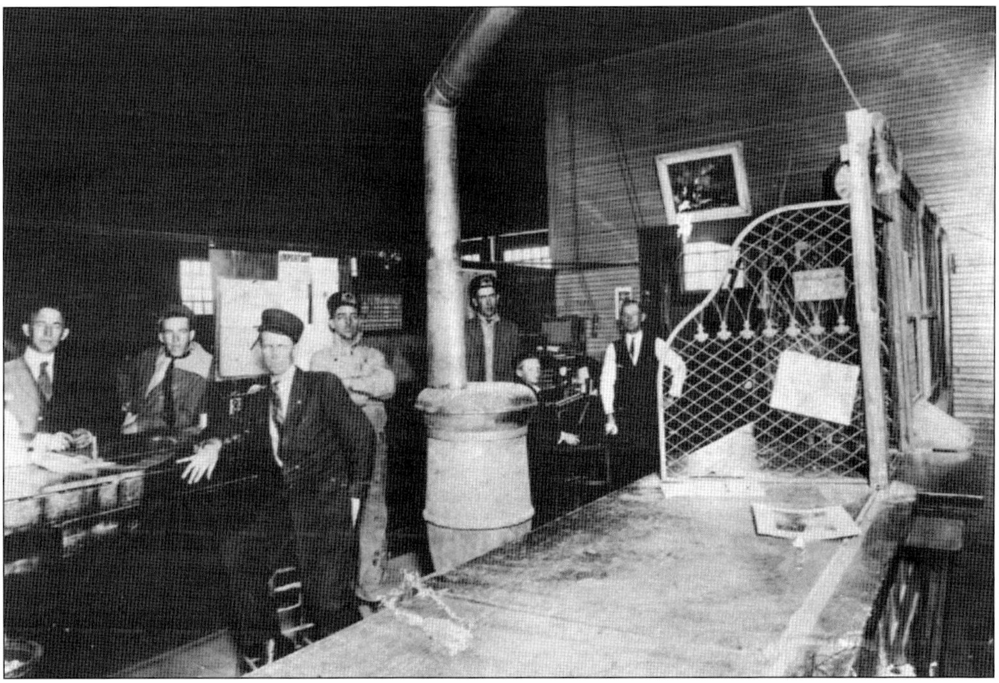

The inside of the Texas & Pacific Railway depot is seen around 1883. It was the first train depot in Sweetwater. The first Texas & Pacific Railway car moved into Sweetwater on March 12, 1881, marking the town's long history as a railroad town. Much in the same way that catering to buffalo hunters spurred the creation of Sweetwater, the railroads spurred its development. Hotels and saloons pandering to railway workers popped up before any other businesses.

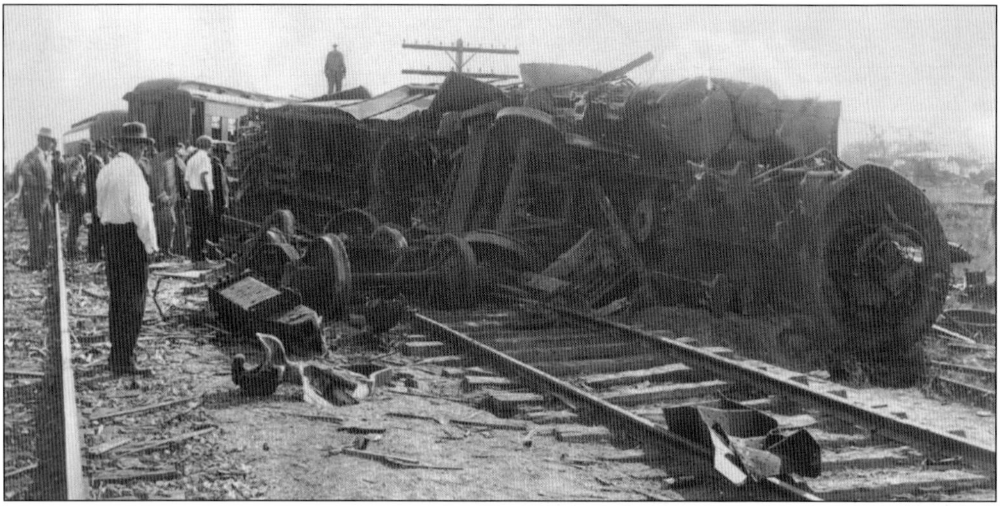

Common sights early on in the development of the railroad were train wrecks, such as this 1909 one. Passengers tell tales of new tracks vibrating so badly that every passenger was required to secure any luggage before reaching new portions of track. This wreck occurred due to a horse getting his hoof caught in a culvert just ahead of the train, which could not stop. The train was known as the "Sunshine Special," and two people were killed, including engineer Mac Weisen and an unidentified fireman. The engine was rebuilt and put back in service during World War II.

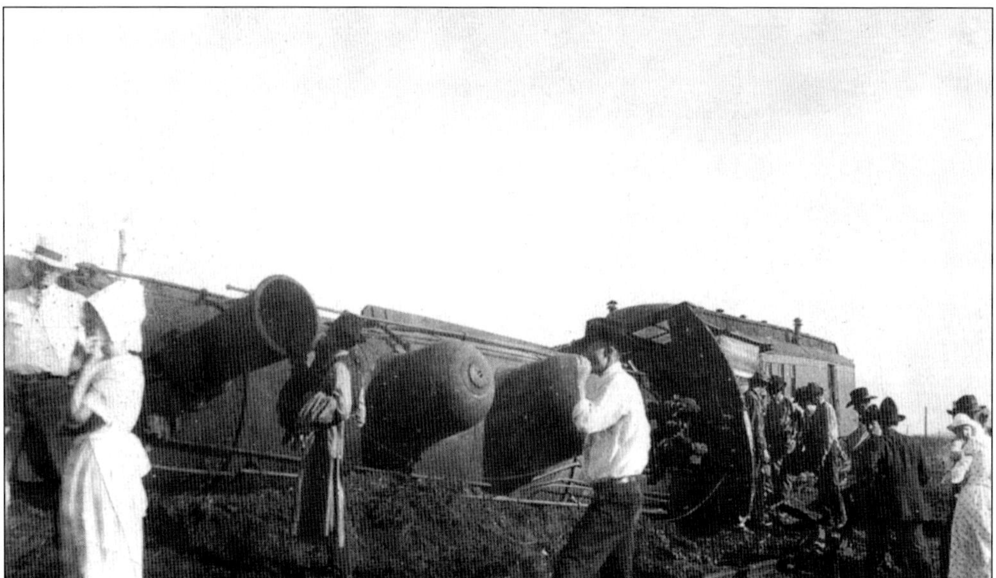

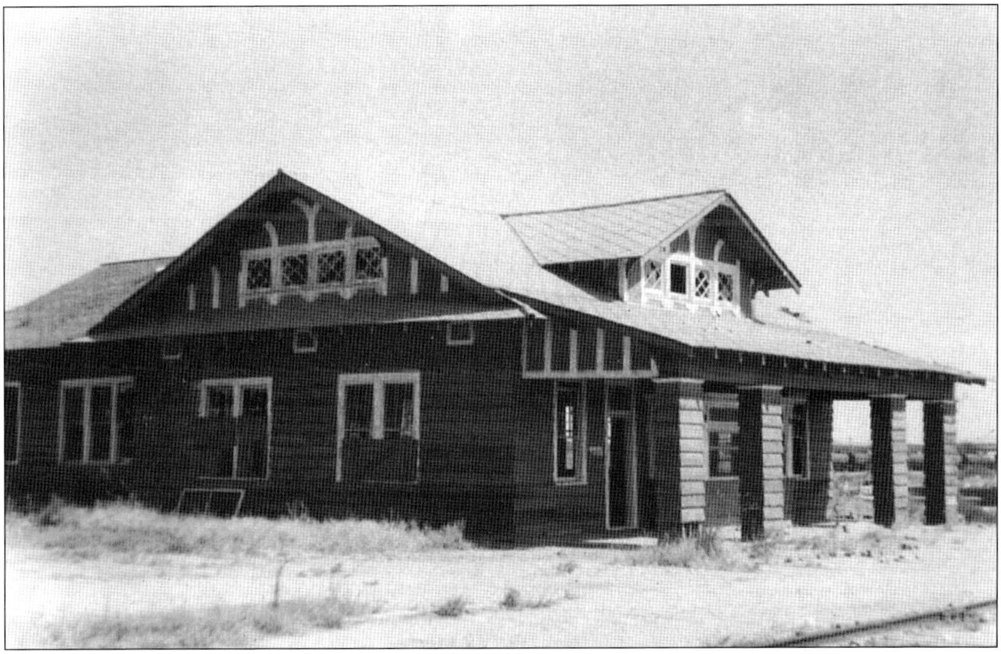

The Harvey House located on the Santa Fe Railroad just north of Seventeenth Street served as the rooming house for Santa Fe employees as well as for the passengers on their trains. On weekends, when a passenger train brought new people to town, citizens of Sweetwater would don their finest and head to the Harvey House for drinking, dancing, and all-around merriment.

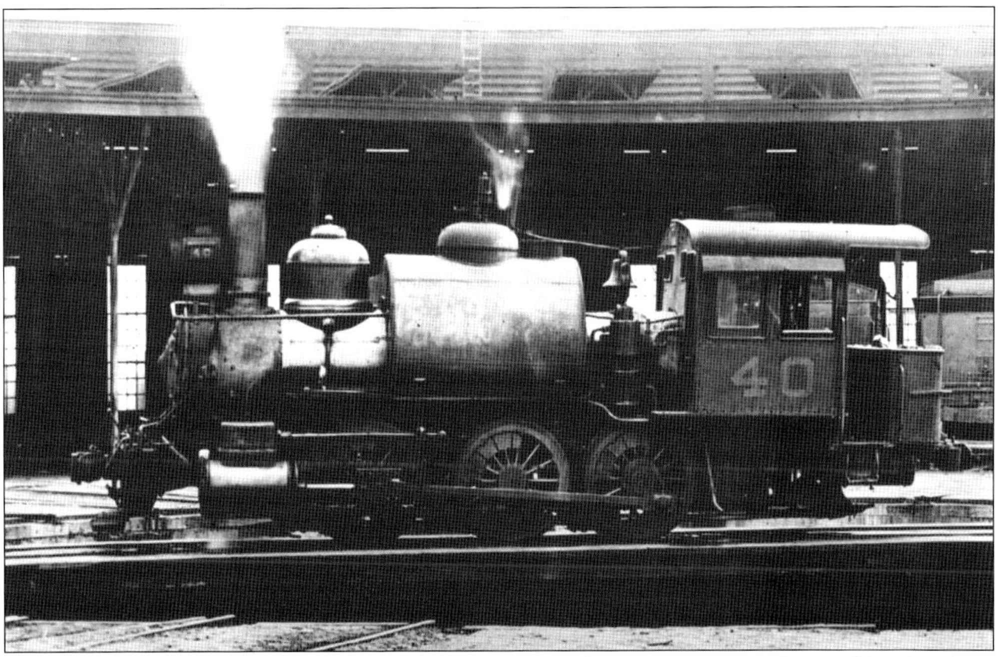

Here is a typical steam engine, built in 1876 by Pittsburgh Locomotive Works, used by the Texas & Pacific Railway in its switching service. Steam Engine No. 40 weighed 68,000 pounds and had a tractive power of 11,500 pounds with a steam pressure of 120 pounds. Steam engines were used until the mid-1950s.

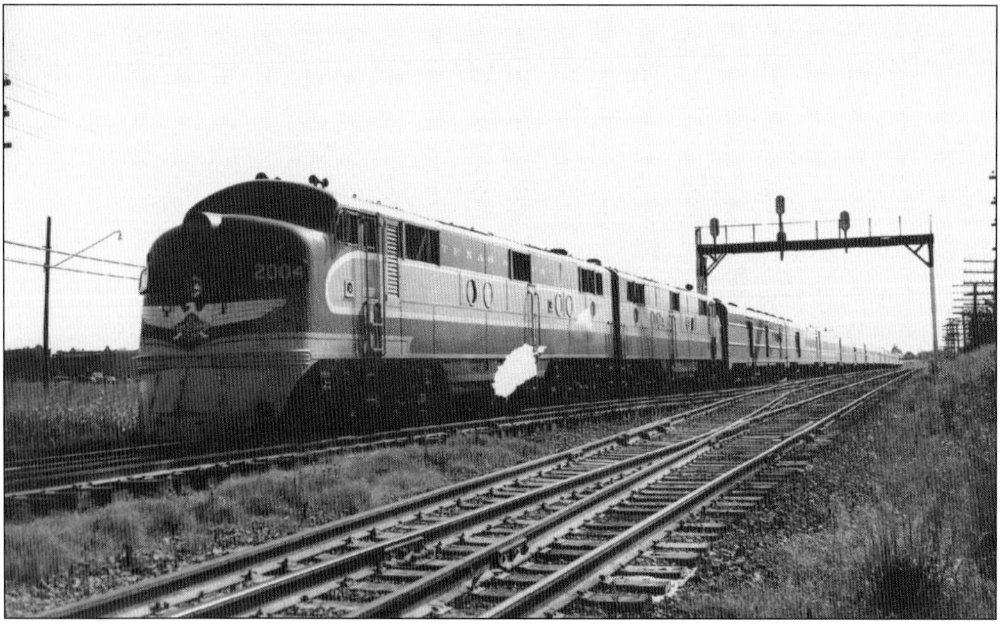

Here is Texas & Pacific Railway's Texas Eagle passenger train, which operated between St. Louis, Missouri, and El Paso, Texas, with connections to the east and west. Passenger trains brought various celebrity acts to the small town of Sweetwater, including Elvis Presley twice. Any acts that played in Dallas and El Paso played in Sweetwater, as it was one of the main passenger train stops.

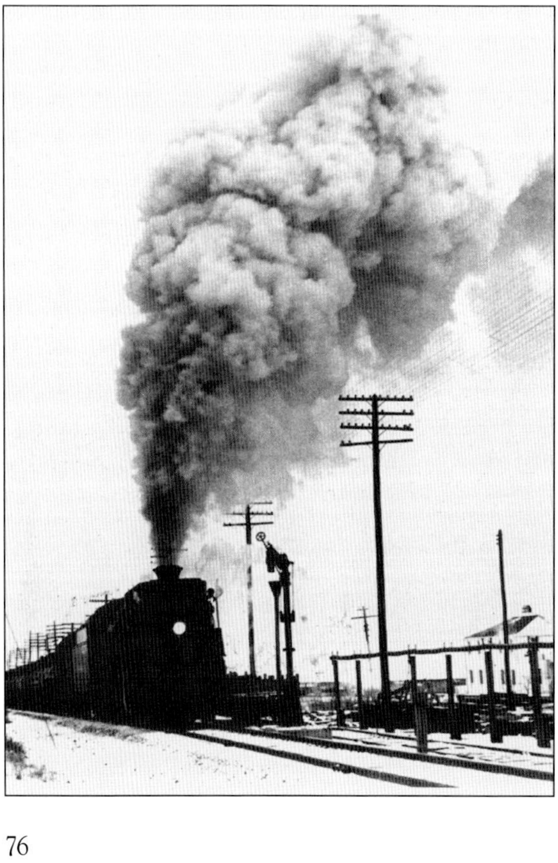

Here is the last steam engine coming through Sweetwater in 1955. Beginning in the early 1900s, steam engines were being phased out and replaced with electric and diesel engines due to the decreased costs of maintenance and improved locomotive ability of the latter. World War II slowed the replacement of steam engines, but by the 1950s, dieselization had picked up steam, and the year 1960 is typically considered the last year of steam engine use.

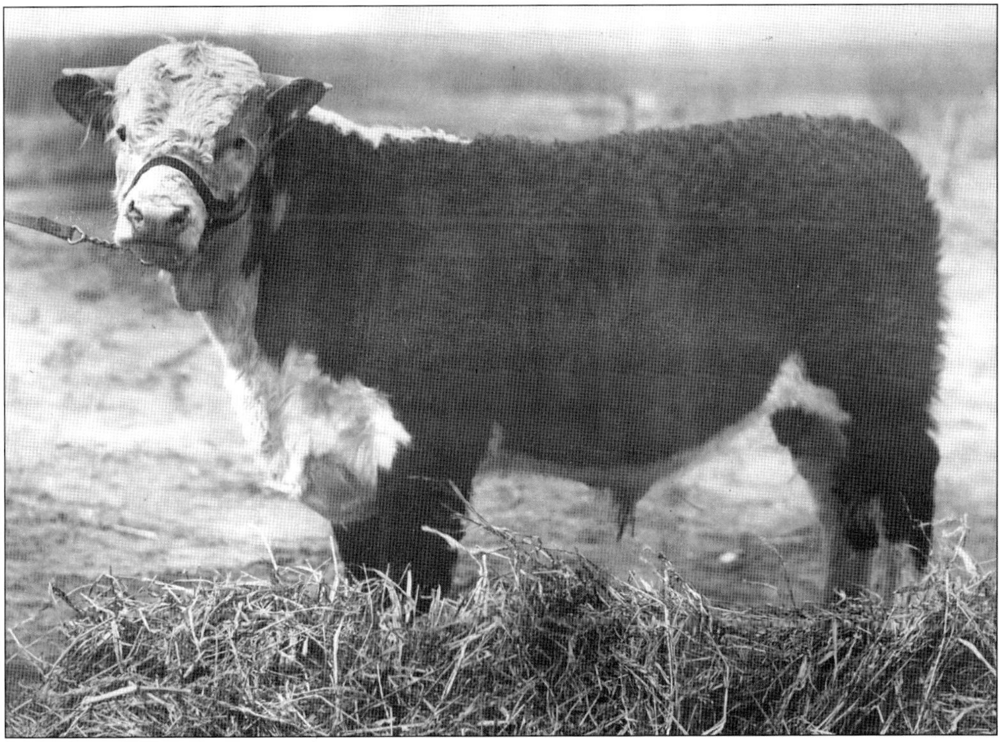

The Hereford first arrived in Texas from western England by way of Kentucky in about 1876. The Hereford quickly replaced the Longhorn as the major range breed, being better suited to open range than their predecessors. Charles Goodnight was instrumental in introducing the Hereford into the Panhandle and West Texas in about 1883, and it continues to be one of the cattle of choice for this area of Texas.

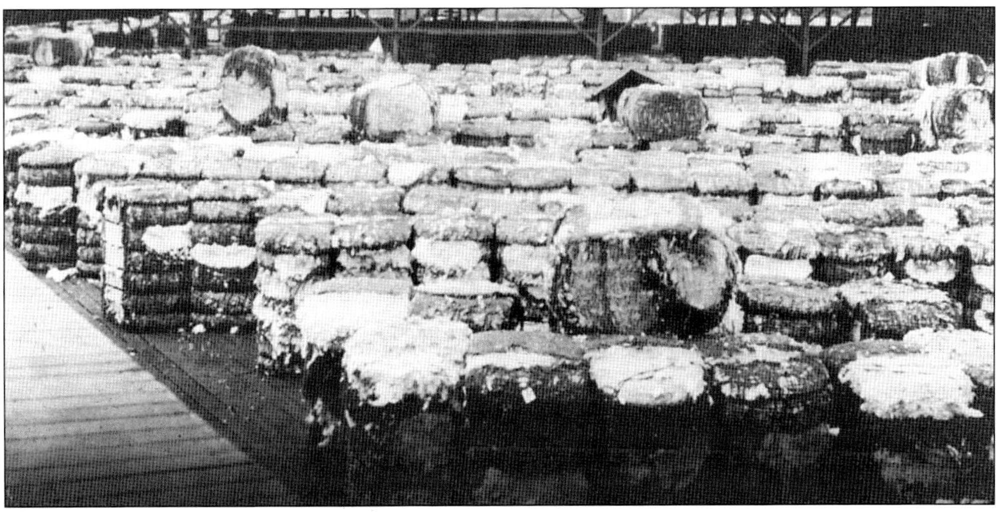

First introduced by Spanish missionaries in the early 1700s, cotton cultivation was taken over by Anglo-American colonists in the mid-1800s. The introduction of the barbed-wire fence increased production of cotton by keeping free-range cattle off the cotton fields. The boll weevil ravaged the cotton industry in the 1890s, but new technologies helped eradicate the pest and cotton remains one of Texas's greatest exports.

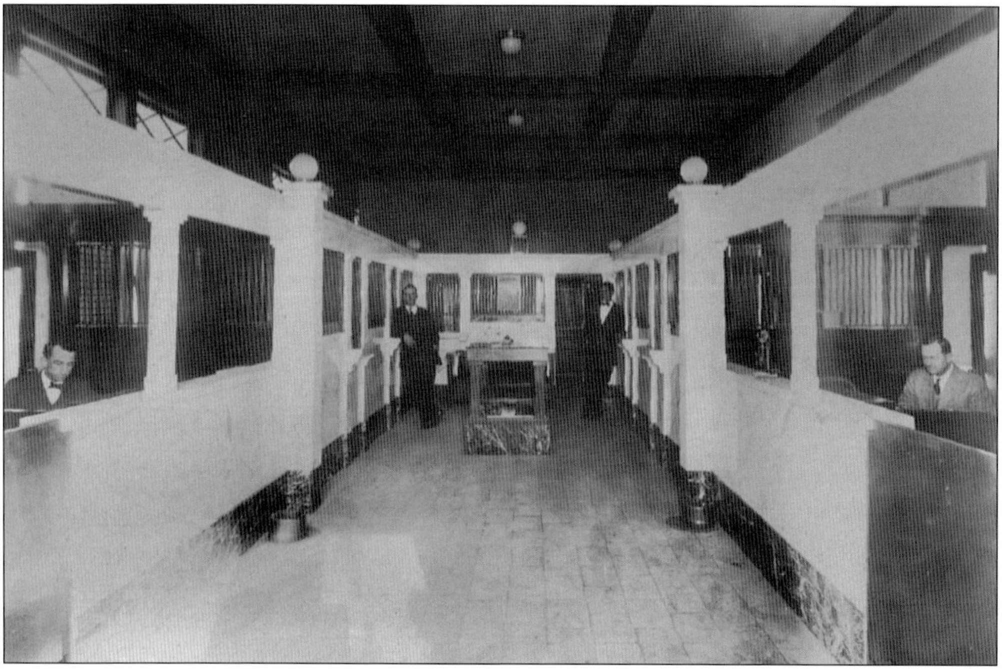

Here is a c. 1917 interior view of the Texas Bank and Trust Company, owned by Thomas Trammell. Texas Bank and Trust was created after the murder of two saloon owners in 1883 whose saloon had been serving as a bank. N.I. Dulaney was also injured during the raid on the saloon.

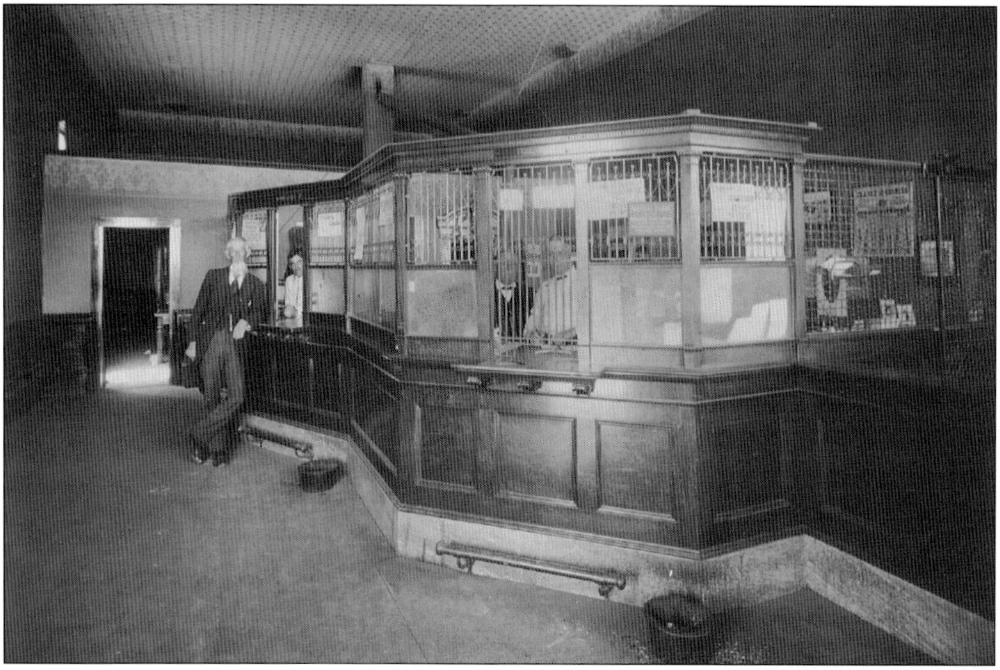

This photograph of First National Bank was taken around 1902 and shows R.H. Fitzgerald, president of the bank at this time, and his son, Gerald, at the front window. At the rear window is Mr. Buchanan; the man standing outside the window is unidentified. First National Bank was the second bank in Sweetwater and was located on the west side of the square.

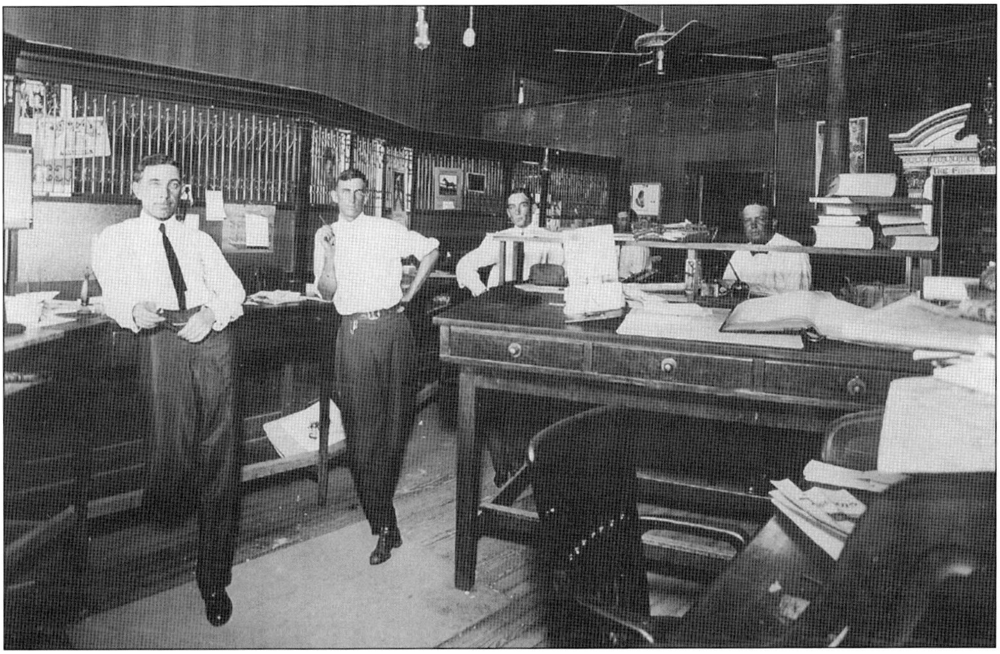

Here is a view of the back part of First National Bank, as it appeared in September 1914. On the far left is R.K. McAdams, president; at the desk facing the camera is Mike Fitzgerald, bookkeeper; the rest of the men are unidentified. At this time, First National Bank was located approximately where present-day Beall Abstract and Title Company is found.

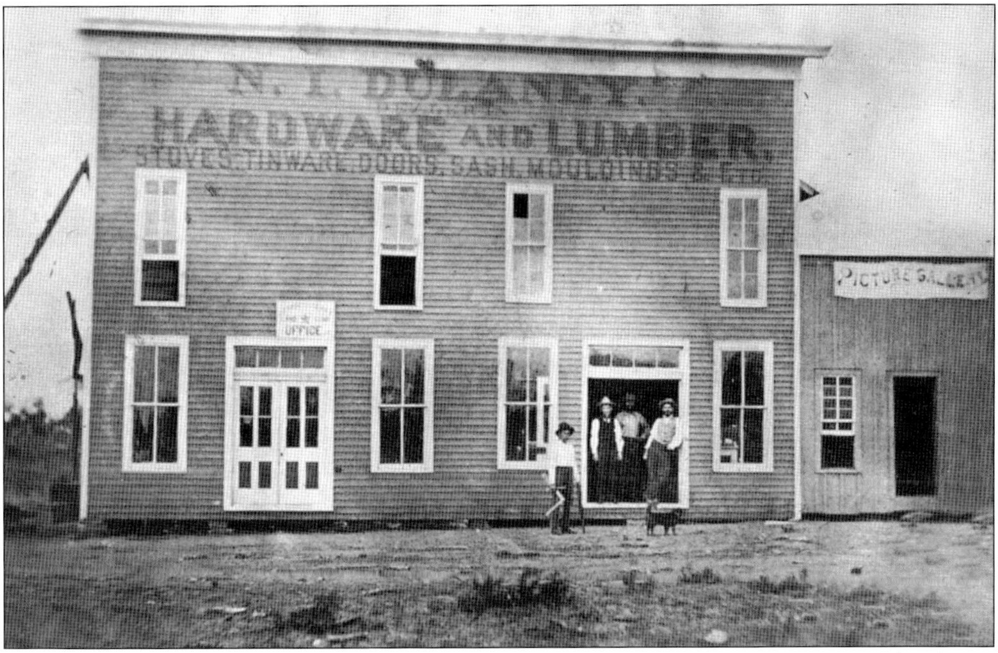

This store of N.I. Dulaney and his brother Jefferson Davis Dulaney was the first to sell lumber in Sweetwater and was built of wood on the site of the old Starr saloon, which was the first house of business built in town. Starr saloon stood just south of the Commercial Hotel. Note the Picture Gallery to the right.

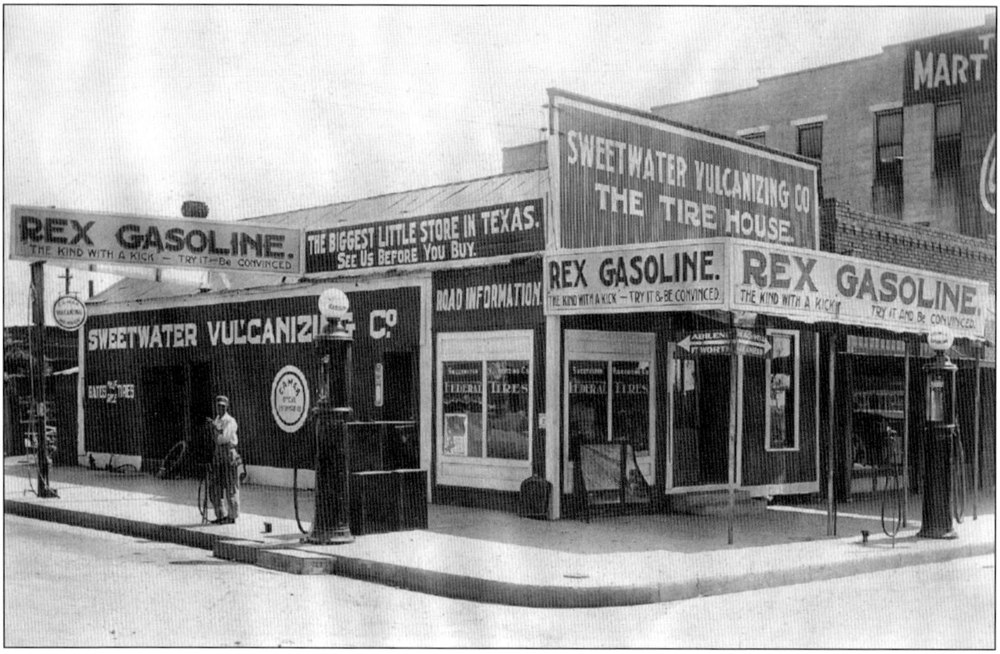

The first filling station in Sweetwater was located where the Woolworth Building once stood at the corner of Locust Street and Broadway Avenue. It was owned by Guy Morris and carried Rex Gasoline, which was manufactured in Sweetwater. Morris was instrumental in keeping the US Gypsum plant in town by buying water from the city and selling it to the plant.

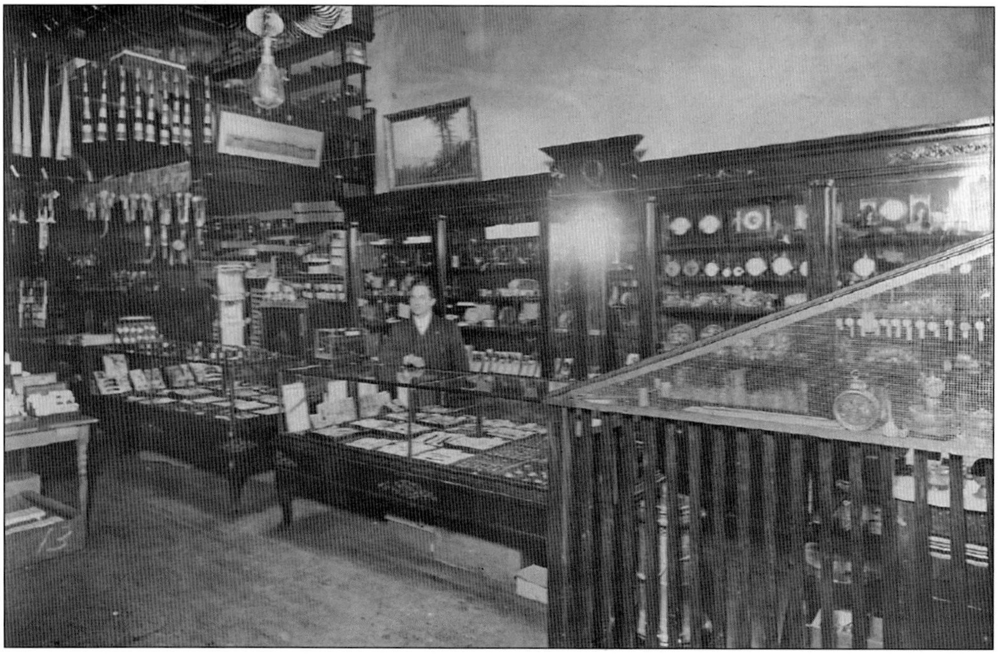

The jewelry store of P.T. Quast was located on Oak Street in downtown Sweetwater. This store also had an optometrist working in the back of the building. At this time, many jewelers worked as optometrists until 1921, when Texas legally recognized optometry as a medical profession and placed more strict regulations on the practice.

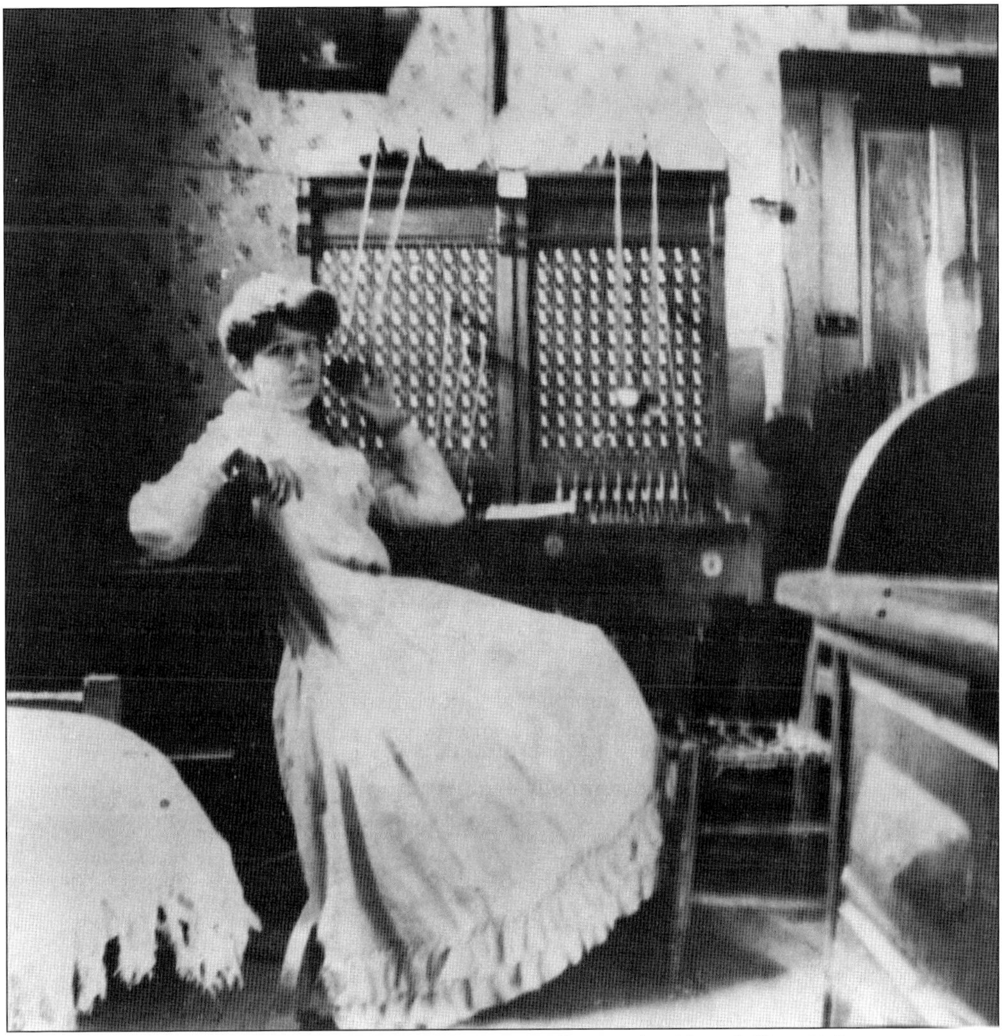

The first telephone exchange in Sweetwater is pictured around 1897 with Kate Eidson as operator. Before the instantaneous exchange of information via today's cell phones, people were required to call an operator to connect their phone calls to their desired parties. A switchboard similar to the one pictured is located at the Pioneer Museum.

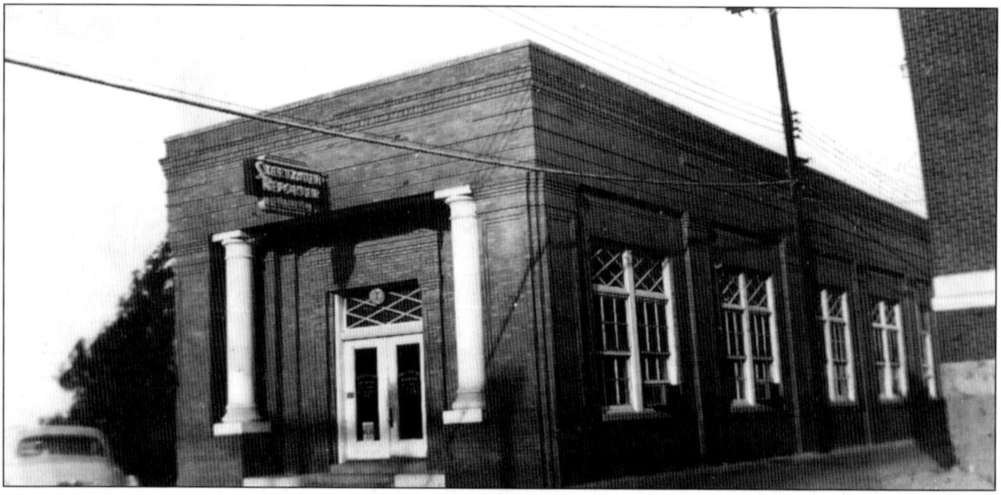

The *Sweetwater Reporter* was established in 1881. It is shown here on January 20, 1951, on the same site as the present-day office. The first newspaper was called the *Sweetwater Advance* with A.J. Wilson as editor. In 1882, R.A. Musgrove bought that paper and changed the name to *Nolan County Record*. It began being called *Sweetwater Reporter* in 1911; today, Tatiana Rodriguez is editor.

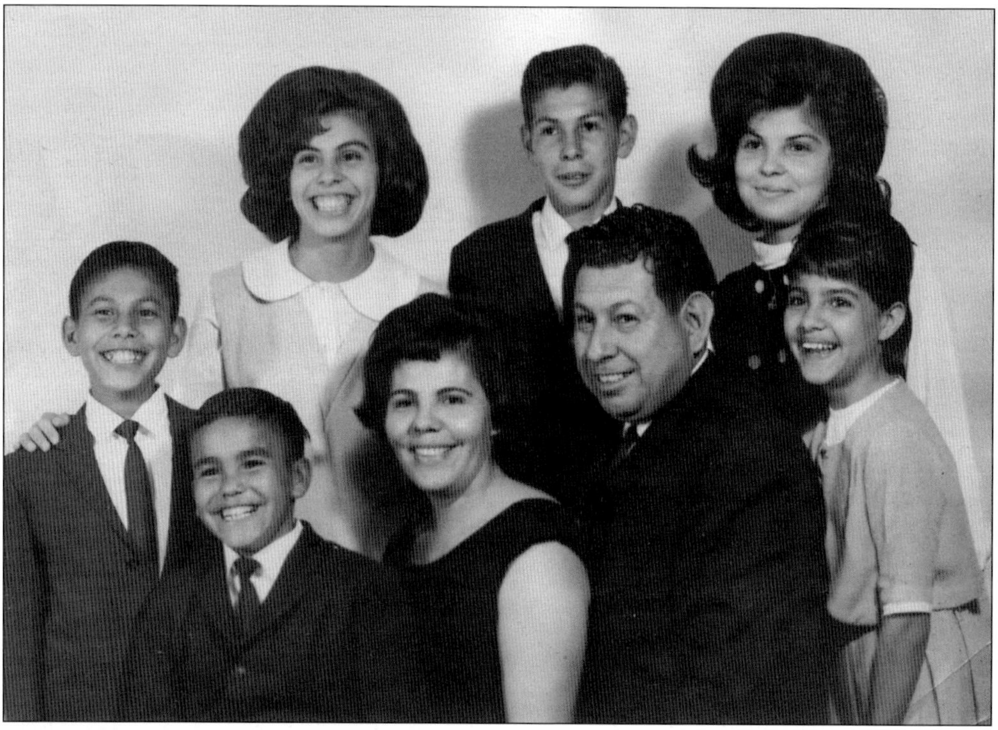

In 1961, Nolan County was considered a wholly dry county, meaning no alcohol could be legally sold. Thankfully, Ruben Palma Sr. and several others stepped in to help as bootleggers, and according to his wife, Nicolasa Palma, "everyone in town knocked on [their] door." Pictured around 1961, the Palma family included, from left to right (first row) Arnold Palma, Nicolasa Palma, Ruben Palma Sr., and Ermelinda Palma Hernandez; (second row) Tony Palma Sr., Odelia Palma, Ruben Palma Jr., and Ofelia Palma Sandoval.

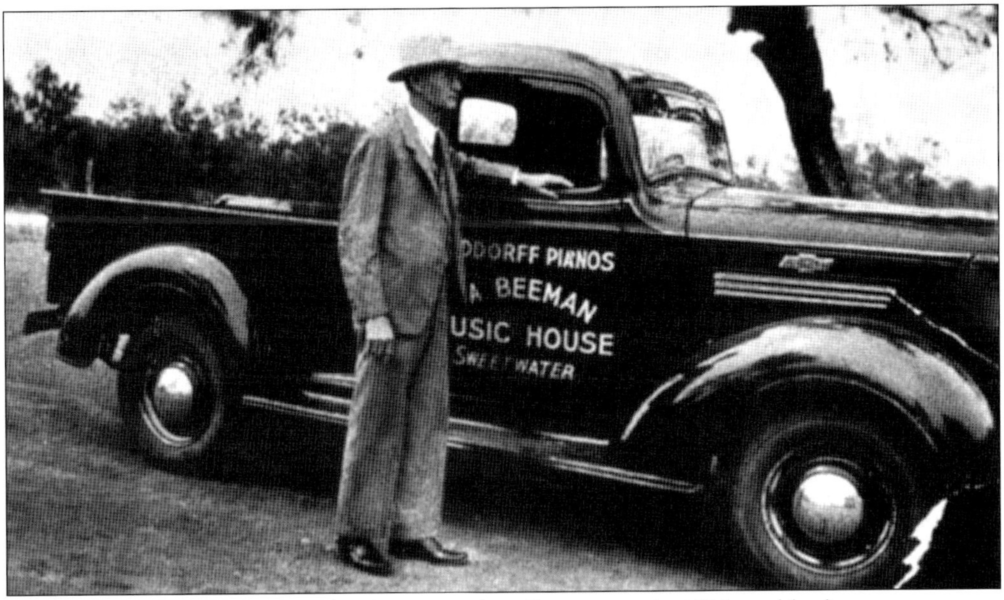

G.A. Beeman and his wife, Lula Mae, moved to Sweetwater in 1924, and he became manager of the George Allen Music Store on the north side of the square. In 1925, G.A. Beeman traded a farm in New Mexico to George Allen, and the store became the G.A. Beeman Music Store. Today, one can find music supplies at Michael's Music on Lamar Street.

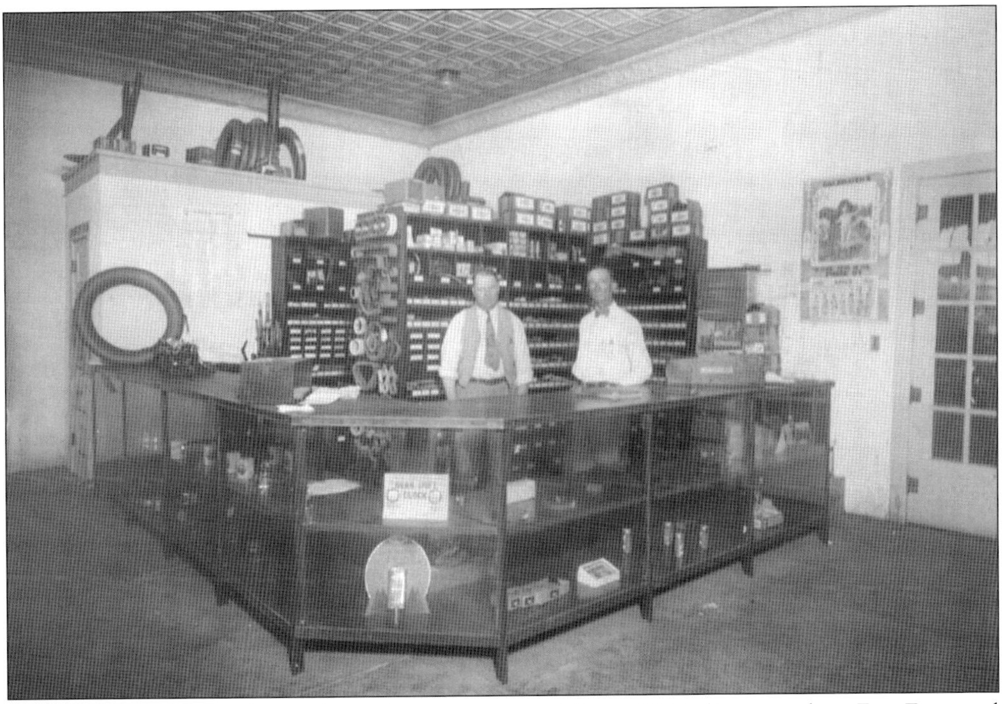

Steakley-Carter Chevrolet was located on the corner of Elm and Third Streets where First Financial Bank now sits. The Steakley family continued in the Chevrolet business for many years with Dan L. Steakley owning dealerships in Knox City and Temple, Texas.

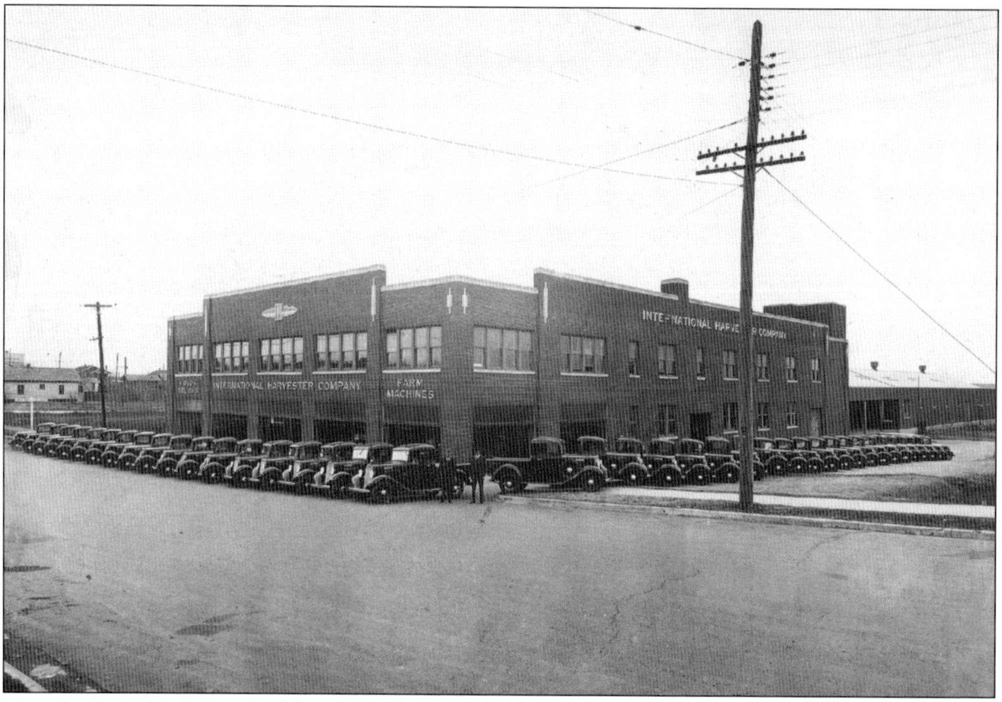

This was the distribution center for the International Harvester company, which served 58 Texas counties, half of New Mexico, and the state of Chihuahua, Mexico, and operated in Sweetwater from the 1920s to the 1950s. International Harvester is now part of Navistar International; the old building still stands on Fourth Street.

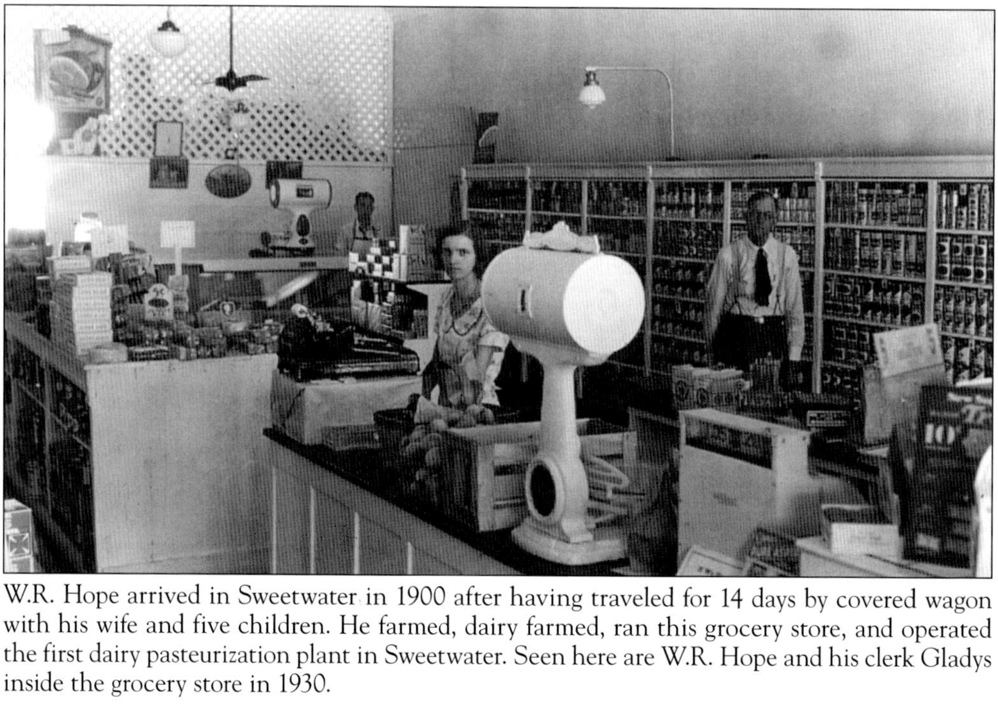

W.R. Hope arrived in Sweetwater in 1900 after having traveled for 14 days by covered wagon with his wife and five children. He farmed, dairy farmed, ran this grocery store, and operated the first dairy pasteurization plant in Sweetwater. Seen here are W.R. Hope and his clerk Gladys inside the grocery store in 1930.

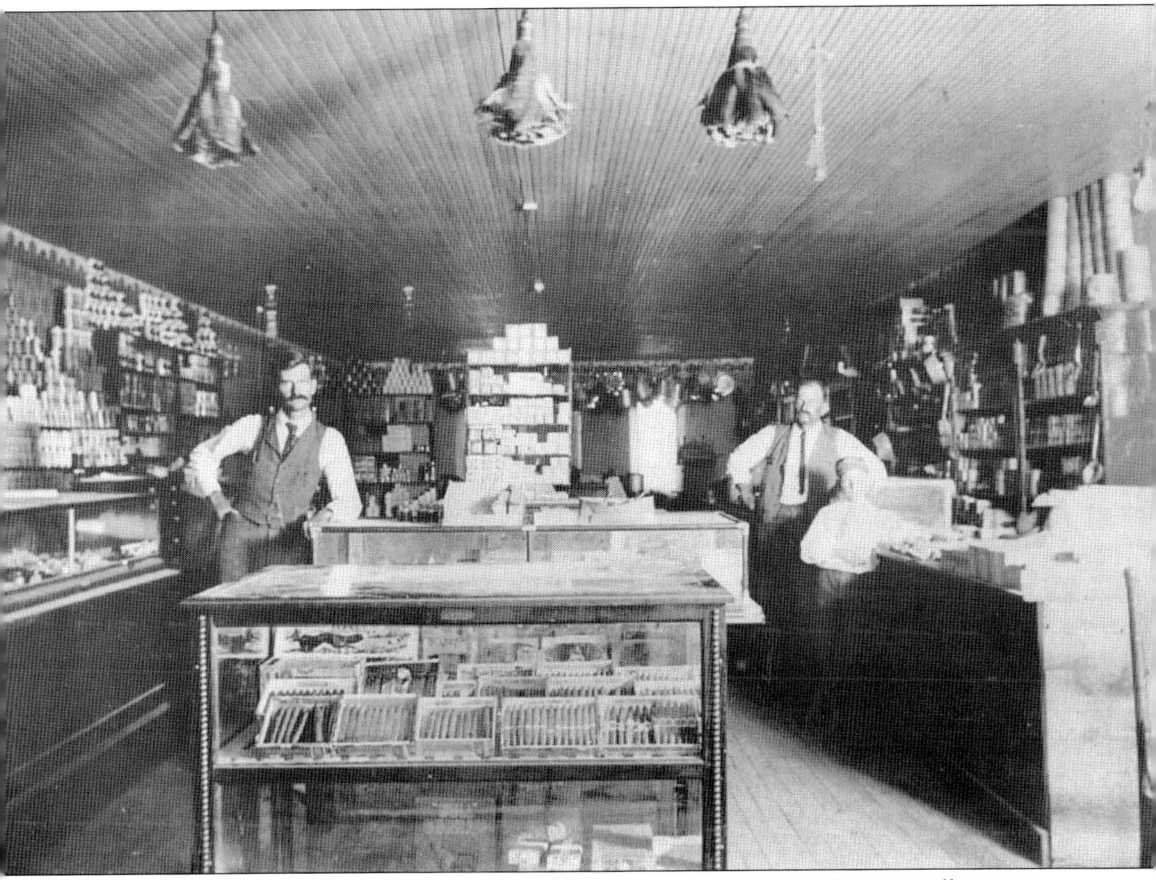

The J.C. King store, opened in 1891, was typical of most dry goods stores of the time, selling items such as cigars, seen in the front display case, wool sacks, and tobacco sheep dip. Note the feather dusters hanging from the ceiling. The men and boy in the photograph are unidentified.

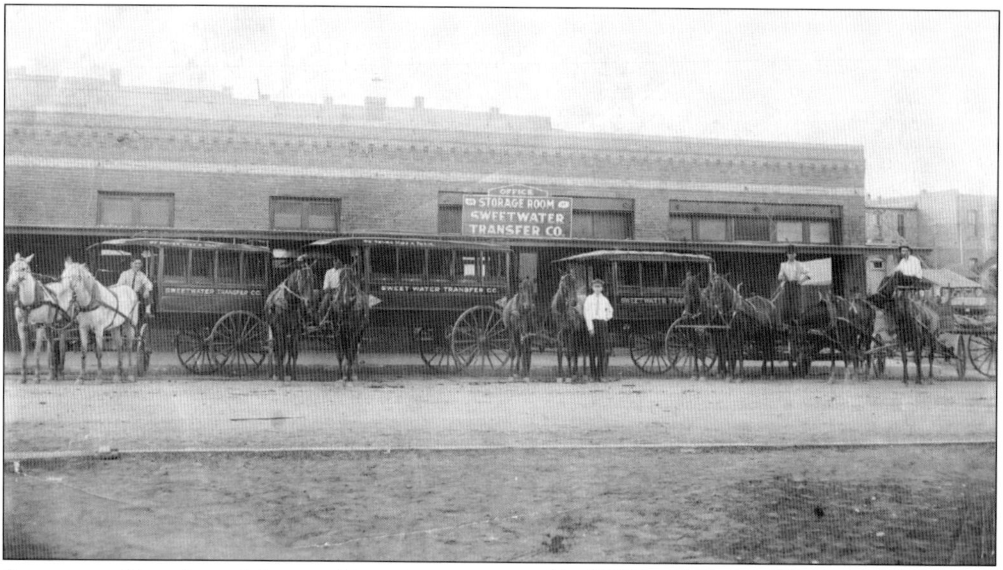

Sweetwater Transfer and Storage Company was opened by W.W. and W.E. Gibson in approximately 1912. Although the company also transferred living passengers, the Johnson Funeral Home and undertaker J.I. Payne used the company to transport the deceased. Black horses would pull one hearse while bay horses pulled the other hearse. The third man from left is W.E. Gibson Sr., and last man on the right is W.W. Gibson.

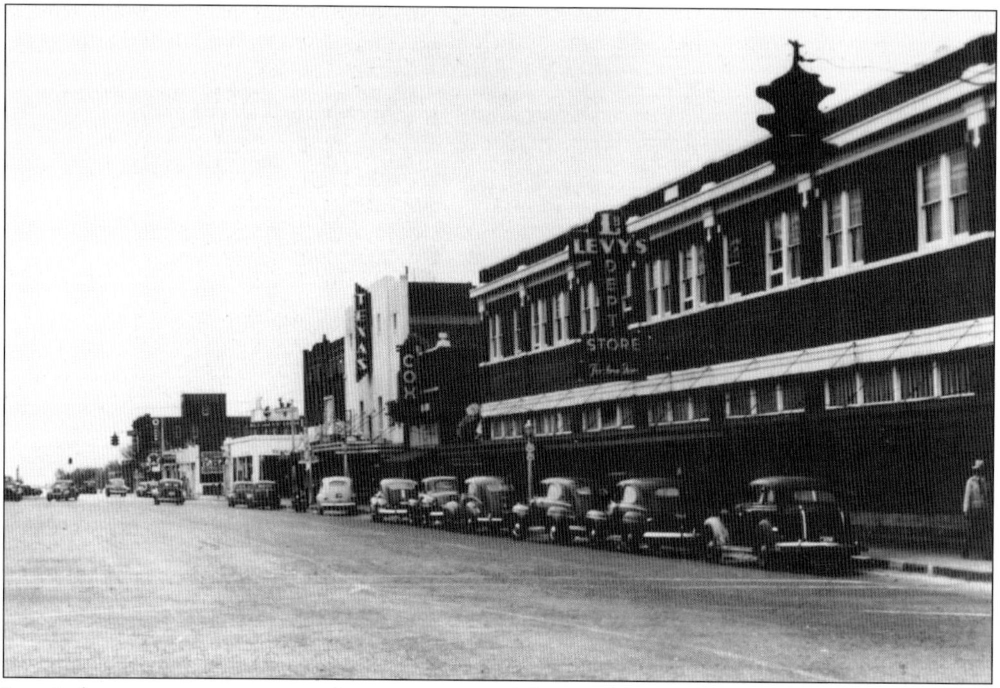

Levy's department store sat on the current site of Azteca Sports Bar and Grill at the corner of Oak Street and Broadway Avenue, which is next to the Texas Theater. One man who worked at Levy's department store, James Garrett, who took out the trash around 2:00 p.m. on Saturdays, made a lasting impression on many young children who attended the 2:00 Saturday movie, as he was the only black man many had contact with in their young life.

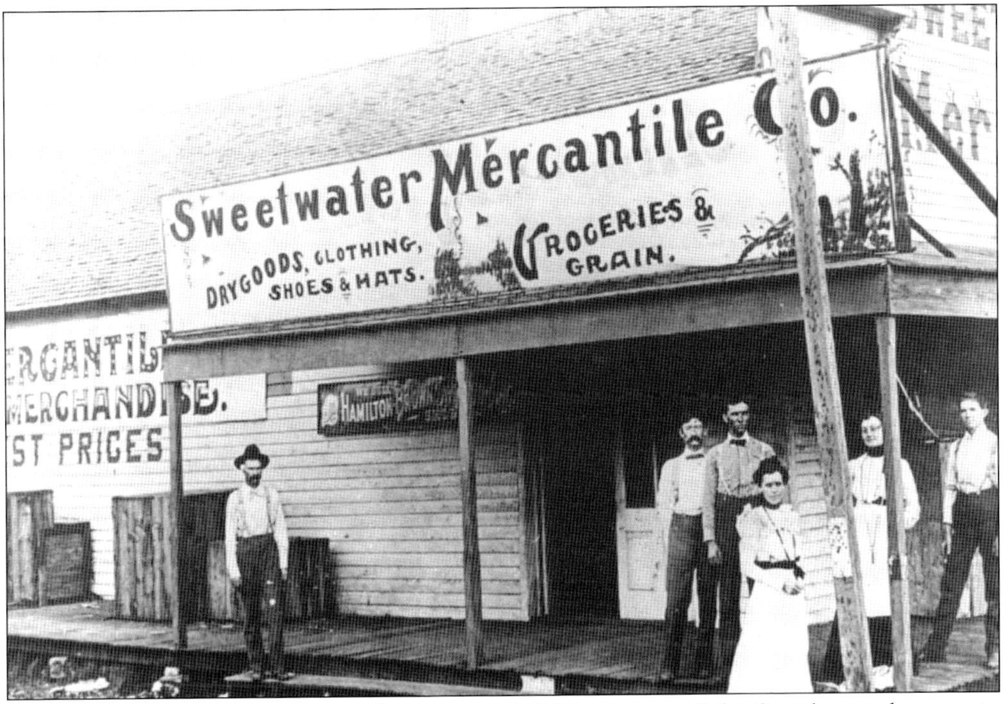

Sweetwater Mercantile Company, shown around 1900, was one of the first dry goods stores in town. W.E. and G.H. Connell of Fort Worth established the business. Ranchmen would send in four-horse teams to buy supplies, and some of them would come from more than 100 miles away to restock.

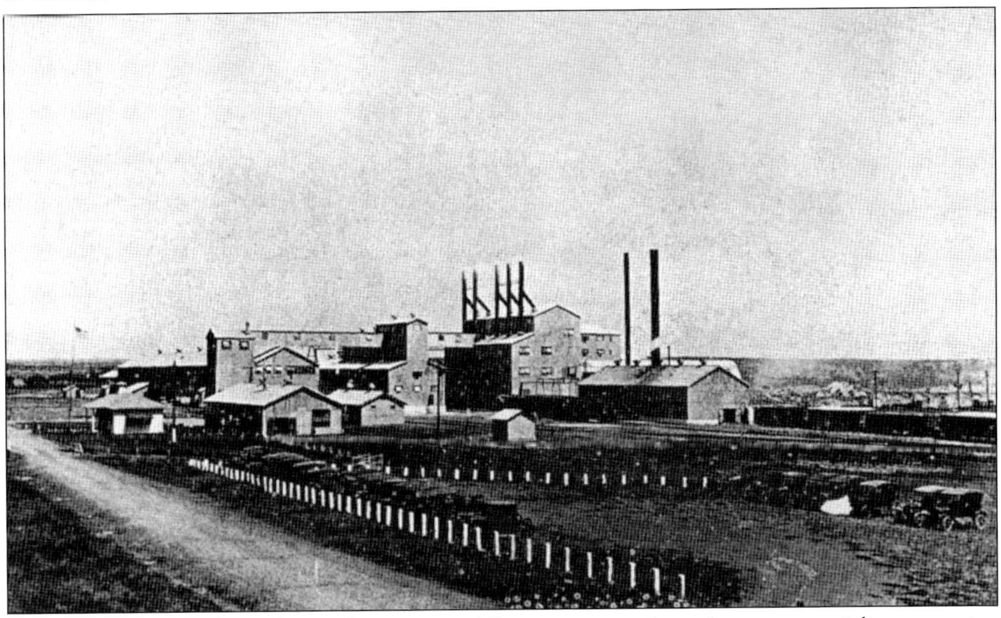

The US Gypsum Plant, located just east of Sweetwater, mines the gypsum-rich mountains surrounding the town, making products such as sheetrock, roofing, and various construction materials. Gypsum has been a part of the town's history since cowboys in the 1800s drank "gypwater," which relieved malaria, chills, and fever, and cleared up their skin.

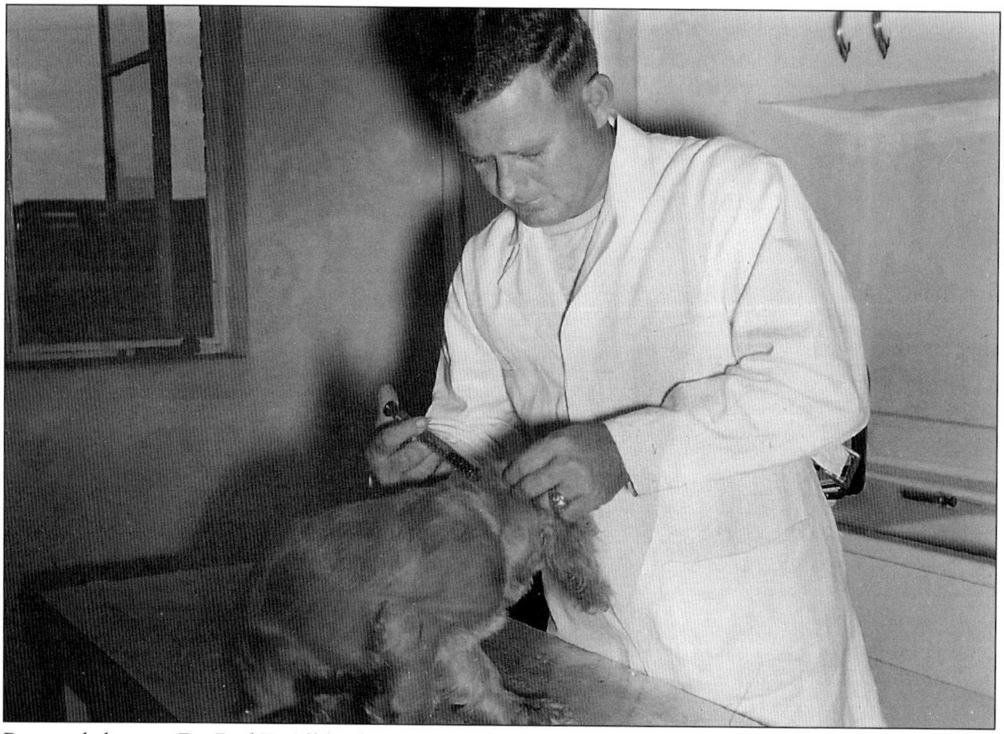

Pictured above is Dr. Bud E. Alldredge, who had the first animal hospital in town. Red Alston built the animal hospital in 1947 on East Broadway, next to the present-day clinic. Recently, Sweetwater Veterinary Hospital was recognized by the Texas Veterinary Medical Association as a Heritage Clinic for its more than 50 years of continuous service to the Nolan County area. Before this first hospital was built, many regular doctors were also responsible for their patients' pets. Dr. Bud E. "Buddy" Alldredge Jr. joined his father in practice in 1969. Today, Sweetwater has two veterinary clinics, including East Ridge Veterinary Hospital, also on Broadway and owned by Dr. Jerod Peek. Note the open window above, a testament to Dr. Alldredge's ability to handle animals.

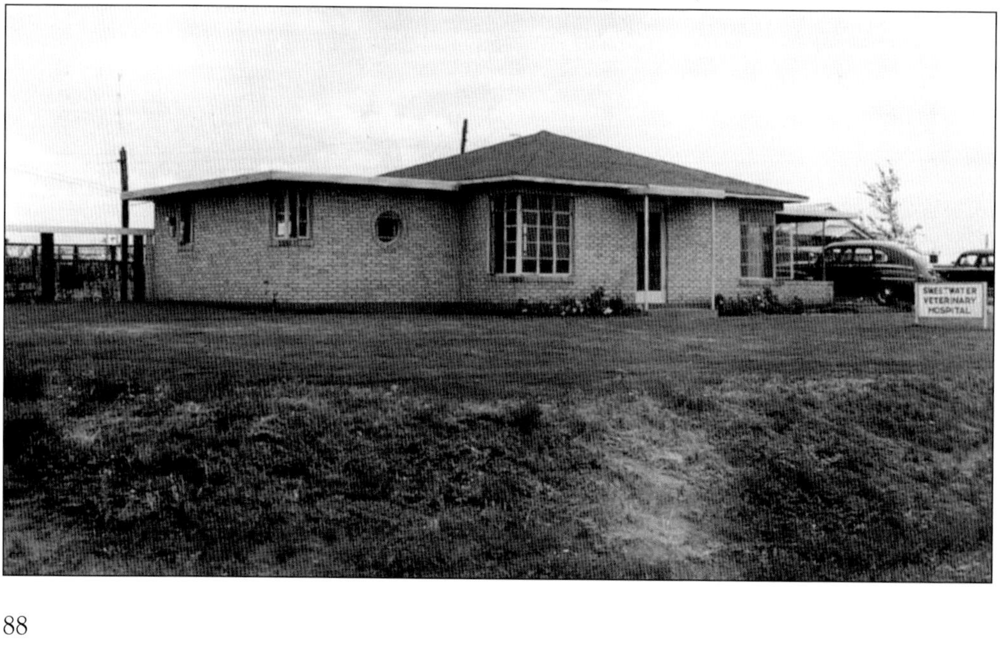

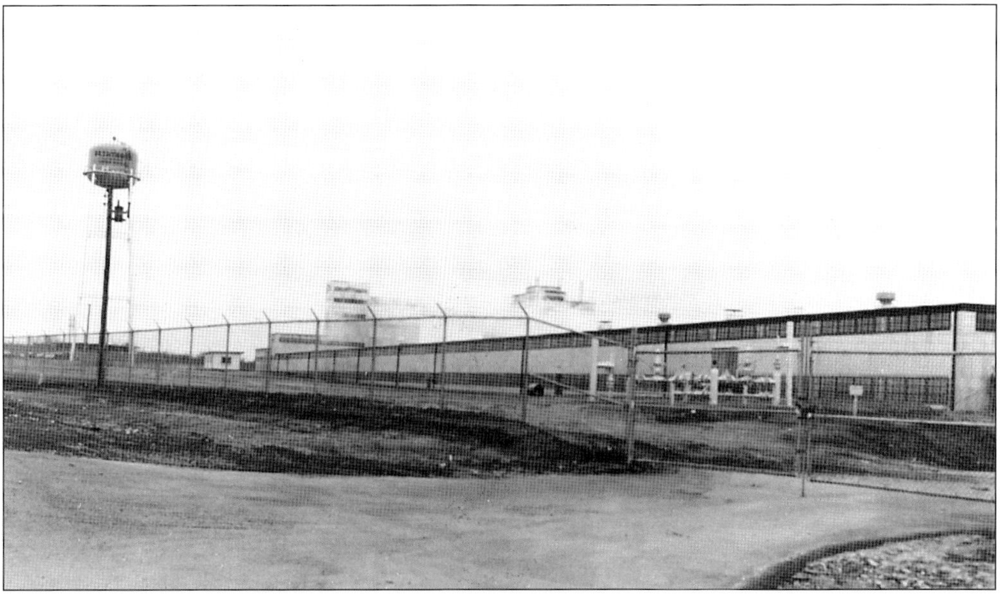

Flintkote Gypsum Company is now known as the Georgia Pacific Gypsum Corporation and is located southeast of Sweetwater. The mortar of Nolan County's first courthouse was made from gypsum, and as gypsum is slowly water soluble, the walls of the courthouse soon fell down. Children in the early 1900s would break up gypsum rocks and make dolls and masks out of the resulting plaster.

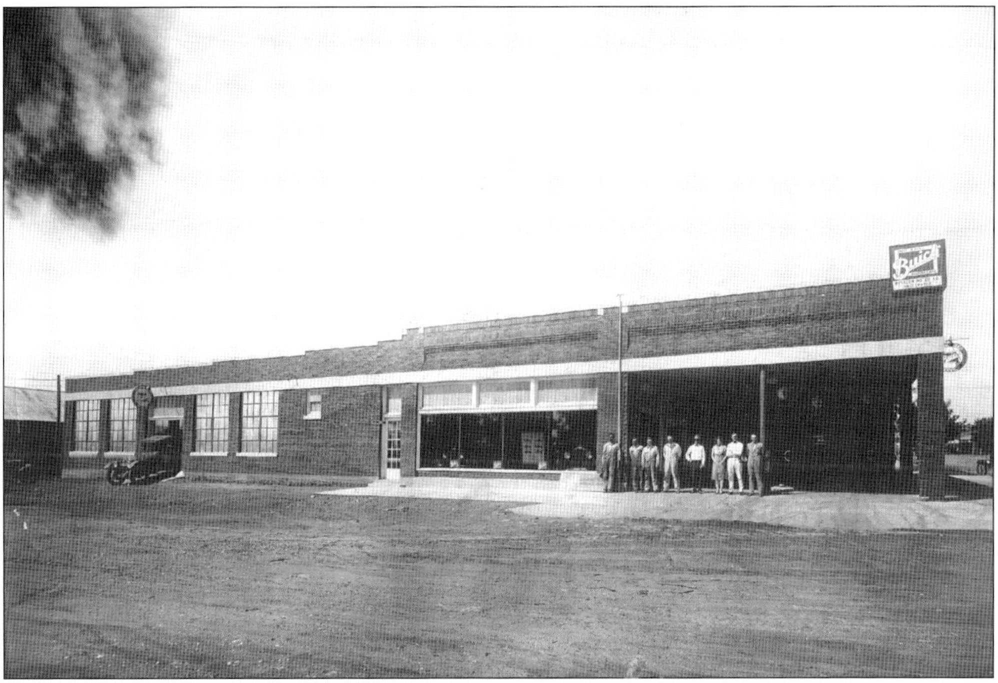

Here is Carl Ragland's Buick dealership on Broadway Avenue in 1920. Carl Ragland was the son of Judge R.A. Ragland, who built the home in which the Pioneer Museum is now housed. Judge Ragland purchased a 1928 Buick from his son, which is currently on display at the museum.

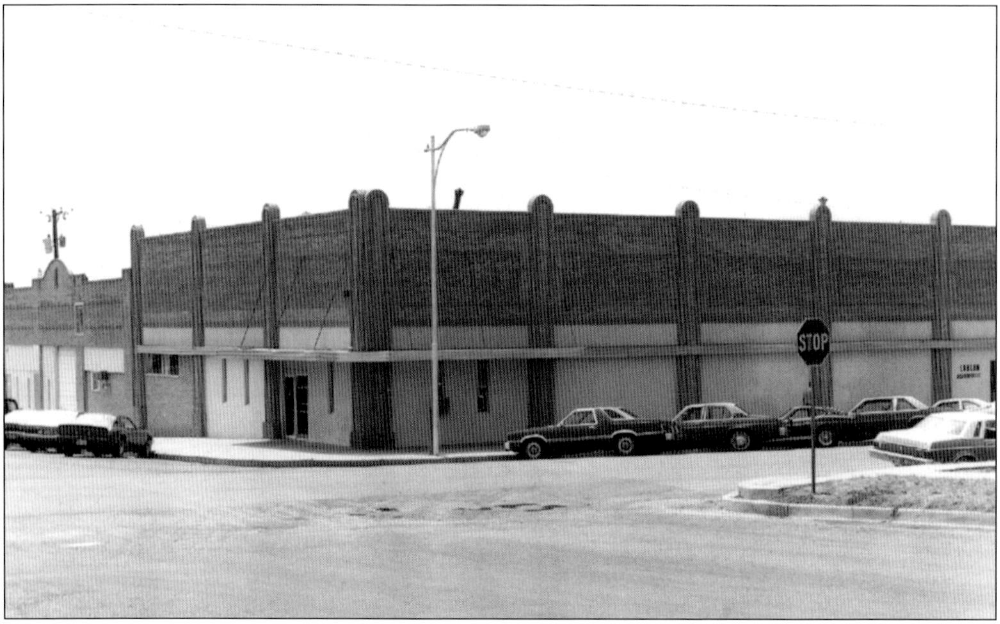

Ludlum Measurements Inc., established in 1962, designs, manufactures, and supplies radiation detection and measurement equipment. Ludlums, as it is locally known, is the largest employer in Sweetwater and has its main office on Oak Street with several sub-offices located around town. Don Ludlum and his son Larry, who live in Sweetwater, remain at the helm of the company.

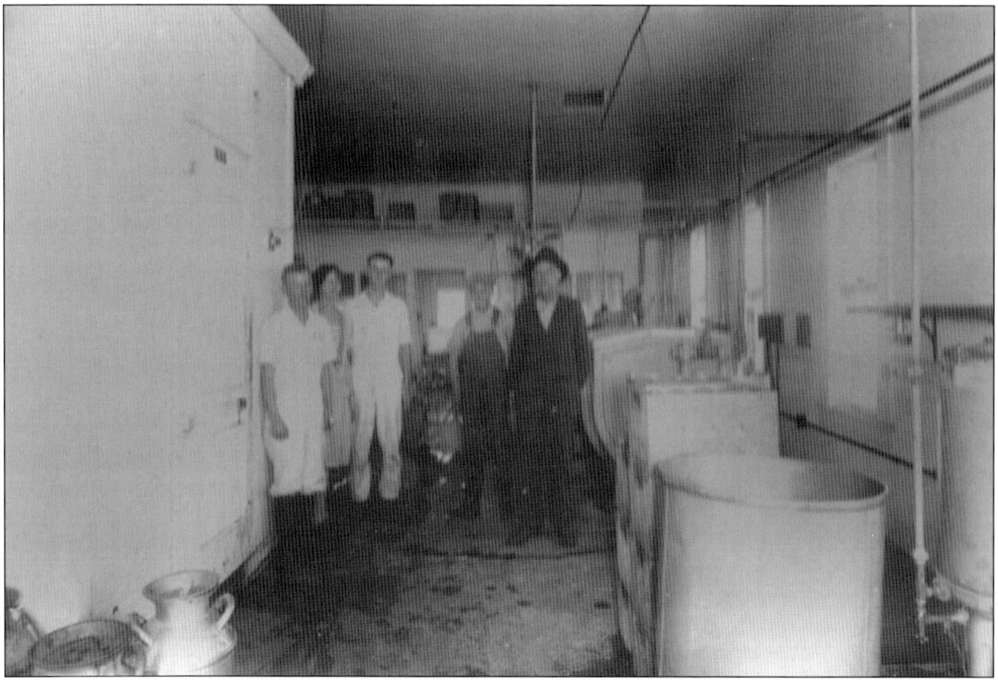

Pictured around 1901, W.R. Hope owned Sweetwater's first dairy pasteurization plant. The motto of Hope's dairy was "Give the babies a fair chance. A careful feeding from Hope's pure milk is a positive assurance of a healthy baby." Pictured in unknown order are Hazel and Claude Hope, Luther Pence, and W.R. Hope.

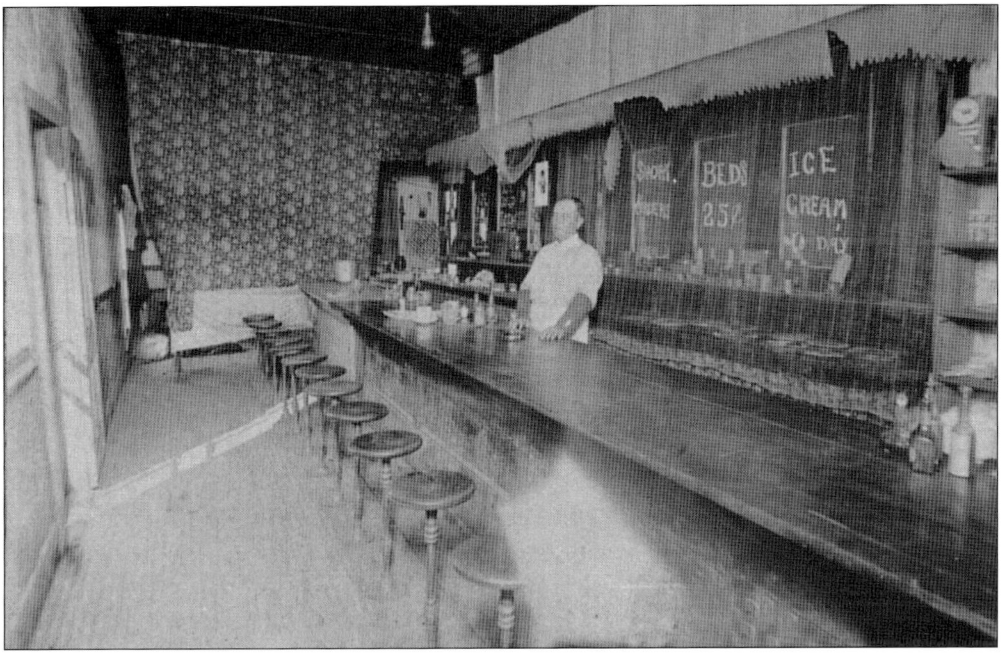

Here is a picture of the inside of an early Sweetwater hotel. Ice cream was reserved for specific days not only because of cooling issues but also because of blue laws, which stated that ice cream could not be served on Sundays. However, if a topping was placed on the ice cream, then it became a conveyance rather than a main dish, and thus, the ice cream sundae (Sunday) was born. Its birthplace continues to be disputed.

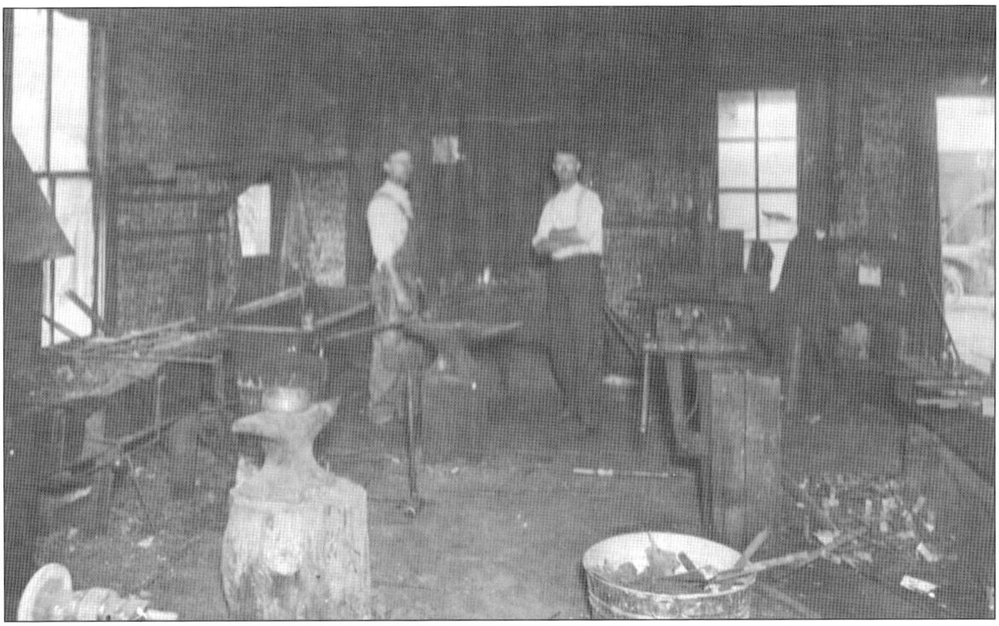

This blacksmith shop was located on the corner of Elm Street and Broadway Avenue on the site of the Baker Hotel. The men in the photograph are S.R. "Red" Reavis and R.C. "Bo" Darr. Blacksmiths create objects from wrought iron and steel by forging the metal using tools like hammers. Blacksmiths also forged horseshoes, and in the past, they also acted as farriers.

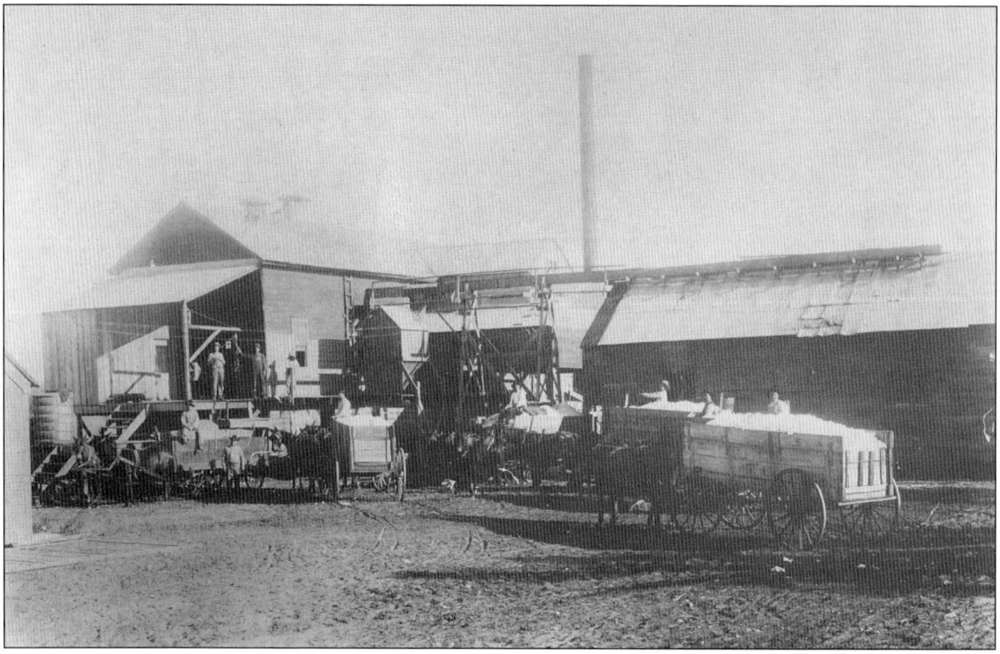

As one of the major exports of the area, cotton has helped to support the economy of Sweetwater and created the need for both gins, as seen here, and a cotton oil mill. Cotton oil is used in the manufacturing of paint and soaps and can be used for cooking. The cotton oil mill just north of town put off the sickly sweet smell of cotton oil every spring.

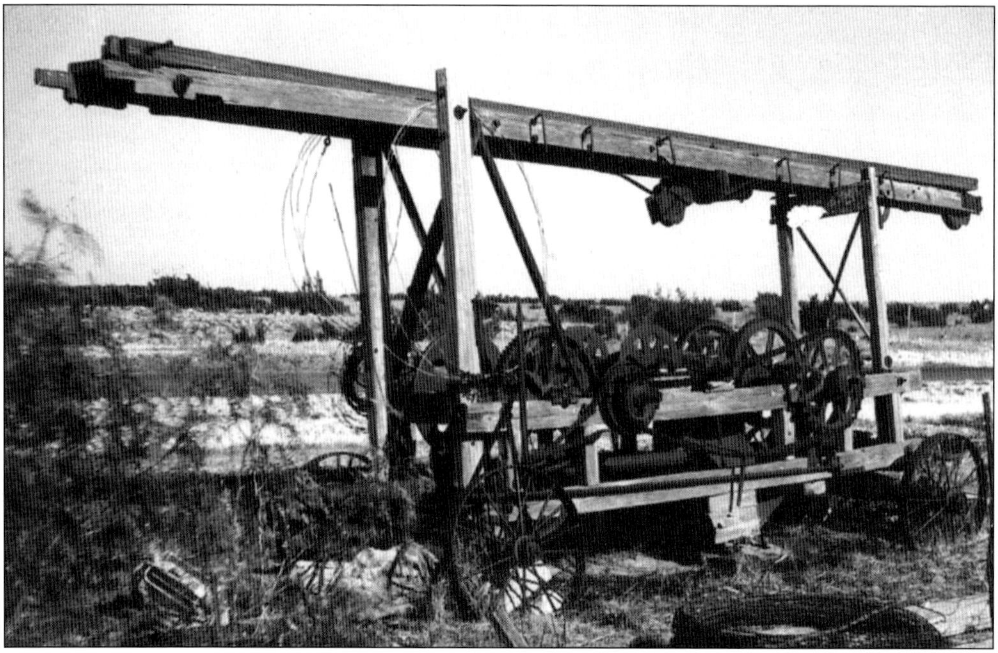

An oil well driller from the early days of the oil industry is on display at the museum. The first boom to hit was in the 1950s in the Sweetwater and Snyder areas. In the mid-1970s, this area experienced the second oil boom of the Permian Basin; Sweetwater profited from it until the bust of the 1980s. Oil found in the Cline Shale puts the area on the verge of another boom.

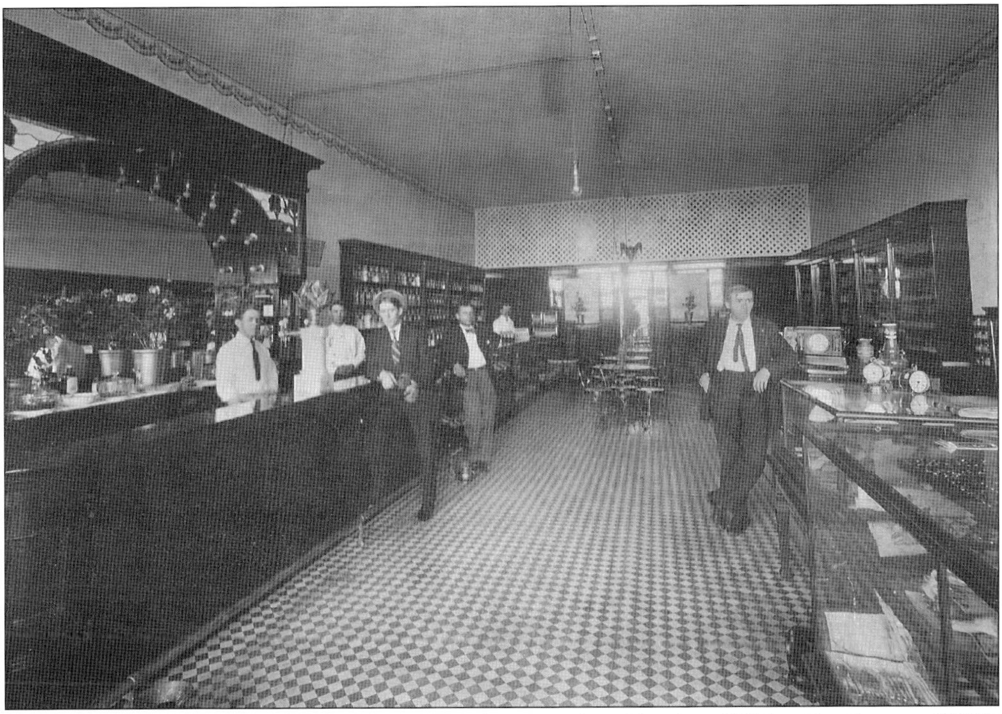

Here is the John Cox Jewelry Store around 1895. Pictured are Floyd and Walter Beall, sons of W.W. Beall, on the left in what served as Beall's Drugstore; on the right in what served as Cox Jewelry Store is John Cox. Beall's Drugstore was also known as Starr and Bowen Drugstores. Later, Cox Jewelry moved into its own building between the Ritz Theater and Levy's Department Store.

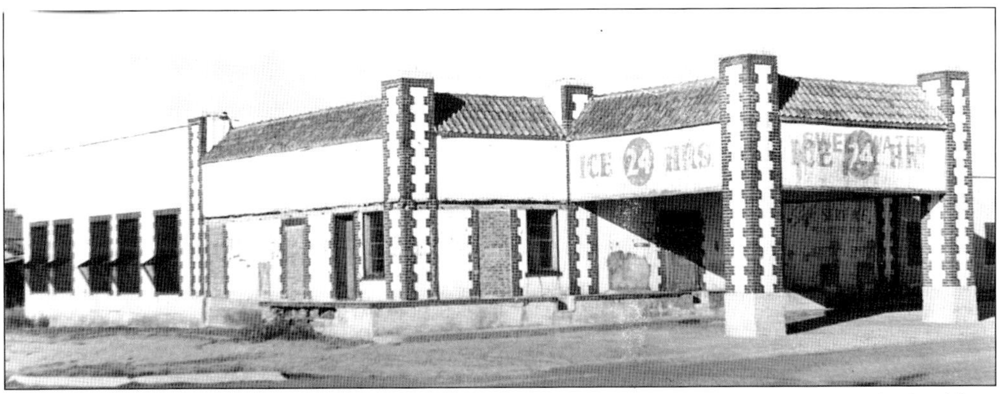

Sweetwater Icehouse was the last ice plant in the area and closed in the late 1950s. The building still stands today. Before the common use of refrigerators and freezers, most homes contained iceboxes. Homeowners would hang a sign in the window or on the front door indicating the size of ice block they needed. Icemen also delivered gelatin to homes that kids enjoyed as a Sunday dinner treat.

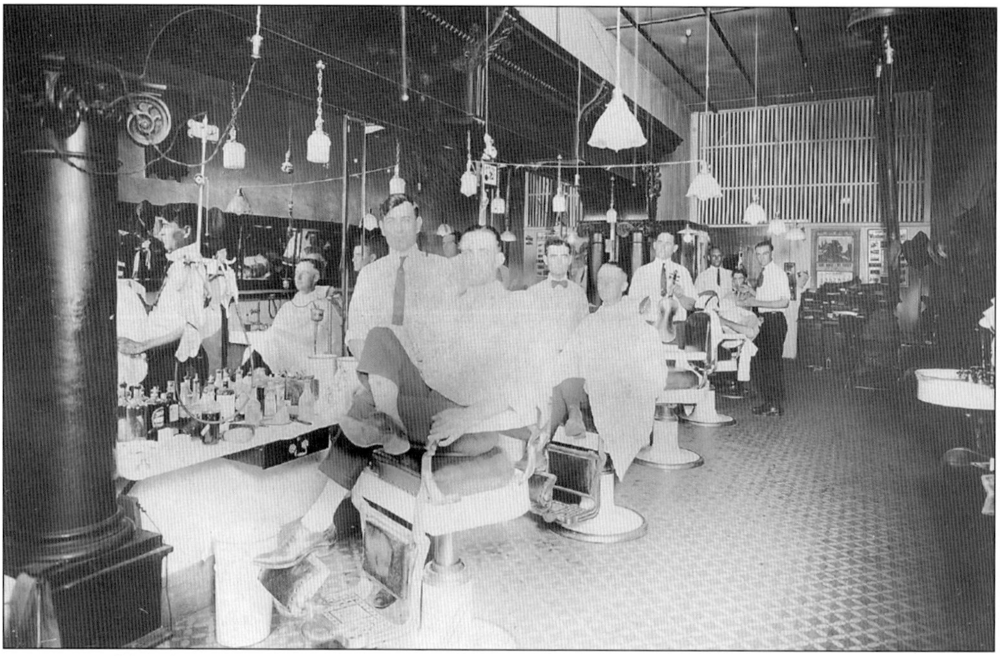

Murray Hubbard's Barbershop, as it appeared in 1922, was located in the Doscher Building at the corner of Locust and Third Streets. The barber to the front of the photograph is Lane Hardy, and the third barber standing with the violin is Murray Hubbard. At the time, Hubbard's barbershop was the longest standing barbershop in town.

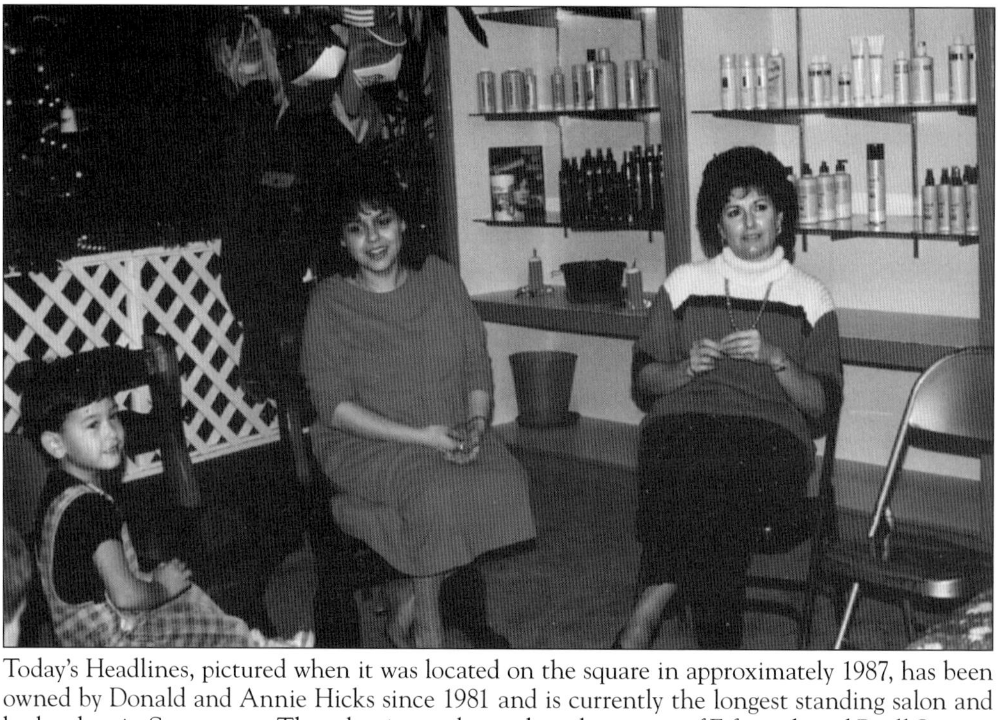

Today's Headlines, pictured when it was located on the square in approximately 1987, has been owned by Donald and Annie Hicks since 1981 and is currently the longest standing salon and barbershop in Sweetwater. The salon is now located on the corner of Fifteenth and Beall Streets. Pictured from left to right are Derek Hicks, Debra Palacios, and Judy Little.

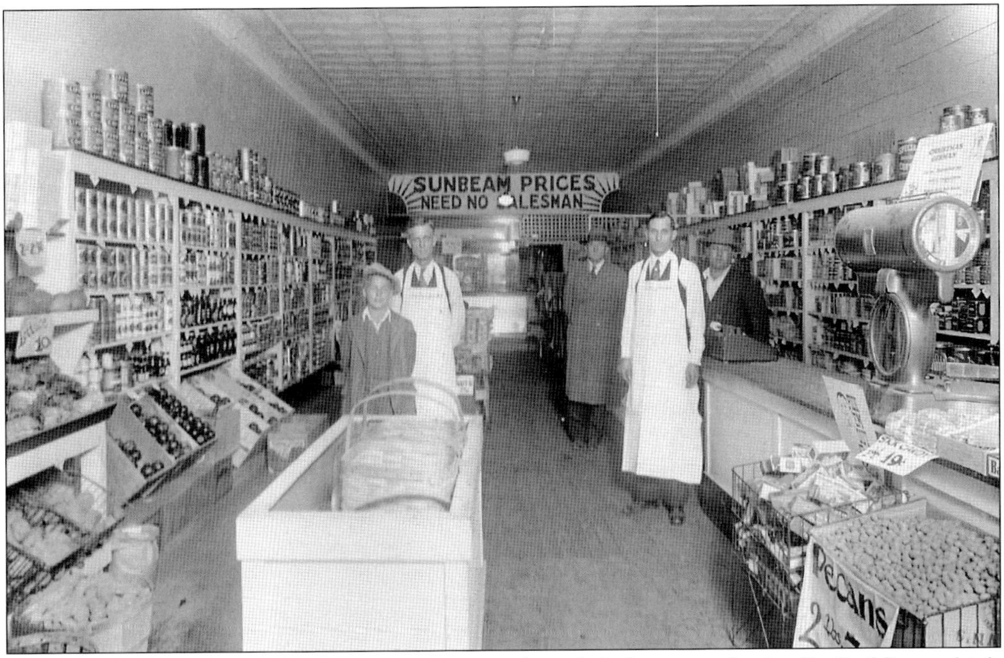

The first store of Sam Leland Glass in 1927 stood on Oak Street in the Luella Building, which still stands today. From here, he moved up the street to the former building of the Hendrix Motor Company. Sam Glass had a bigger vision for his small store, and before he retired, he owned 11 super stores throughout Texas.

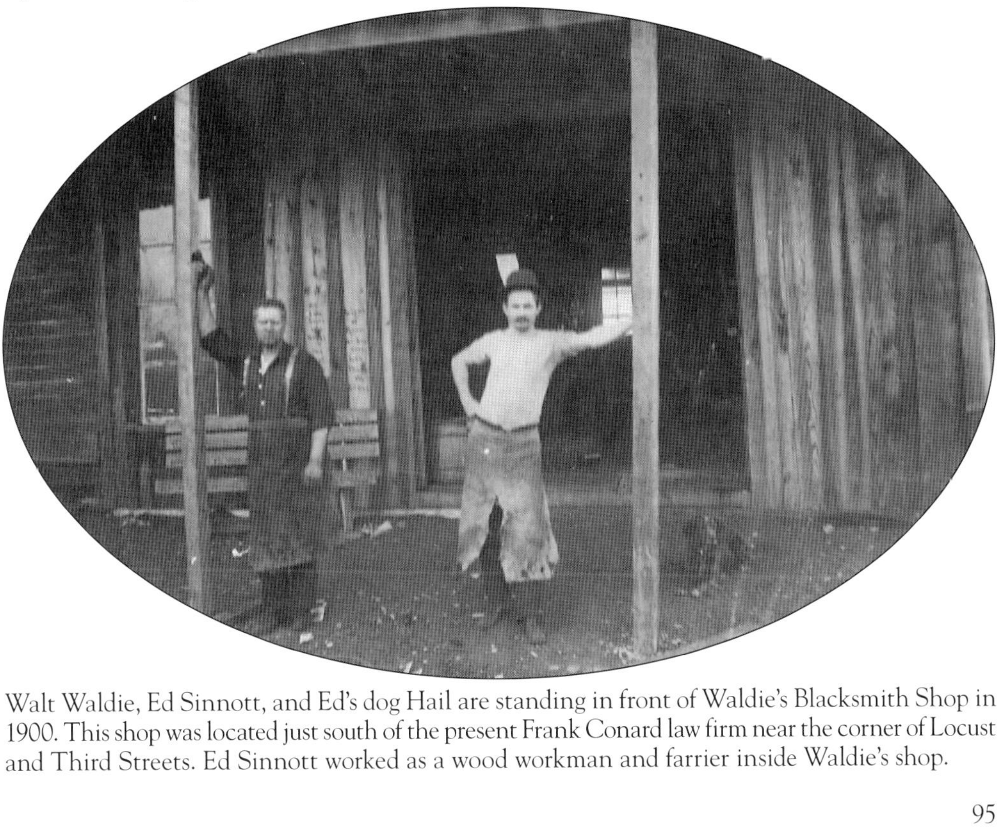

Walt Waldie, Ed Sinnott, and Ed's dog Hail are standing in front of Waldie's Blacksmith Shop in 1900. This shop was located just south of the present Frank Conard law firm near the corner of Locust and Third Streets. Ed Sinnott worked as a wood workman and farrier inside Waldie's shop.

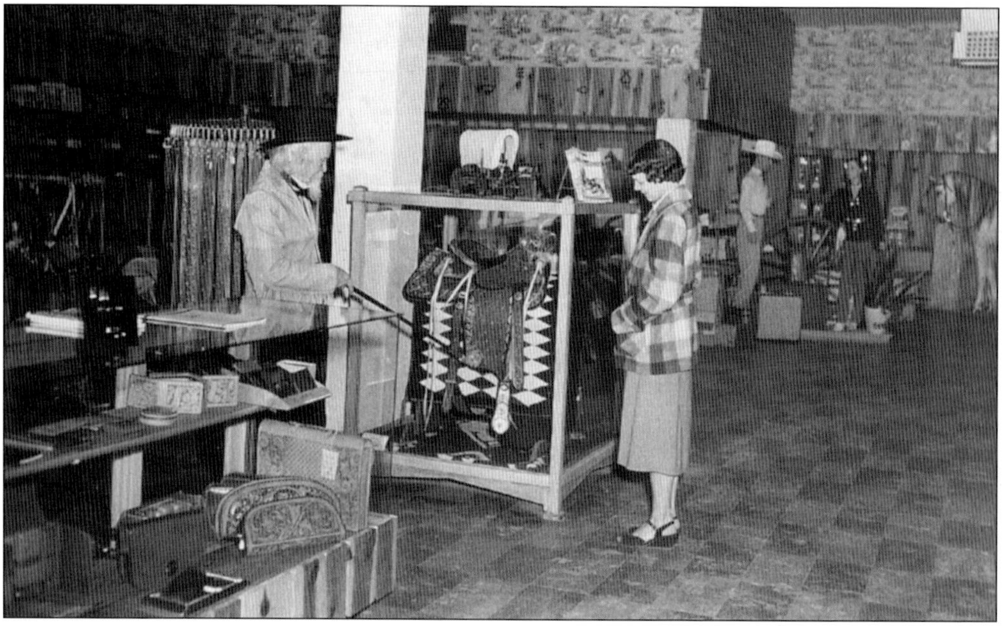

Samuel Dale Myres apprenticed at the T.R. James and Sons Saddlery in Cleburne, Texas, for three years and spent the next five years honing his craft. In 1897, he moved to Sweetwater, and by the fall of 1898, he had bought the saddle and harness business of J.K. Polk, which was located just north of the square across from the windmill. In 1908 and 1911, he was elected mayor of Sweetwater and, during this time, was a known confidant of Pancho Villa. One of S.D. Myres's greatest contributions to his town was bringing the Santa Fe Railroad directly through Sweetwater, making travel and shipping easily accessible for its citizens. Many of his saddles, holsters, and accessories are also on display at the museum.

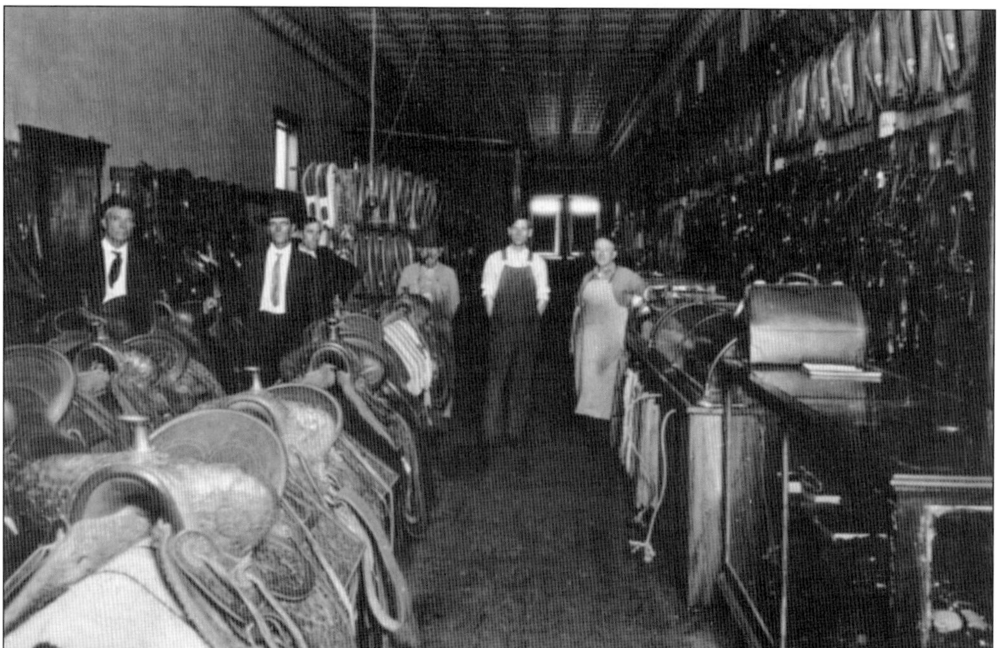

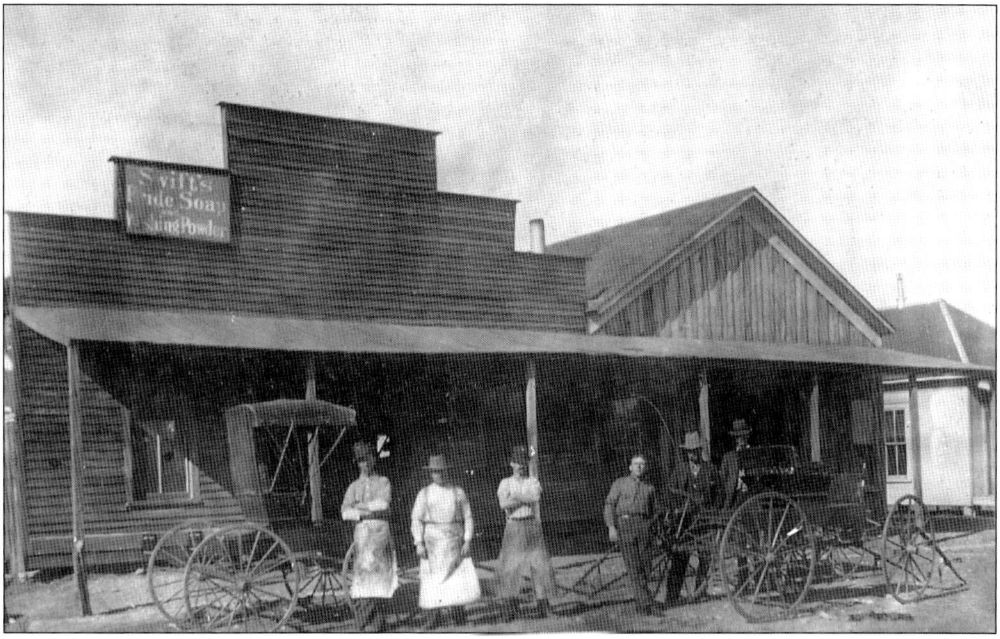

Swift's Pride Soap and Washing Powder were sold at this unidentified dry goods store. In 1915, Swift and Company of Chicago began offering a line of soap products. By 1925, the company's line of products expanded from fresh, cured, and smoked meats to products such as washing powder and wool soap. The cartoon slogans on the company's products have ensured they remain collector's items.

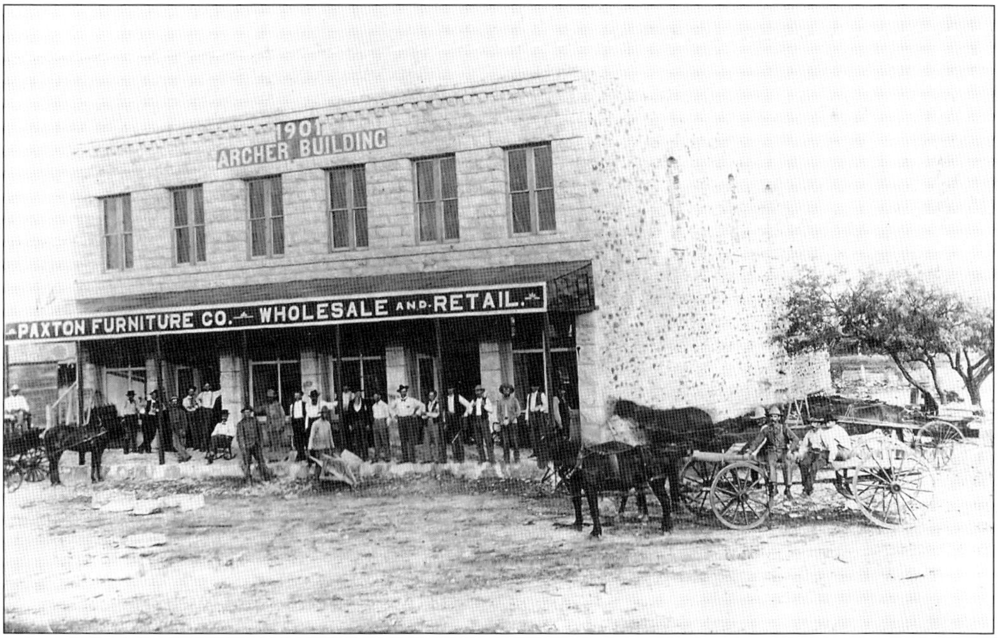

The Archer Building was erected in 1901 and, in this photograph, housed the Paxton Furniture Company. The building stood on the site of what would become the Ritz Theater, later Texas Theater, and John Cox's Jewelry Store. The Archer Building was also once the home to Hubbard's Dry Goods Store and was located next to Shook Realty and the office of Cowen and Tidwell.

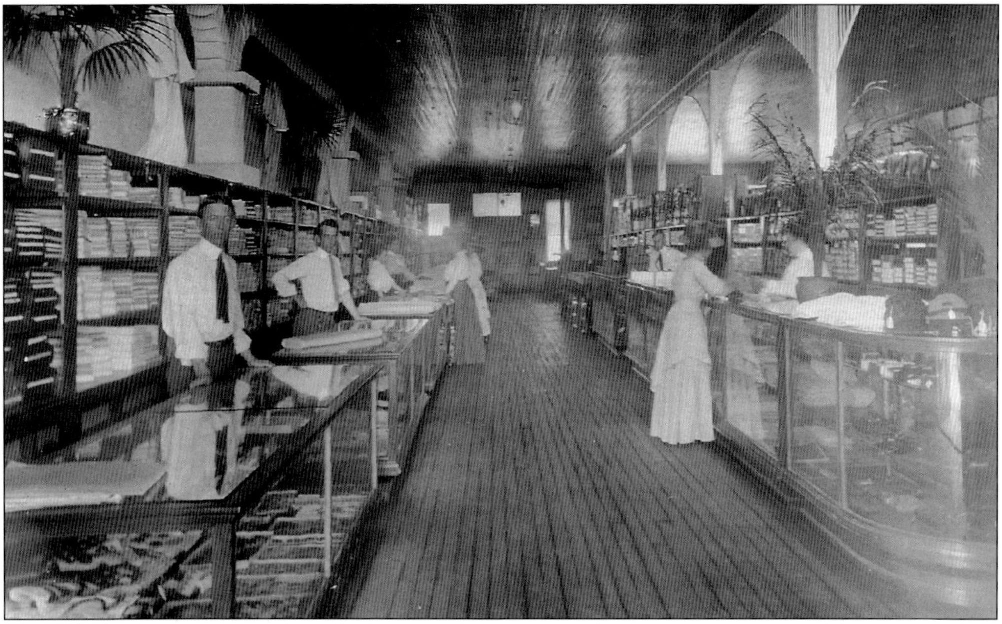

John Howard Hubbard moved to Sweetwater in 1906 at the age of 17 and opened a dry goods store; a year later, his brother William joined him in the business. John married Shirley Elise McCarty on October 22, 1910, and ran Hubbard's Dry Goods until 1933. The store's diamond-shaped logo with the words "The Sign of Quality" became well known throughout the area. Seen below is the men's department inside Hubbard's store. Hubbard's was a popular spot for men to shop, and he would often appeal to them with drawings like the one held on April 3, 1922, in which he gave away a New Series Maxwell automobile.

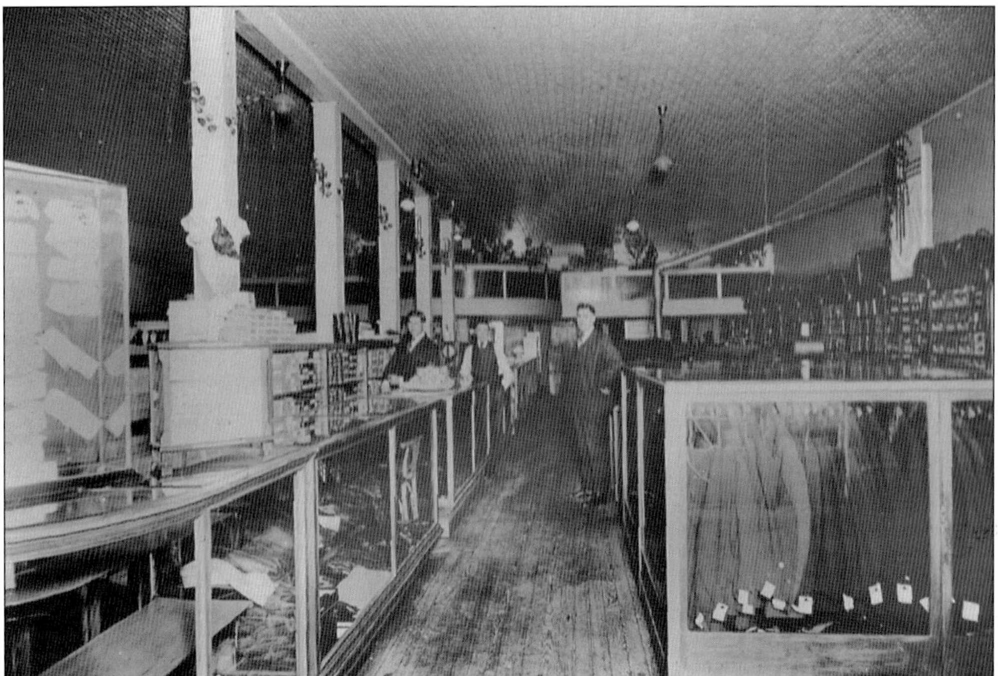

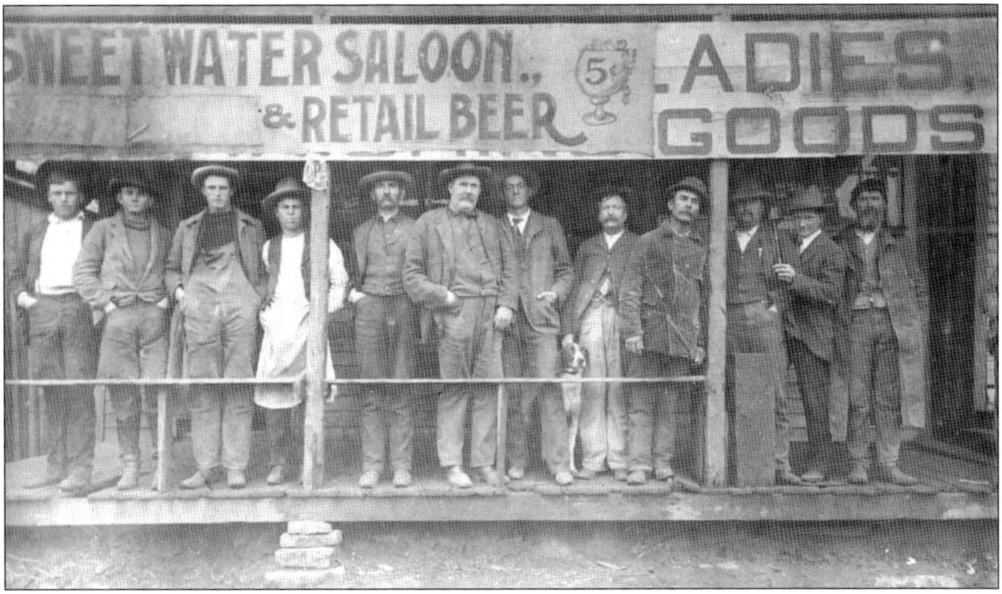

Here is an early saloon located on the west side of the square in 1889. Sometimes, an early county attorney would find himself in a card game at a saloon like this one. He would use the game to get acquainted with the participants and would then proceed to file charges and levy fines against them. The county attorney quit this position the night a few of these men showed up with a rope and demanded his resignation.

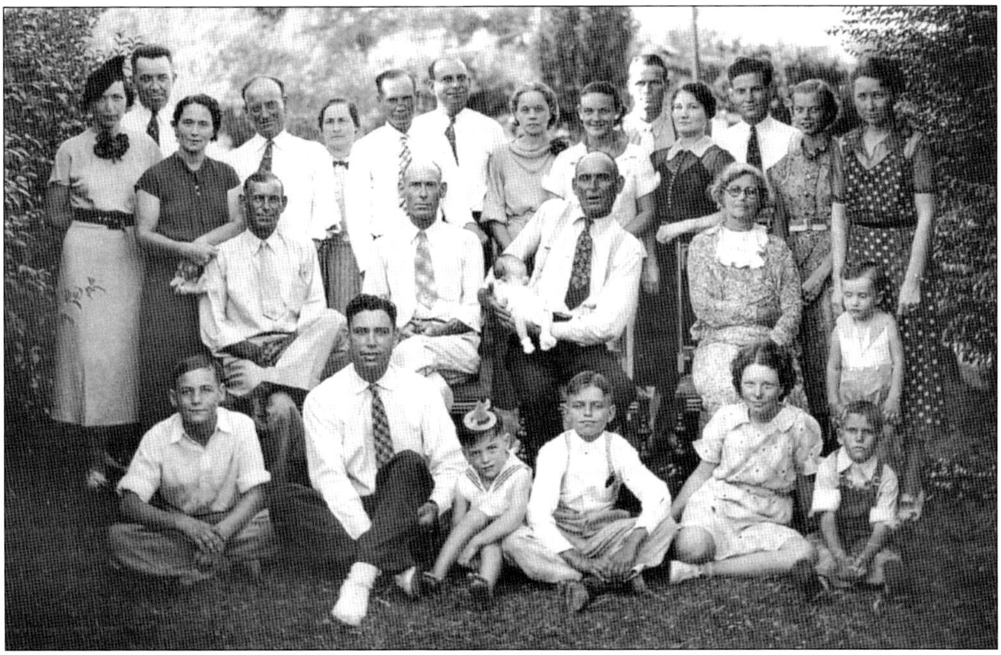
The Pace brothers opened their first grocery store in 1924 on First Street just across from the Texas & Pacific depot; the store was the first in Sweetwater to have an electric refrigerator. In 1927, the brothers moved the business to the east side of the square and called it Hokus Pokus Grocery. In 1931, they moved to Elm Street and operated the first supermarket between Fort Worth and El Paso.

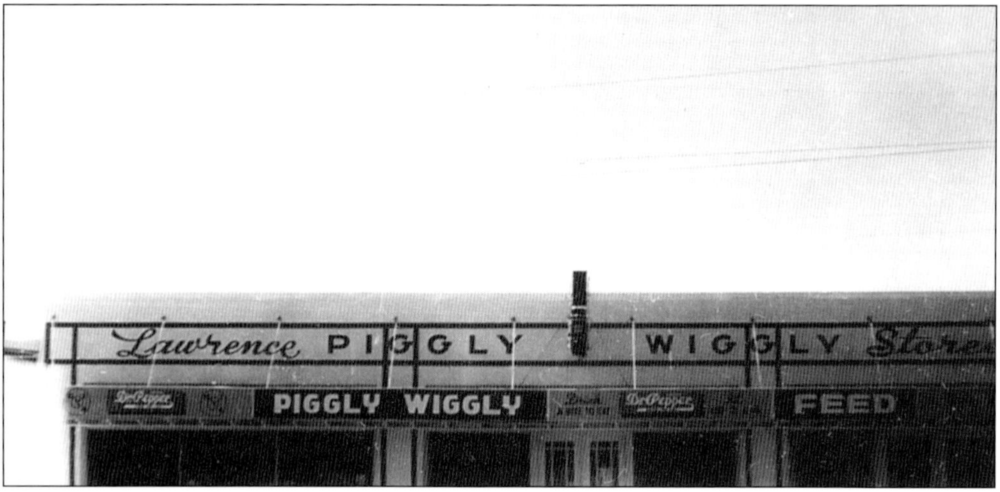

Jonah Mack Lawrence and his wife, Thelma, moved to Sweetwater in 1929 and purchased the Piggly Wiggly grocery store, which they operated for 50 years. J.M. Lawrence was appointed mayor of Sweetwater in 1942. Descendants of J.M. and Thelma have remained in the grocery business, operating their own Piggly Wiggly store, Lawrence Brothers IGA, and now Lawrence Brother's Management, located on the corner of Third and Hailey Streets.

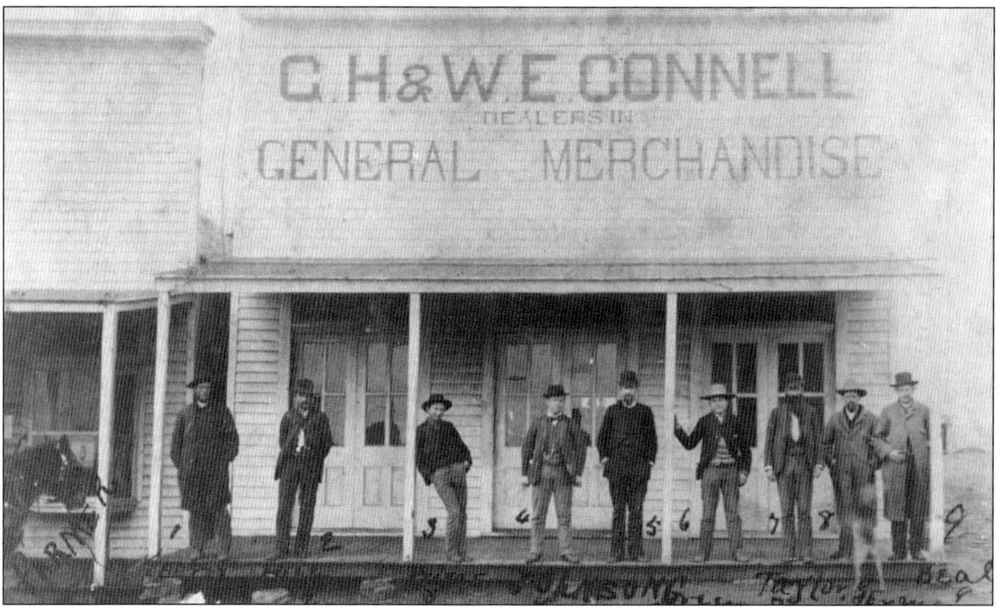

G.H. and W.E. Connell General Merchandise Store handled principally ranch supplies for the surrounding ranches and kept about $25,000 worth of goods in stock at any given time. The Connells were one of the first advertisers in the *Sweetwater Advance*. In cold or bad weather, the Connells provided a place to sleep for the teamsters who came to purchase their goods.

Six

LIVING SWEETWATER

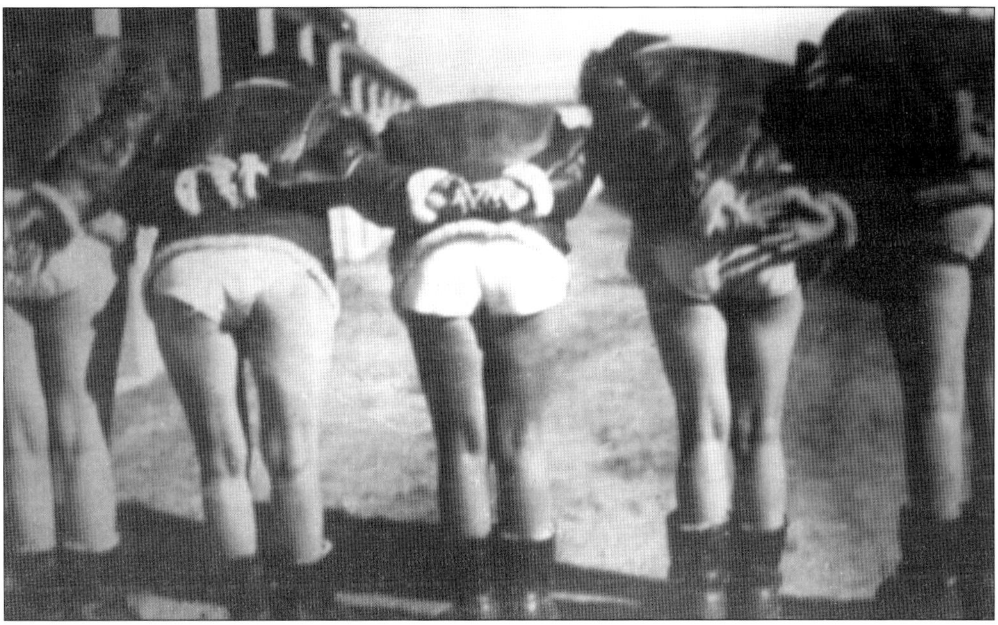

In 1943, the Women's Auxiliary Ferrying Squadron and the Women's Flying Training Detachment joined to become the Women Airforce Service Pilots. These women pilots were trained to ferry planes for the military due to a shortage of male pilots. The women were trained at Avenger Field in Sweetwater in the only program of its kind in the world. 1,830 women were accepted to the program, and 1,074 received their wings.

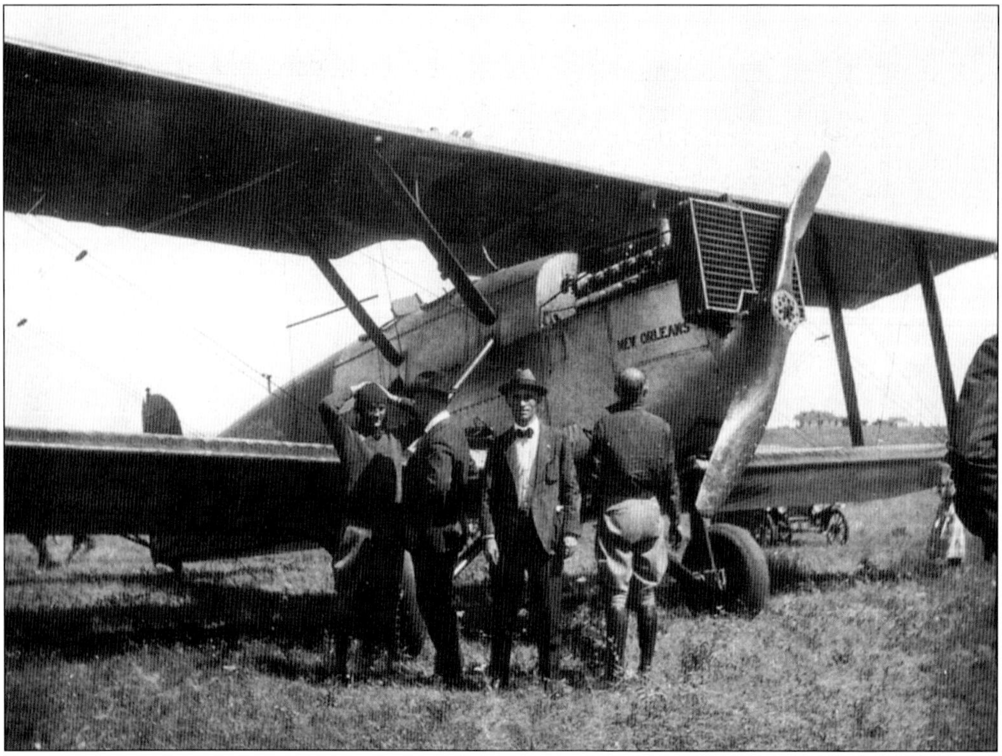

On April 6, 1924, eight US Army Air Service pilots and mechanics in four airplanes left Seattle, Washington, to carry out the first circumnavigation of the globe by air. The *New Orleans*, one of the two planes that completed the flight, landed in Sweetwater to a huge parade. Lts. Erik Nelson and John Harding Jr. flew it. The photograph above shows the globetrotting pilots with Mayor Joe H. Boothe. Later in 1931, another set of world flyers, Harold Gatty and Wiley Post, also stopped in Sweetwater on their circumnavigation of the globe. Below is a photograph of Post's wife, Mae Laine Post, and her mother, Mrs. David Laine.

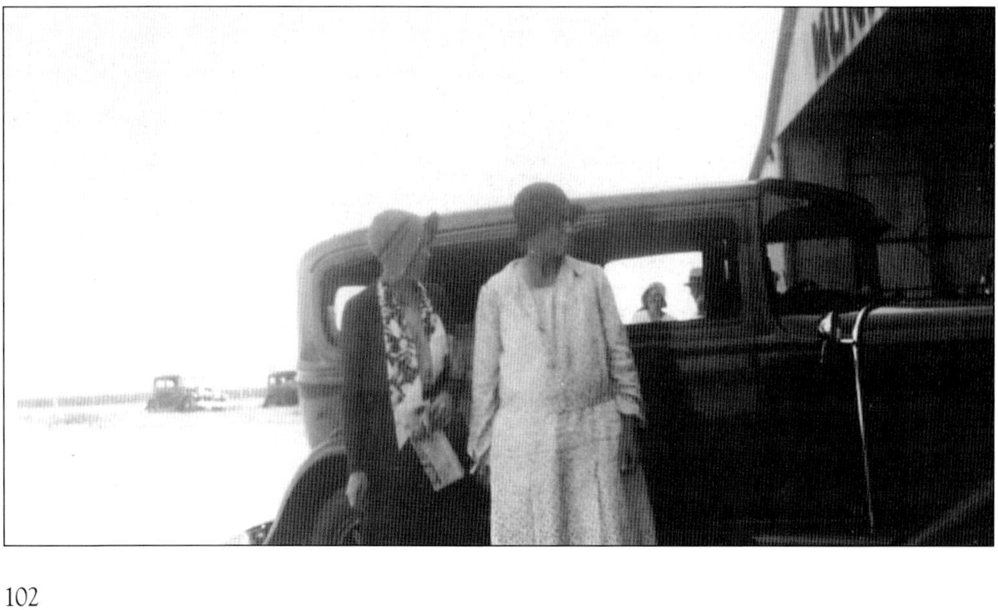

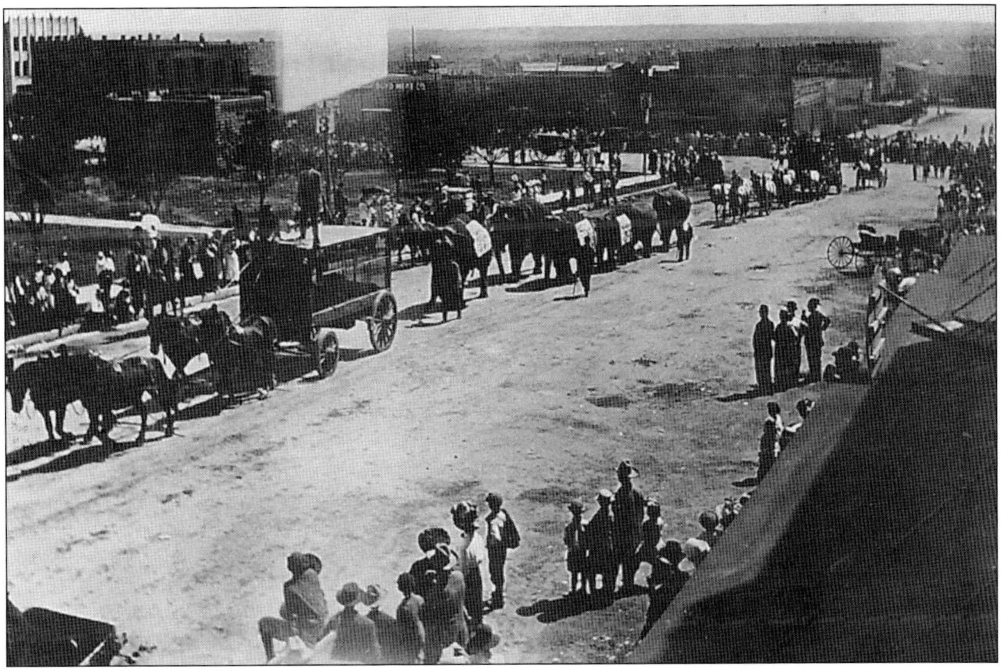

A parade in 1902 near the courthouse square celebrated the arrival of the circus. Like many small towns, Sweetwater loves a parade and has several every year, including parades for the Rattlesnake Roundup, Fourth of July, homecoming, and Christmas. The parade route was the same for every parade and traveled up Broadway Avenue for many years; however, in past years, with the town being smaller than it used to be, the parade route has been changed to follow the path around the courthouse.

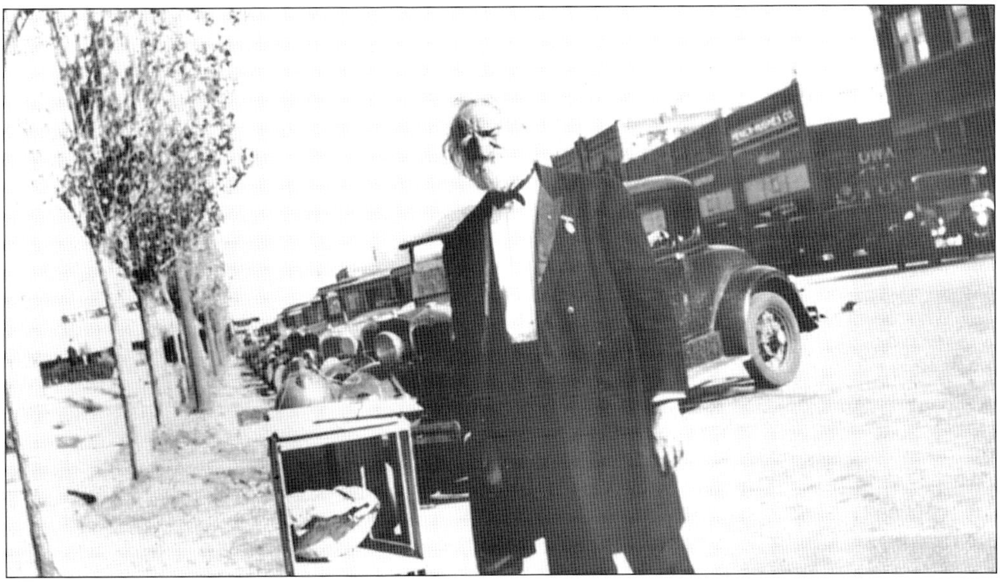

Professor Ned Walker, shown here on the square, was a traveling phrenologist who came to Sweetwater often during the early 1900s. Professor Walker would read a person's character by studying the bumps on his head. A local freight hauler named Mr. Tudor was an ardent student of Professor Walker.

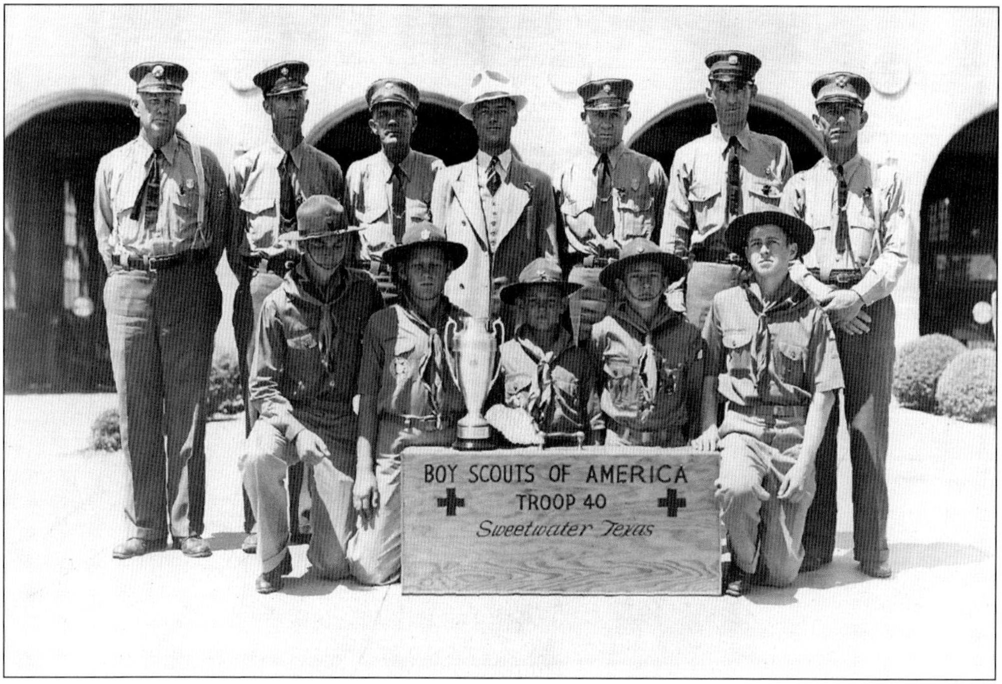

A 1938 Boy Scouts of America first-aid trophy has been polished and put on display at the Pioneer Museum; Jack Harris was scoutmaster of Troop 40, now 140, when the troop won a tri-state first-aid contest in Dallas. Sweetwater's first Boy Scout troop was established in 1914 and had members of the Cox family in it. Troop 40 is the oldest continuously active troop west of the Mississippi and was originally sponsored by the First Presbyterian Church but is now sponsored by the Church of Christ. Some of those pictured above are Jack Fitzgerald, John Simpson, Nelson Boothe, Maurice Reich, DeWitte Conley, and Vance Jobe.

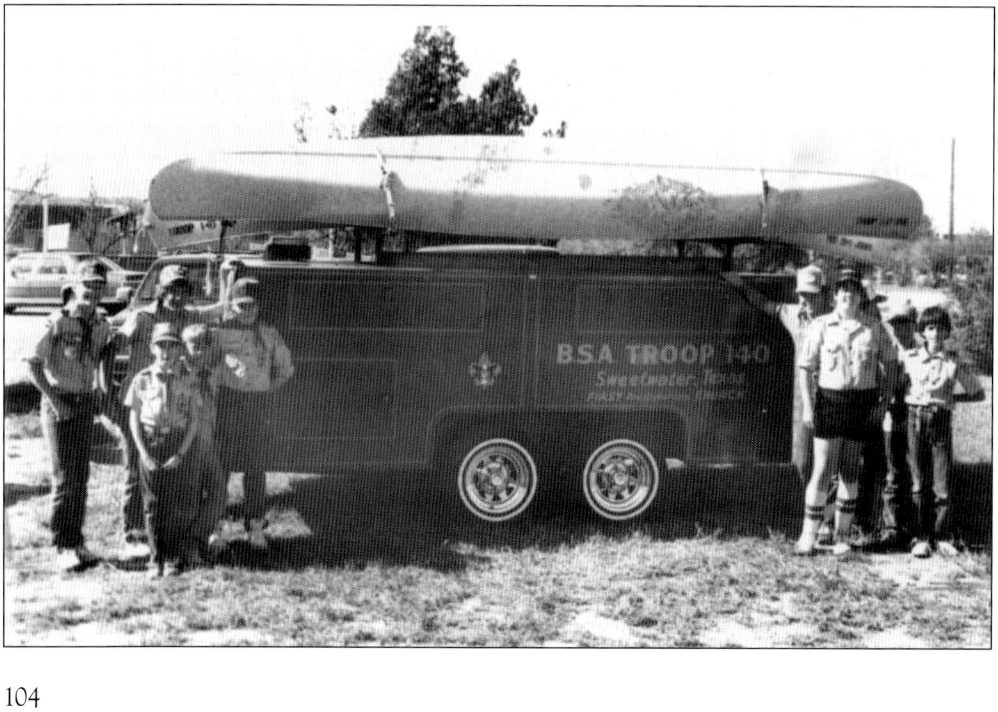

Sweetwater has always supported little league teams in various sports; shown here are six players representing different baseball teams in 1984. Beginning in the early 1990s, Donald and Annie Hicks, seeing a need for little league football, began the Pop Warner program. The initial intent was to have one Sweetwater team, but in a town in love with football, this grew into a full-blown program the first year.

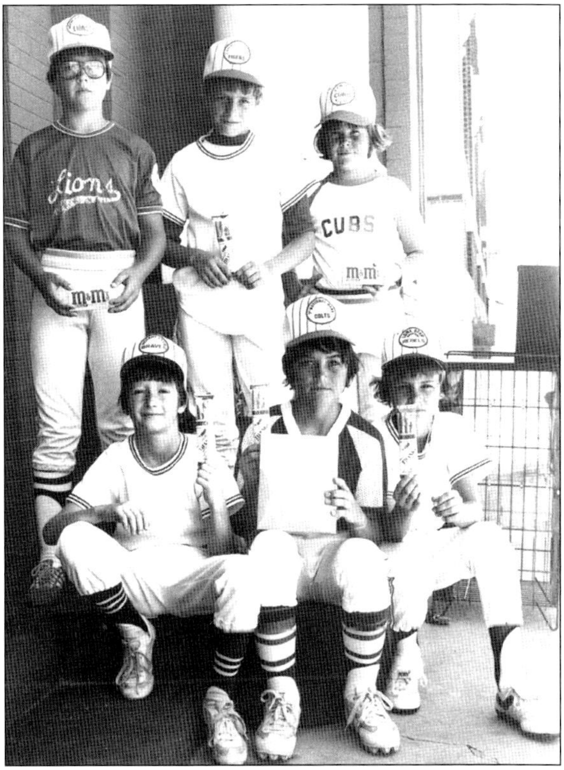

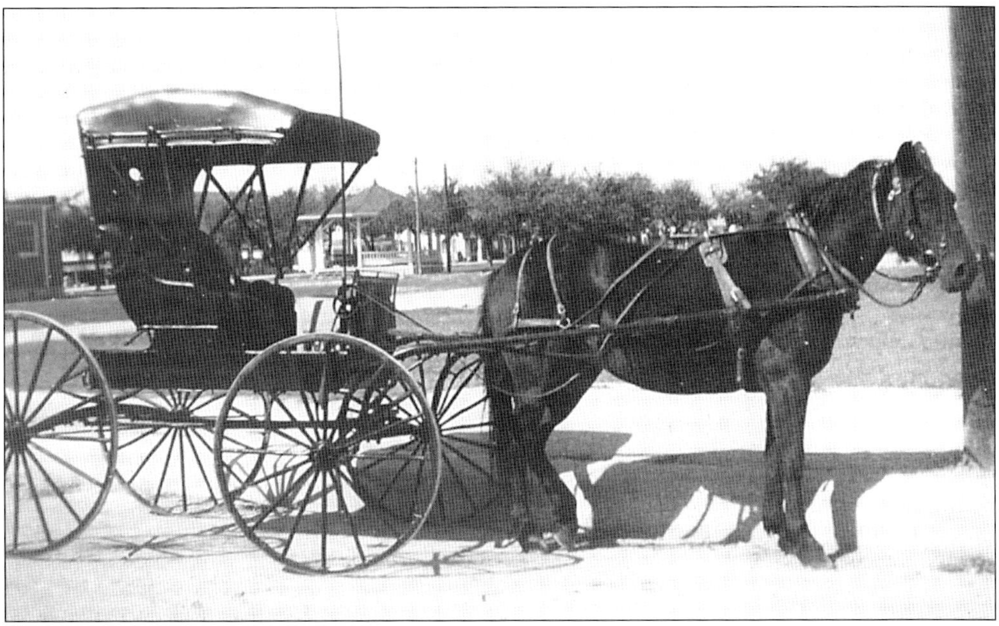

This one-horse buggy belonged to Heinrich and Augusta Hackfeld, who came to Nolan County in 1908. Their oldest son, Otto, courted Emma Heine in this buggy, and the pair married in 1913. Sweetwater descendants of Henry and Augusta include Alma Hackfeld Green, Glenda Soules, David Green, Bernice Patterson, Willie Hackfeld, and Marie Leach. Oscar Hackfeld, Otto's oldest son, donated the buggy to the Pioneer Museum in 1989.

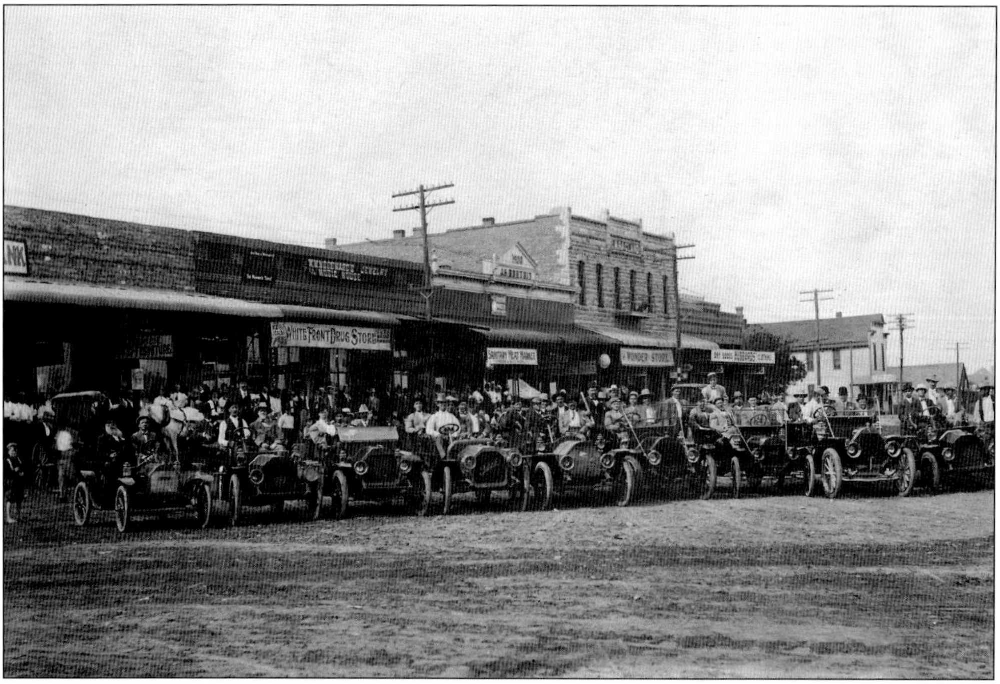

All of the owners of automobiles turned out on the north side of the square in 1910 to show their support of the Republican Convention. In the background can be seen Hubbard's dry goods store, located at this time on the corner of Locust and Third Streets next to the Ragland Building, built by R.A. Ragland in 1901. The Ragland Building still stands today.

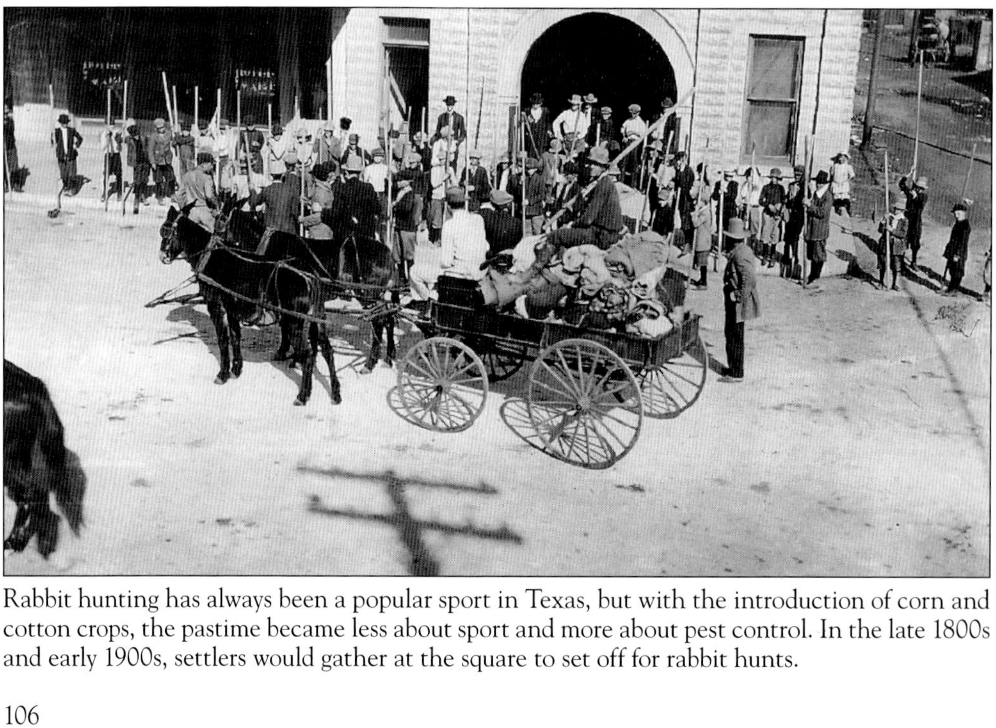

Rabbit hunting has always been a popular sport in Texas, but with the introduction of corn and cotton crops, the pastime became less about sport and more about pest control. In the late 1800s and early 1900s, settlers would gather at the square to set off for rabbit hunts.

At right is an aerial photograph of Nolan County from around 1940 by the US Army. Pictured is the Newman family racetrack just on the other side of City Lake. To the right of the racetrack are the horse barns, and below these on the other side of the lake is the baseball field of the Sweetwater Swatters, the minor league baseball team once housed here. Legend in Sweetwater has always told that the Mustang Bowl was built on the site of the old racetrack, but as this photograph shows, the track sat at about the present location of Nolan County Coliseum. Below, racers are trying out new shoes on horses shod for Mose Newman. (Right, courtesy of the US Department of Agriculture.)

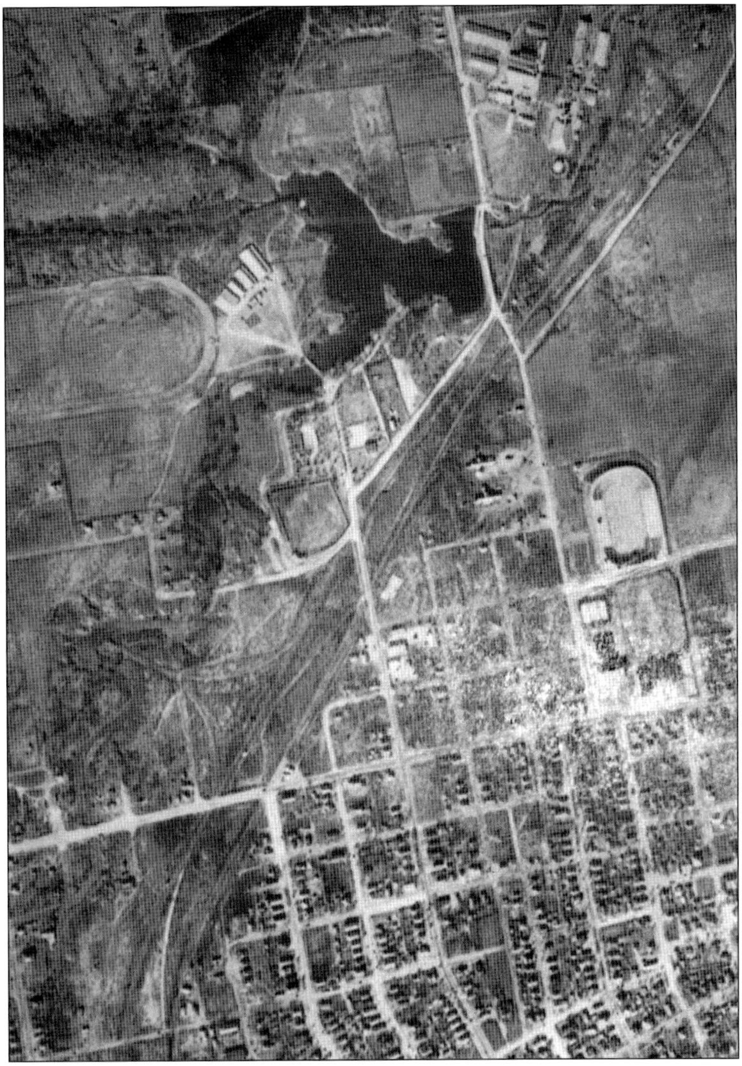

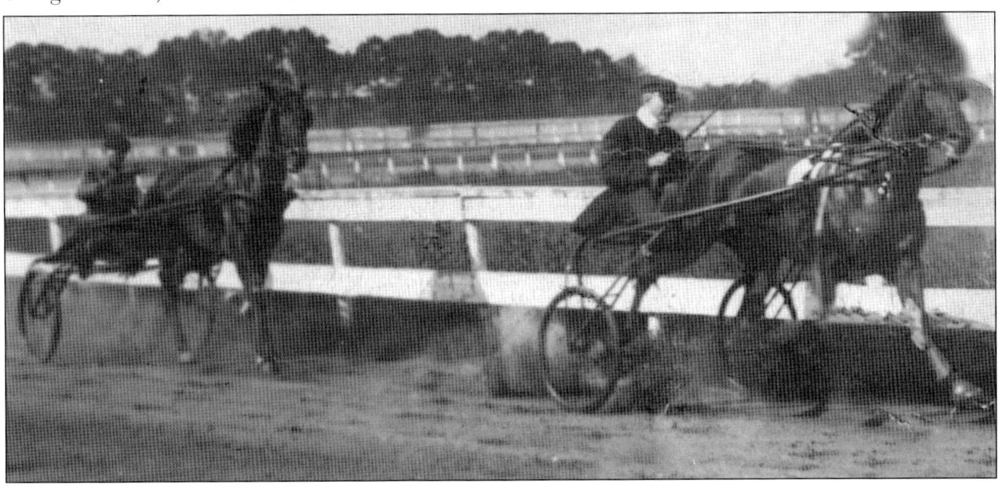

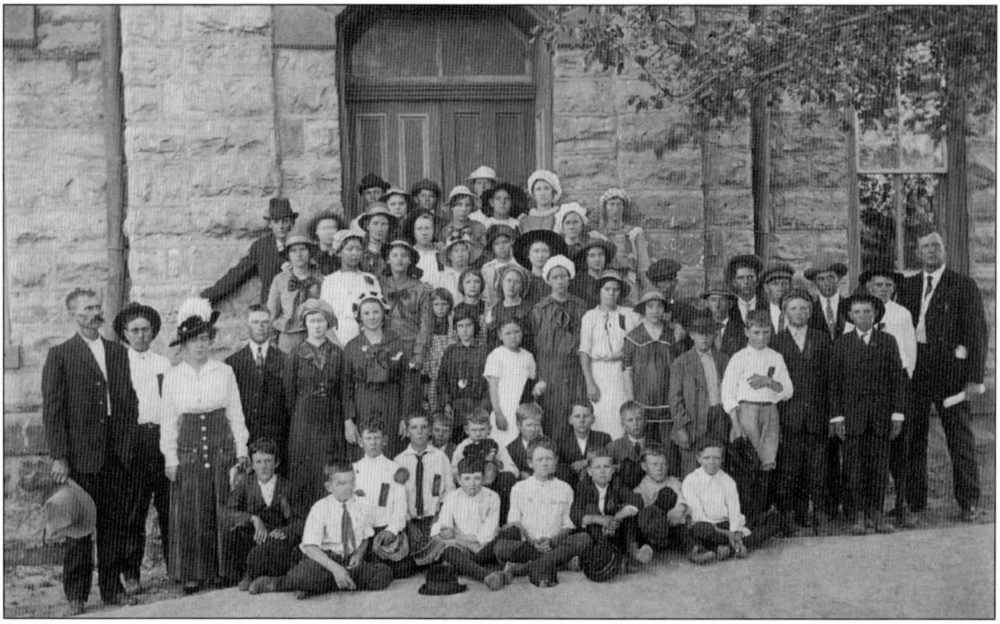

Agriculture and 4-H has always been a big part of Sweetwater and Nolan County's histories. Shown here is an early 4-H club in 1915. Members of this club included Bob Carson, Doc Scott, Mrs. Earl Scott, Ozella Brown, Ruth Scott, Ola Eidson, May Eidson, May Eidson, Lillie McReynolds, Gertrude Witt Christopher, Judd McReynolds, Carl Brown, Mr. and Mrs. Bill Scott, Charley Fry, Wesley Lynch, and Jane McReynolds.

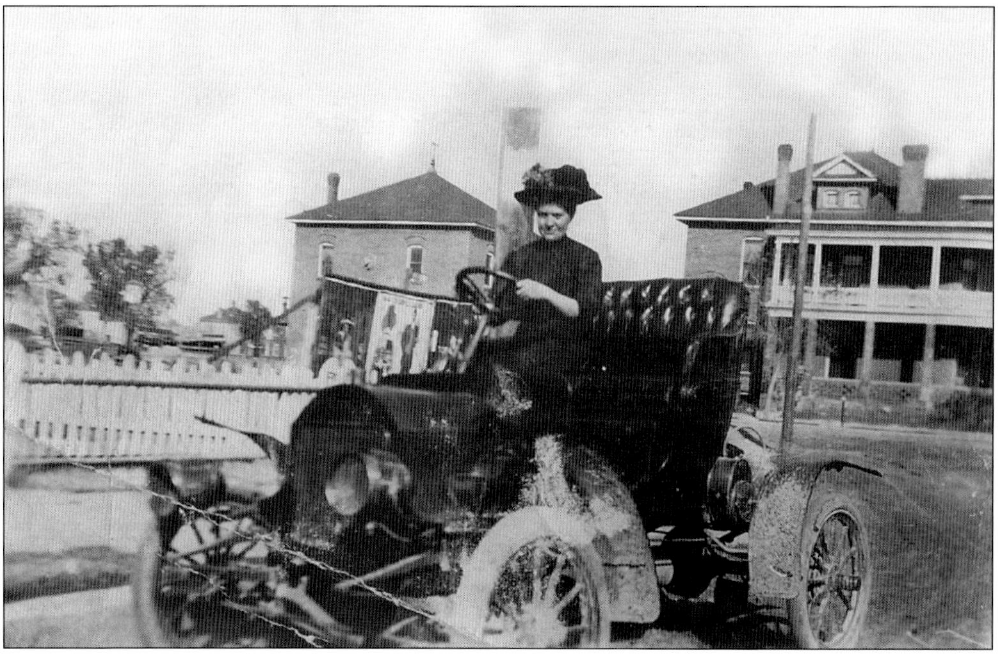

Mrs. A.O. Bennett, in the early 1900s, was one of the first women to drive in Sweetwater. Once automobiles came into regular fashion, it was still only the wealthy who could afford to own one. Only when Henry Ford's Model T came around did others purchase cars en masse. A 1921 Model T is on display at the Pioneer Museum.

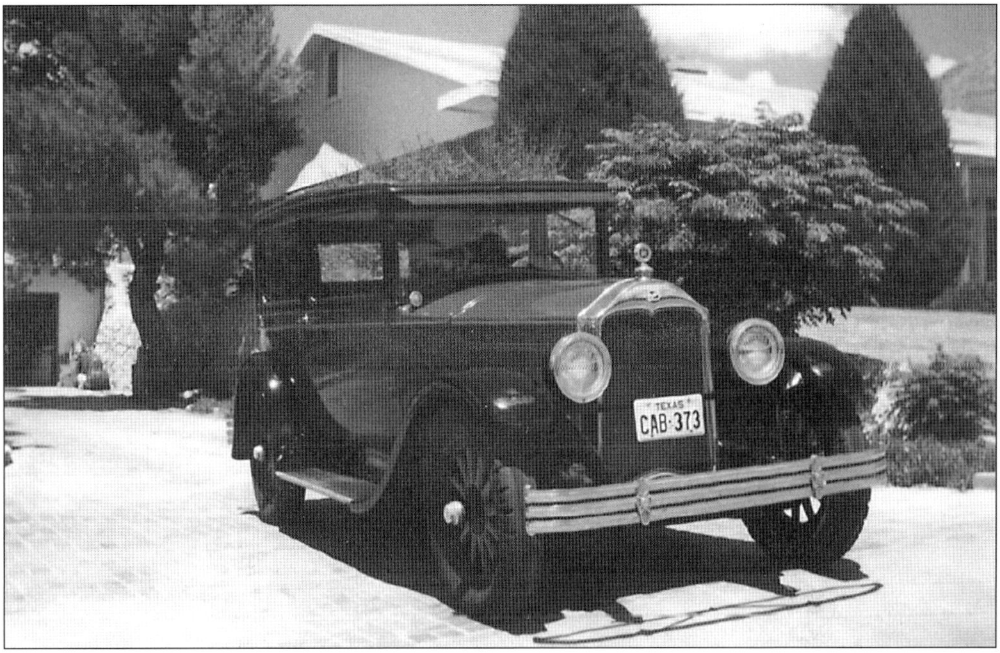

This is the 1928 Buick that belonged to Judge R.A. Ragland. Carl Ragland, Judge Ragland's son, was the Buick dealer in Sweetwater for 25 years. The Raglands were considered one of the wealthier families in the county and built their home in 1906 with running water, electricity, and indoor bathrooms.

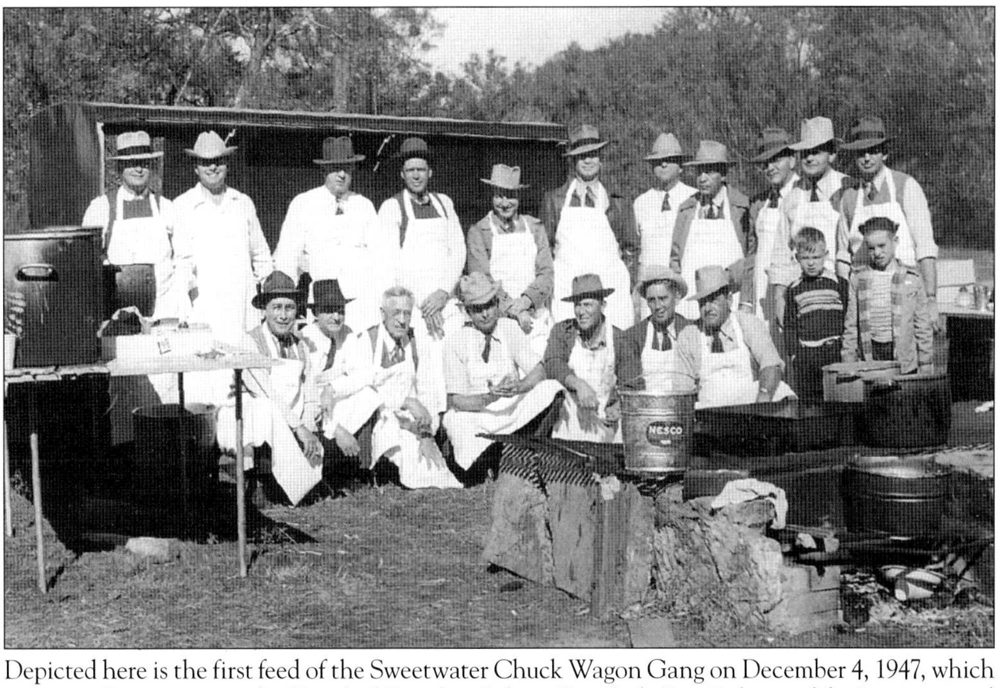

Depicted here is the first feed of the Sweetwater Chuck Wagon Gang on December 4, 1947, which was served to citizens at the Hereford Breeders Sale in City Park. Ben Roberts of the International Harvester company was the gang's first president. Among those pictured are Hans Thorgeson, J.C. Pace Jr., Rig Edwards, Clayton Williams, Guy Morris, and Joe Price Maddox.

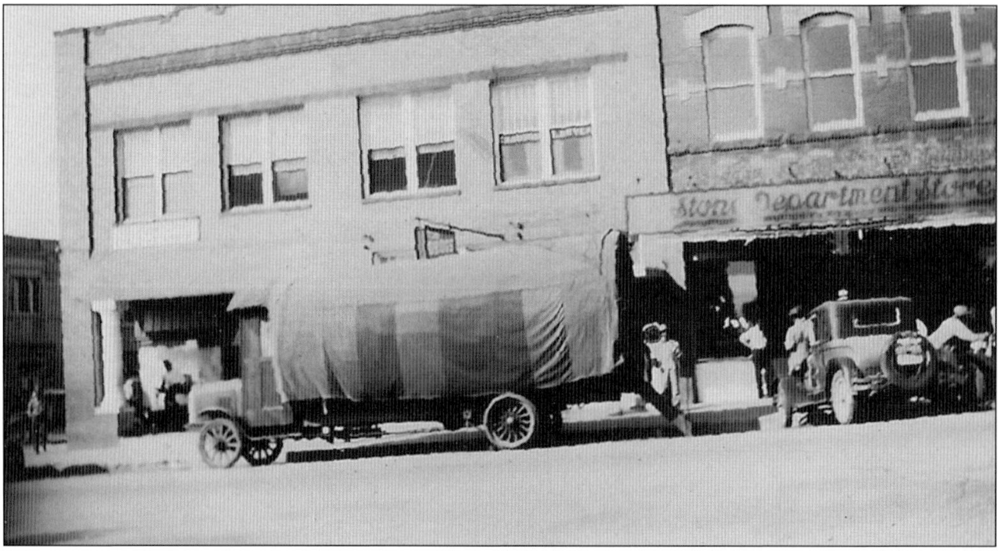

This covered wagon is just one section of a Pacific coast big-tree medicine wagon show, which came to Sweetwater in September 1932. Medicine shows were popular in the 19th century and lasted through World War II. They were known for their miracle elixirs, which are more commonly referred to as snake oil.

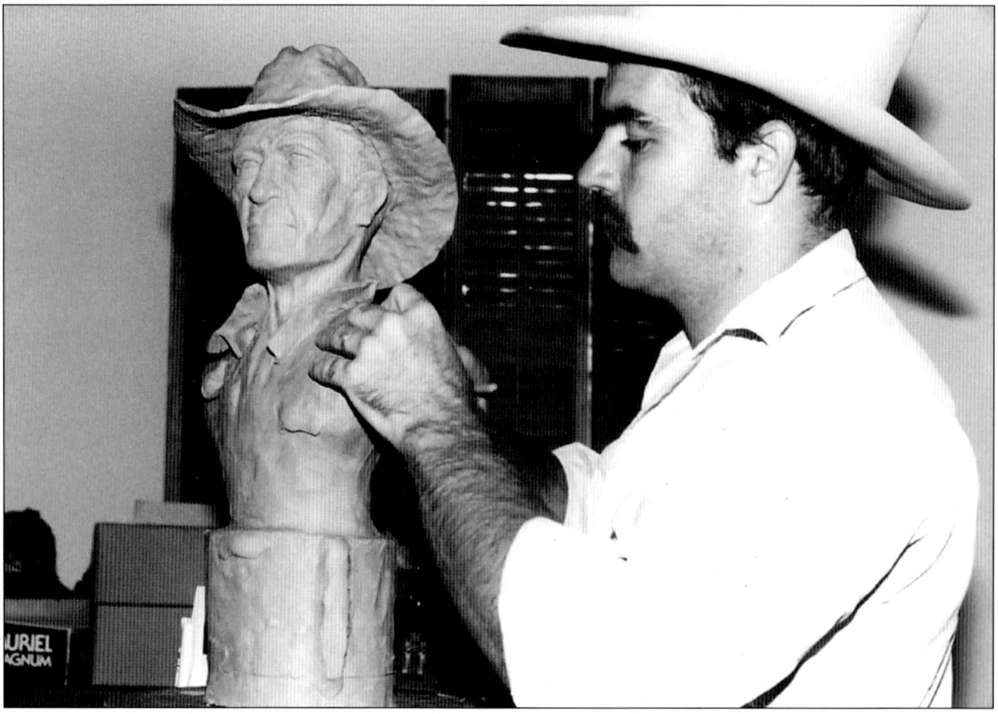

Sweetwater has a long history of artists, from S.D. Myres and Mondel Rogers to Mike Maloney, who is pictured here. All of these artists have works displayed at the Pioneer Museum. The museum also has a section dedicated to writers from both Sweetwater and Nolan County. Also included at the museum is a pictorial of the Jaycees Rattlesnake Roundup by Tom Turner and Colby Hamlin.

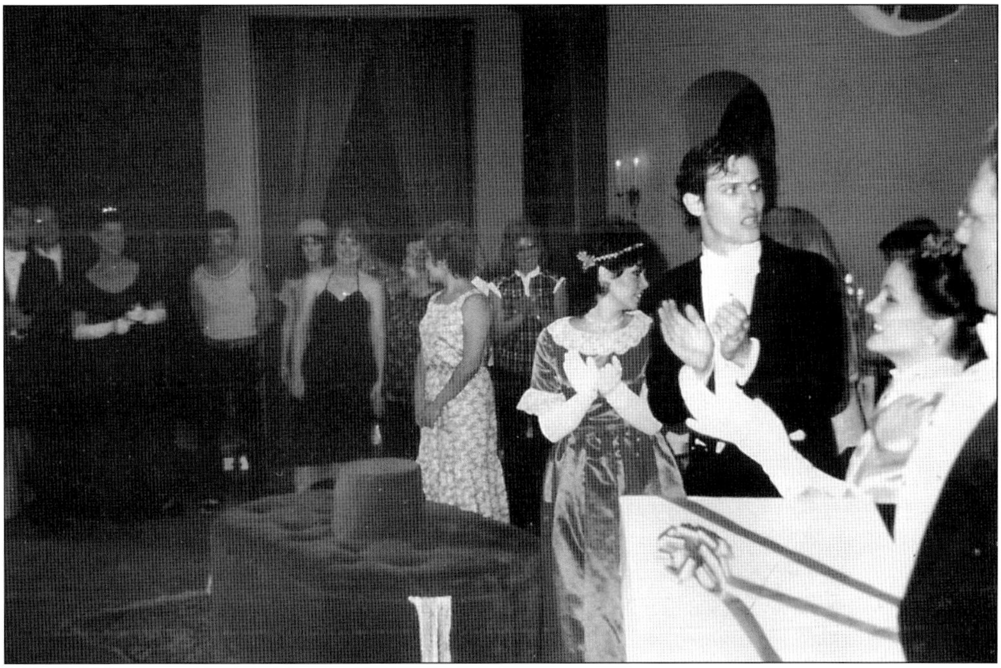

Sweetwater Little Theater was formed in 1979 by a small group of amateur dramatists. This group succeeded the Sweetwater Community Arts Theater, which had been inactive for many years. Originally, the group had no stage home and performed at the Lamp Post Restaurant and the high school auditorium; however, the group finally found a stage at the Municipal Auditorium. The group is currently defunct, but murmurings hint at a reemergence.

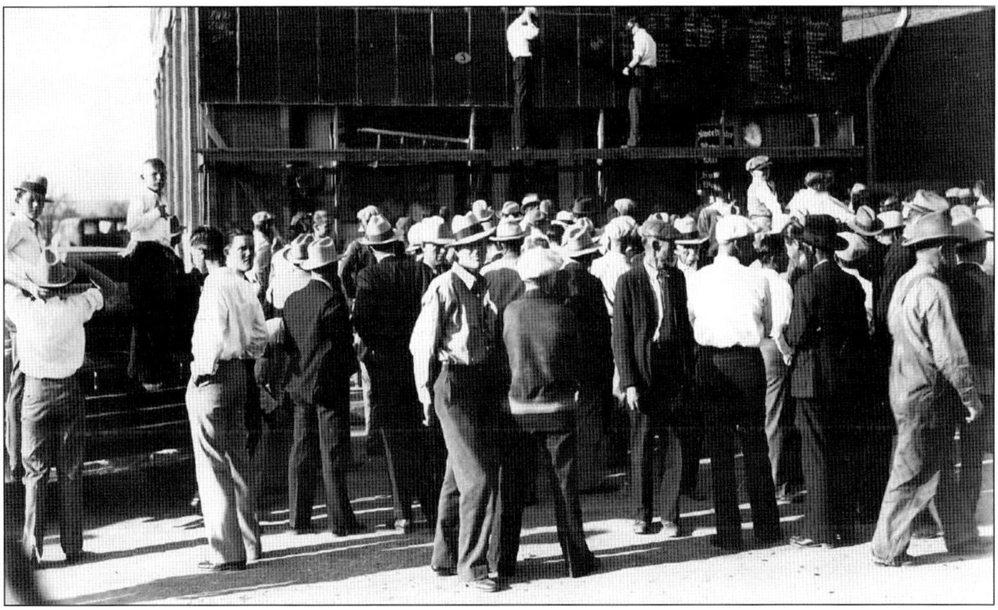

As a community, Sweetwater has tended to lean toward conservative voting in the past few decades, although all points of view are welcome. In this photograph, citizens in the 1930s are outside the *Sweetwater Reporter* building awaiting election results, which were posted on the side of the building as they came in.

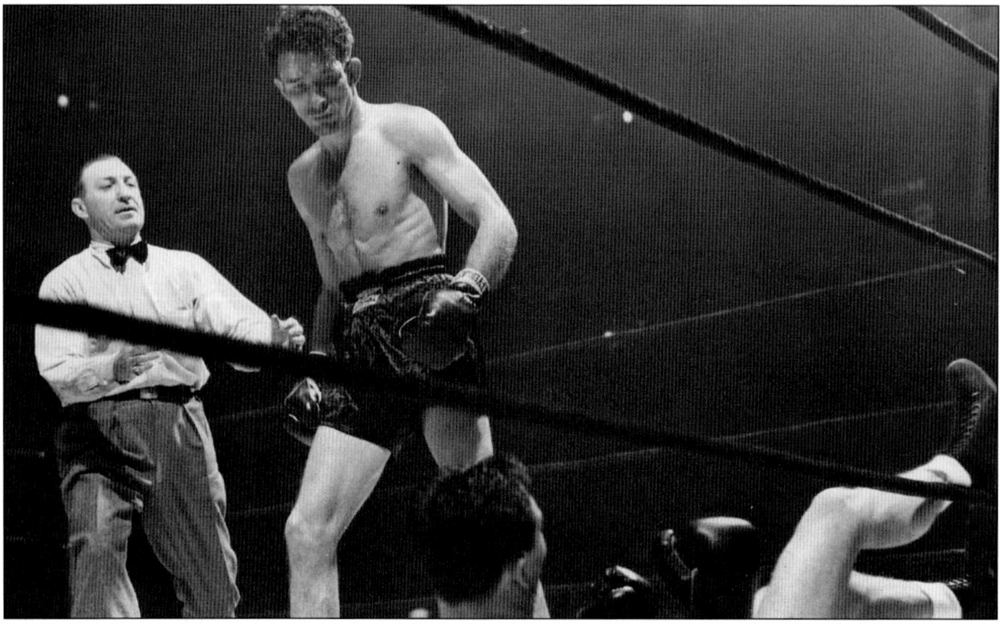

Many professional athletes have been born in Sweetwater, including the "Sweetwater Swatter" Lew Jenkins, seen here standing over an unlucky opponent. Lew was the Lightweight Champion of the World. Other notable athletes include "Slingin" Sammy Baugh and David Terrell, who both played for the Washington Redskins; Clyde "Bulldog" Turner, who played for the Chicago Bears; and Kenneth Norman, who played for the Minnesota Twins.

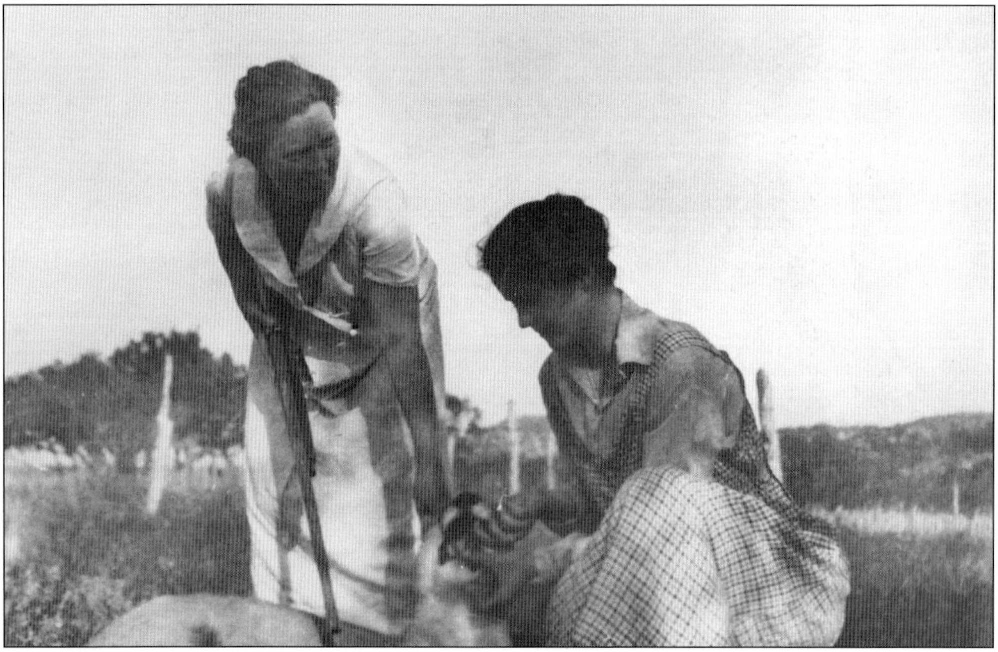

Mountain lions, bobcats, coyotes, and black bears all greeted early pioneers arriving in Nolan County. In 1924, Fred Berfriend killed this mountain lion in First Canyon west of Wall's Point. Gladys Coomber is the woman holding the rifle. In the past several years, there have also been sightings of black Mexican pumas in the area, although none have been killed.

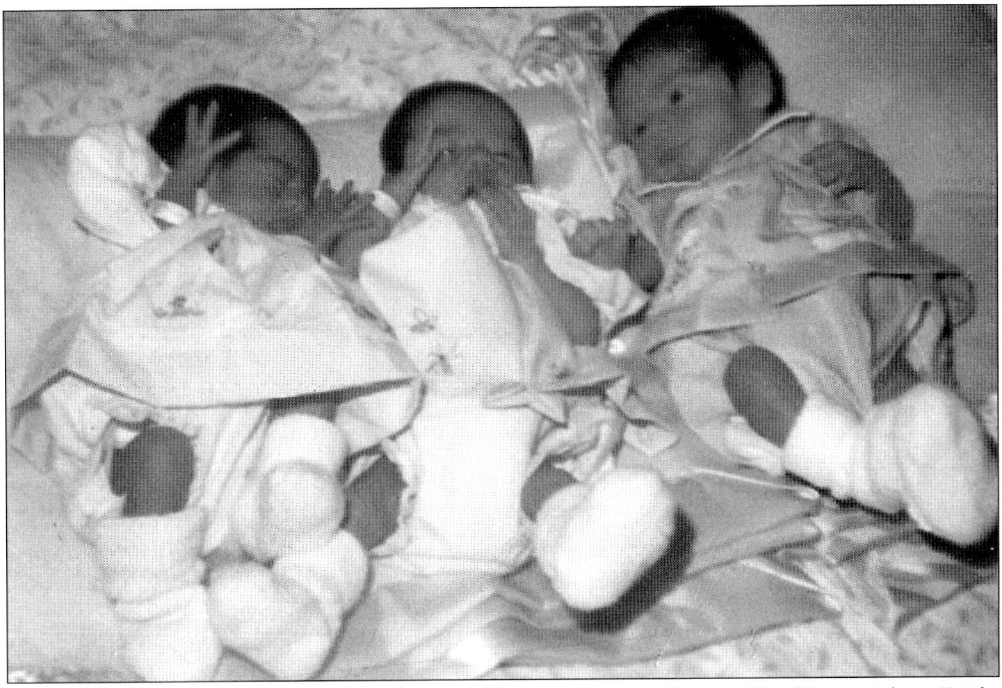

In March 1978, Sweetwater had the honor of being home to the world's oldest triplets, Faith, Hope, and Charity Cardwell, who were so named by Pres. Grover Cleveland's wife, Frances. On March 20 and 21, Sweetwater also had the honor of being home to the world's youngest triplets, Beatris, Christina, and Stevan Bugarin, pictured. (Courtesy of the Bugarin family.)

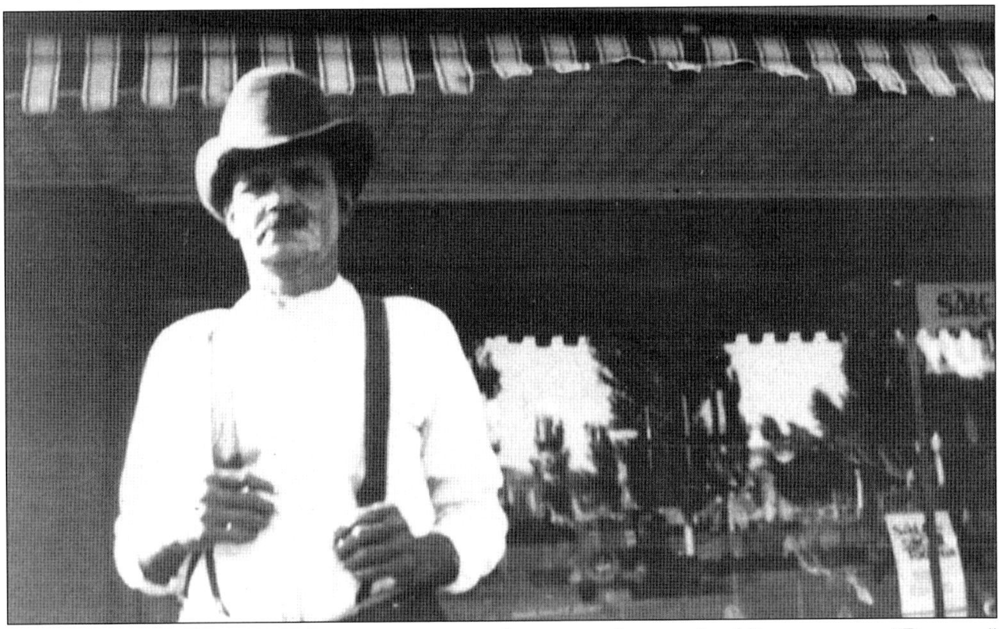

In the late 1800s, this man, who was a mute, was known to the people of Sweetwater as "Dummy." He was a friend to all and sold popcorn on the sidewalk close to the theater in the days before theaters sold their own popcorn. His last name was Moon, and he came to Sweetwater in 1883 and relatively soon after owned property.

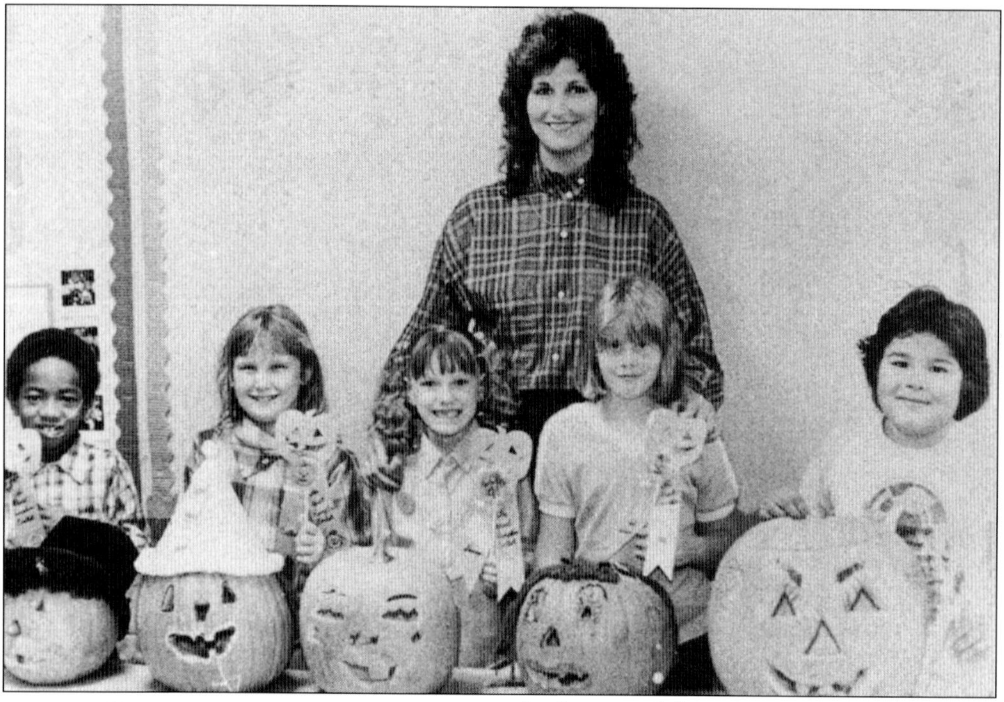

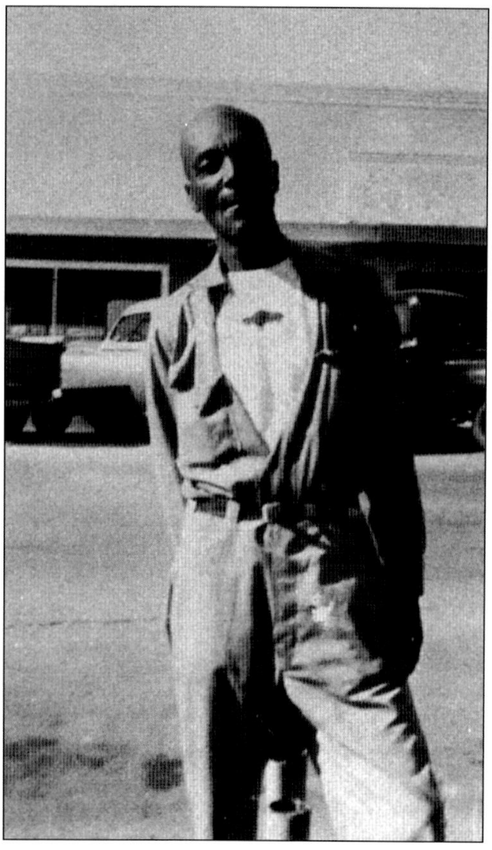

As director of the museum, Franzas Cupp has hosted a Halloween contest dubbed Pumpkins on the Porch, in which area children compete for the most creatively decorated jack-o-lantern. Appearing in this photograph with Vicky Mayberry (back) are, from left to right, Randal Jackson, unidentified, April Brantley, Jamie Gardener, and unidentified. The Pioneer Museum will again host Pumpkins on the Porch in October 2013.

Pete Harvey was the "cook and general ramrod for the Sweetwater Boy Scouts" for over 27 years, according to *Nolan County First One Hundred Years*; he worked with Boy Scout Troop 140. The Pioneer Museum has an extensive Boy Scout display, and the Boy Scouts are honored every February with a special exhibit arranged by Frank Carpenter. This photograph was taken on November 1, 1950, near the square.

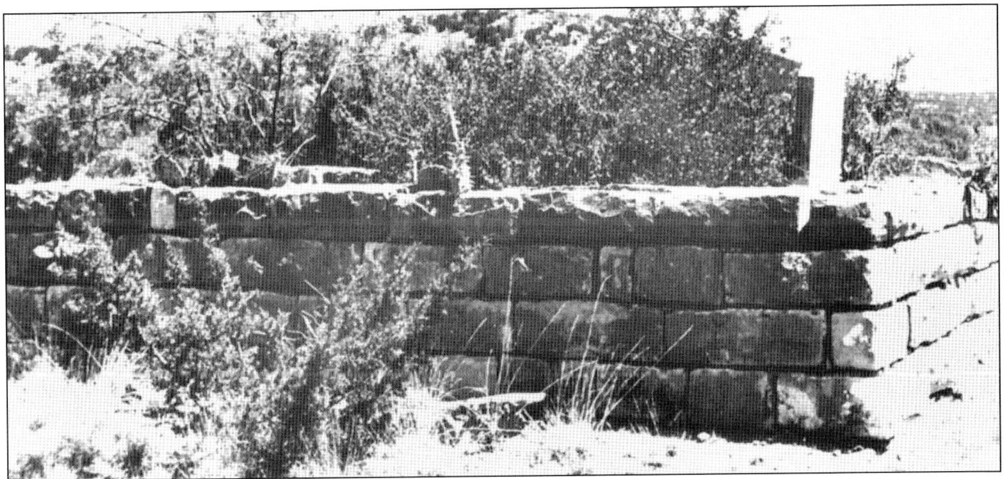

George "Beardy" Miller's grave sits atop a hill overlooking Bitter Creek. Miller died at the age of 78 on September 28, 1892, while roping a bull when it jerked his horse down on top of him. When anyone needed a loan, he or she went to Beardy Miller, who was never seen going to a bank but always had cash. It was rumored he had a hidden treasure on his land.

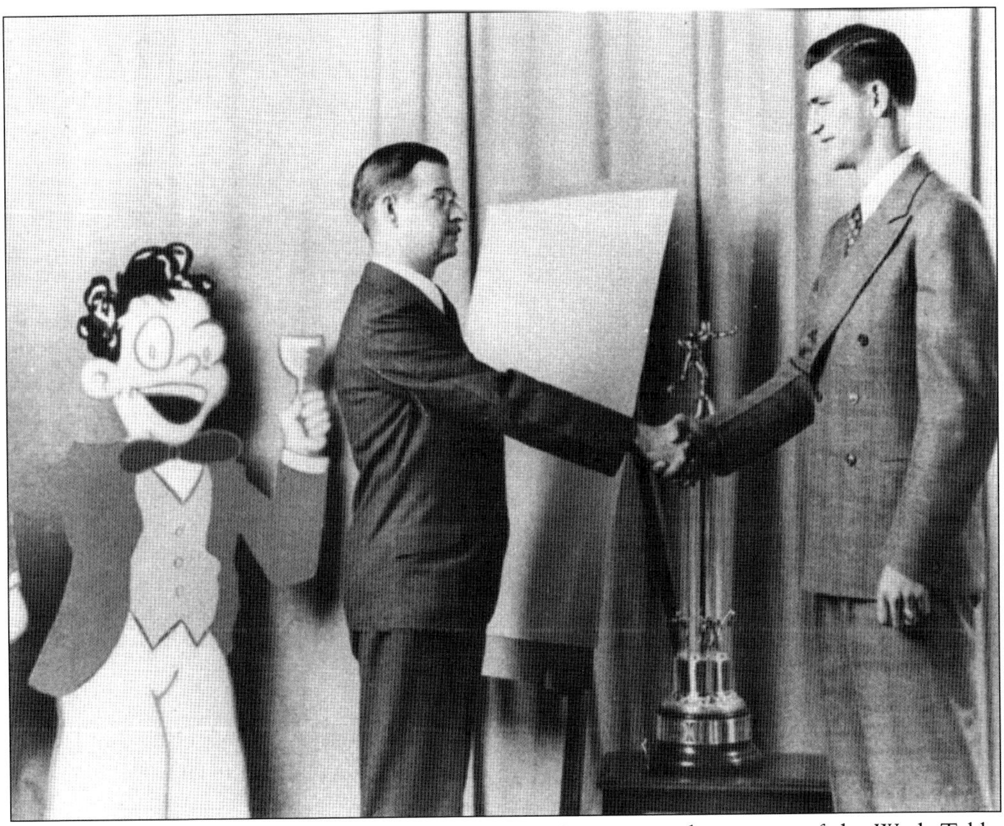

Royston "Roy" Crane, the son of R.C. and Mamie Crane, was the creator of the Wash Tubbs and Easy and Buzz Sawyer comic strips. Roy (pictured at right) took classes at Hardin-Simmons University and the University of Texas but did not stay at either school for more than a year. He rode the rails as a hobo for a while before finding his niche as a cartoonist.

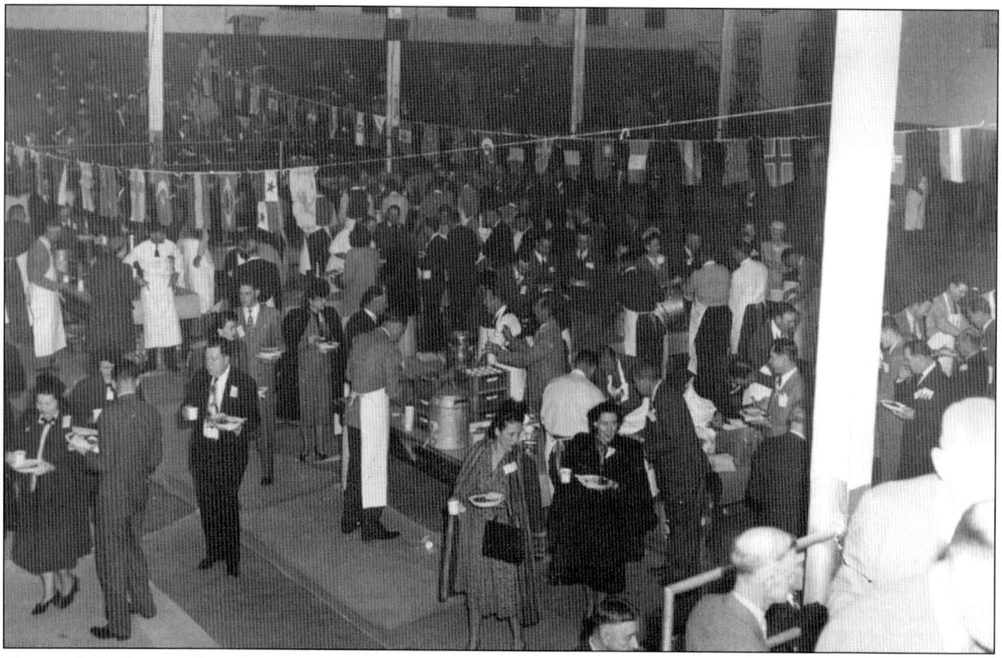

Civic clubs have played a major part in Sweetwater's history and continue to serve its interests today. Some of the current clubs include the Sweetwater Masonic Lodge, the Order of the Eastern Star, Women's Forum, the Kiwanis, the Rotary Club, the Lions Club, Republican Women's Club, Sweetwater Book Review, Sweetwater Jaycees, Sweetwater Gun Club, and many others.

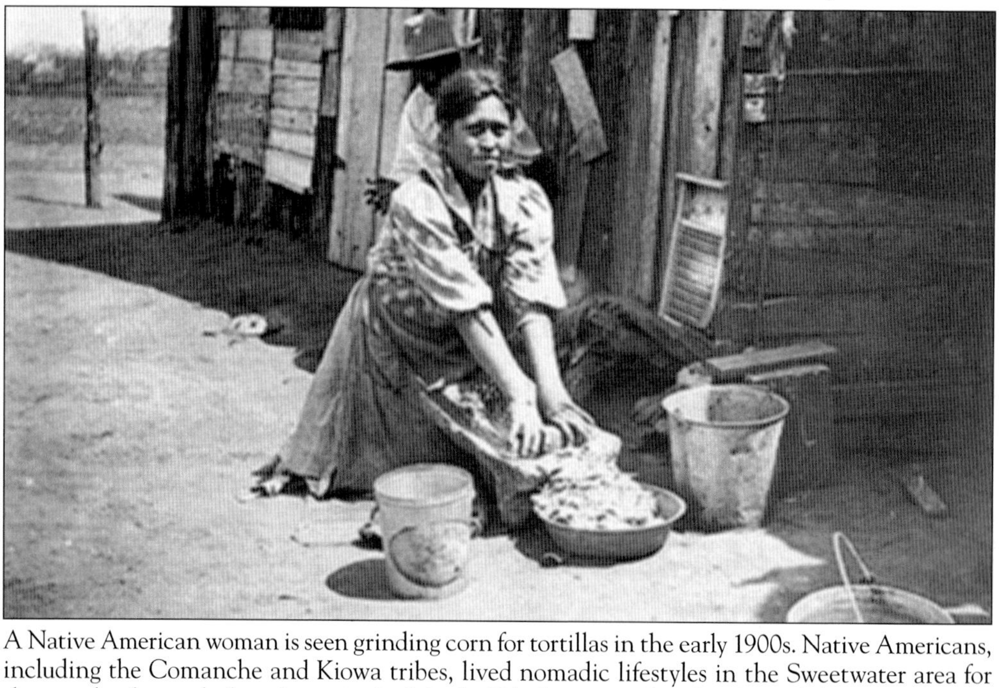

A Native American woman is seen grinding corn for tortillas in the early 1900s. Native Americans, including the Comanche and Kiowa tribes, lived nomadic lifestyles in the Sweetwater area for thousands of years before the arrival of the buffalo hunters, who slaughtered their food supply. Comanches in the area were known as the "Honey Eaters" and would mark trees known to have the lifesaving nectar. (Courtesy of T.W. Beauchamp.)

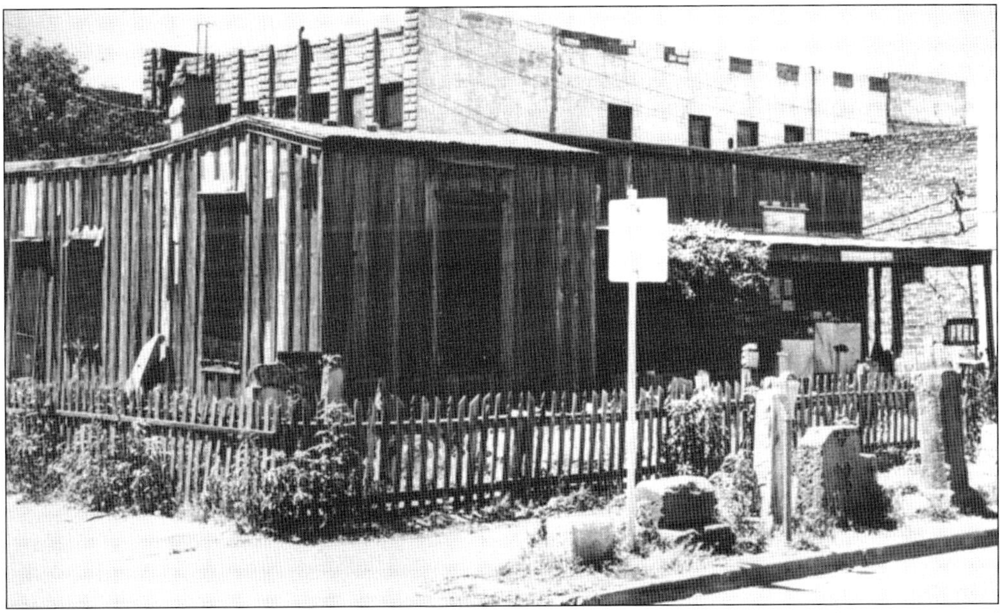

A.A. Prince and his son Newt Prince were collectors, and their home, porch, and yard were filled with various relics, including the noose from the only hanging that occurred in Coleman County. During early years, both Newt and his father had odd jobs around town. Their home was located in the middle of the 200 block of Broadway Avenue.

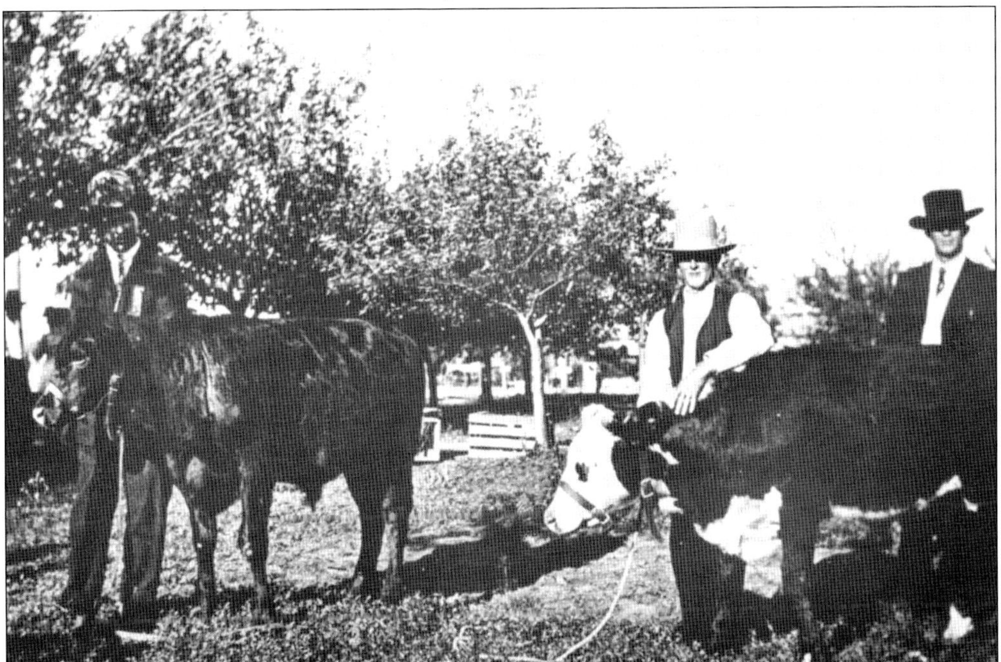

In the late 1800s and early 1900s, cattle and sheep grazing on the courthouse lawn were not an unusual sight. Here, W.C. Calvert, the Nolan County agricultural agent in 1915; Robert Lee McReynolds, the first Nolan County agricultural agent; and G.W. "Judd" McReynolds are shown on the Nolan County Courthouse lawn.

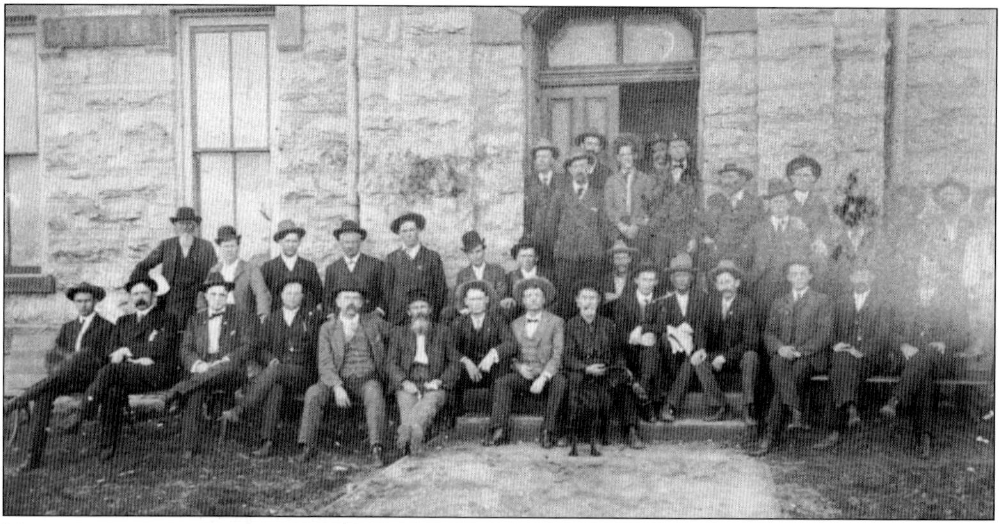

Here, some prominent citizens of Sweetwater are having their picture taken on the south side of the courthouse in 1906. Justice of the peace E.M. Sayle is sitting on the steps with a newspaper in his hand. R.C. Crane is sitting on Sayle's left-hand side. Note the wide variety of hats worn by men of similar social status.

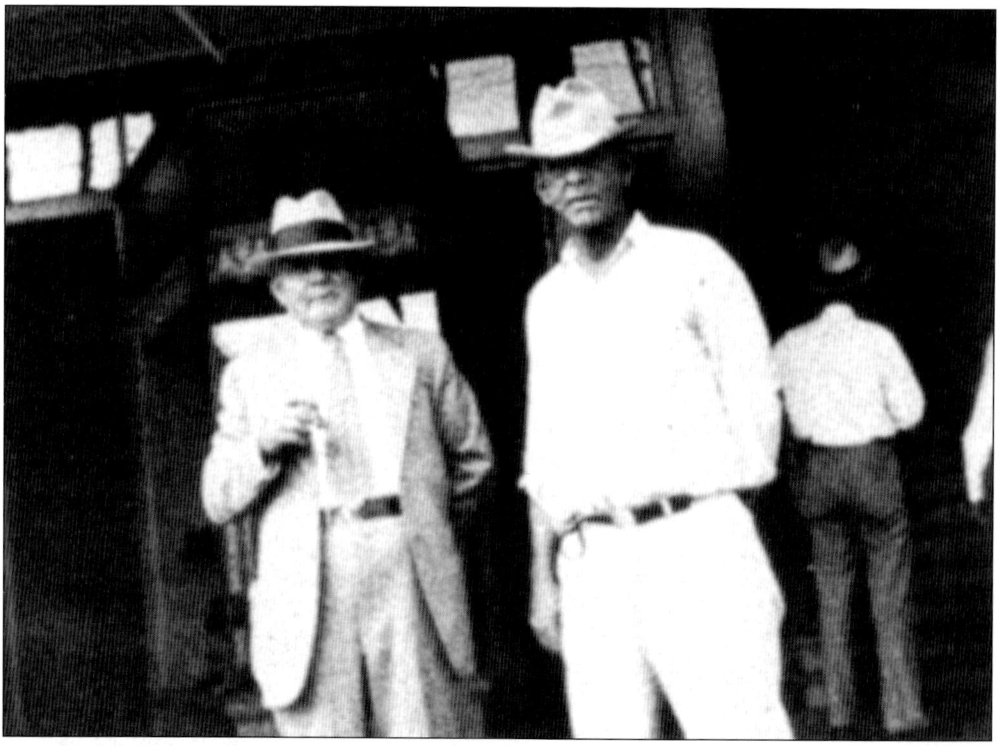

Here are Samuel L. Glass (left), owner of Glass grocery store, and Bert Trammell, a rancher who lived from 1880 to 1946. Trammell had large ranch holdings in Nolan County and was a major stockholder in his family's bank, but his major interest was racing. He once had an encounter with Pancho Villa when racing horses in Juarez and somehow acquired a bridle bit of Villa's.

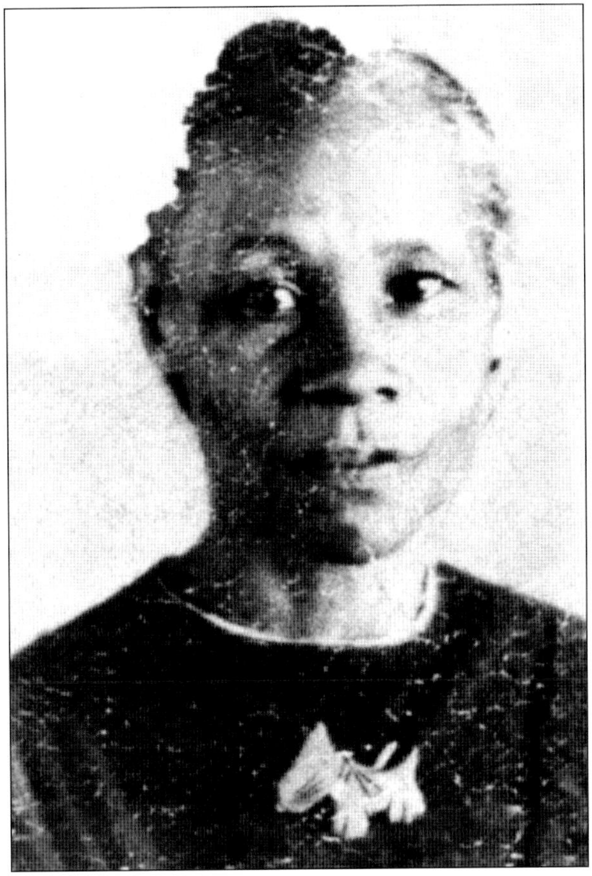

Dr. and Mrs. T.W. Moore taught in several East Texas schools before coming to Sweetwater. Professor Moore helped to organize the West Texas Interscholastic League, which became District 21 in the Prairie View Interscholastic League. The Moores served as teachers at Booker T. Washington School in Sweetwater. Their tenure began around 1934 and lasted until their retirement at the end of the 1945–1946 school year. Both of their sons, S. Darnell Moore and Edgar Watson, served as teachers in the Snyder Negro School. Darnell retired from teaching and went into the postal service, but Watson became principal of Big Spring's Lake View School. Here, he sponsored the Cattle Bowl, which featured outstanding West and East Texas black high school football teams.

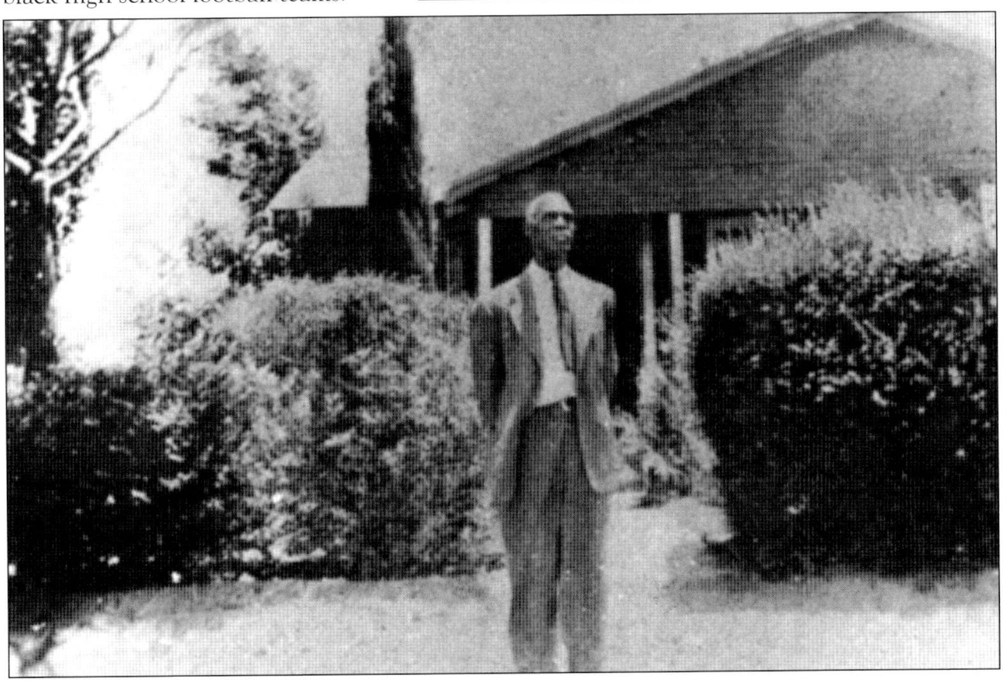

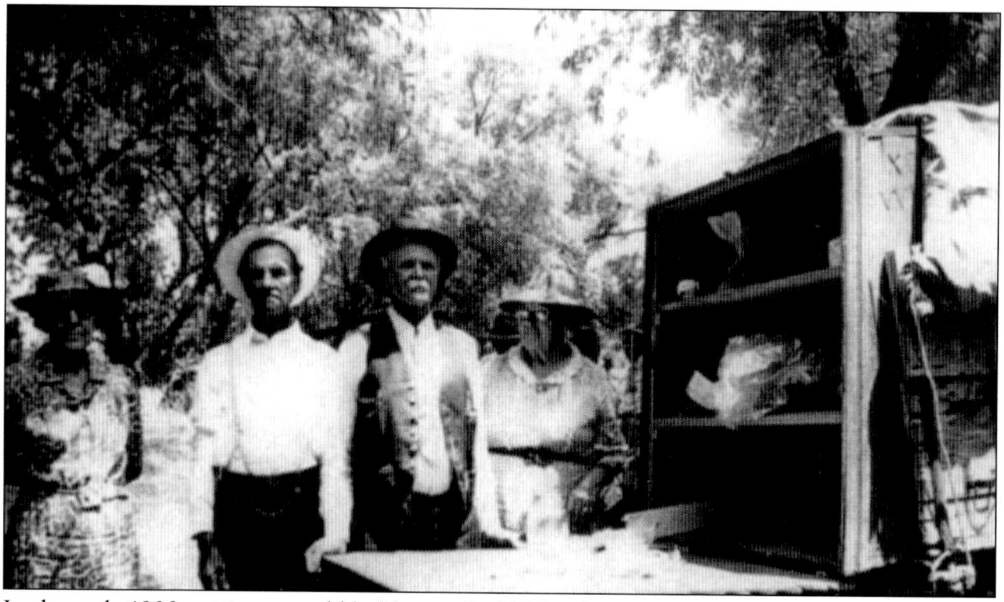

In the early 1900s, citizens would hold a yearly Old Settlers Reunion in City Park. Pictured here from left to right are Bettie George Hopkins, Clint Scott, W.A. "Billie" George, and an unidentified woman. This reunion lasted for several years until there were no old settlers left to reunite.

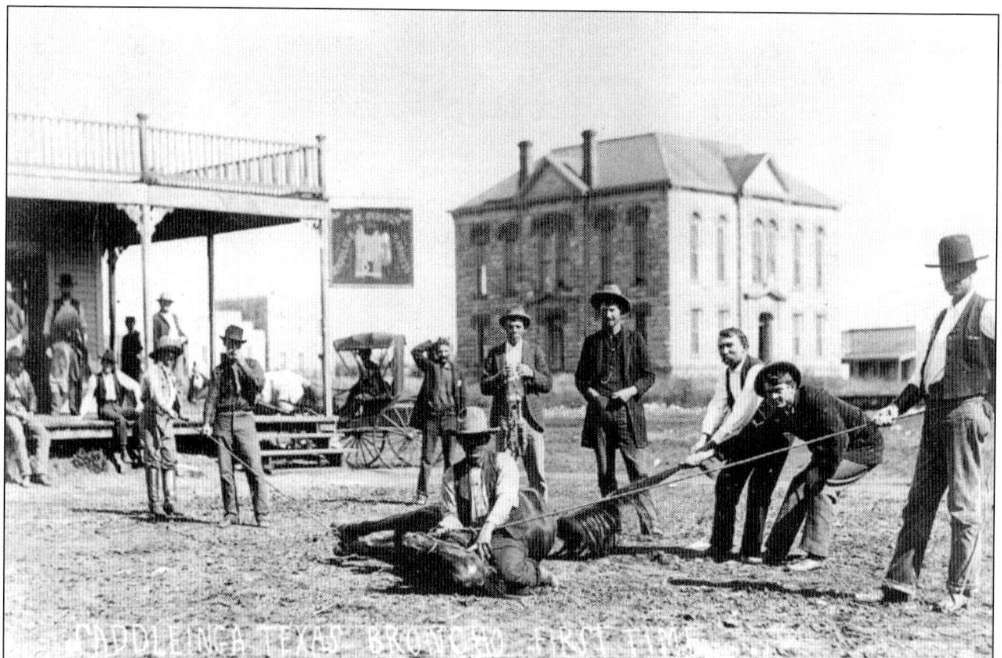

Men on the courthouse square are saddling a bronco for the first time. Shown holding the tail is early saloon owner Lang Aycock. In the foyer of the Pioneer Museum is a bartender's hutch made from the bar in his saloon. A day care memorialized with his name stands today at the corner of Pine and Fourth Streets.

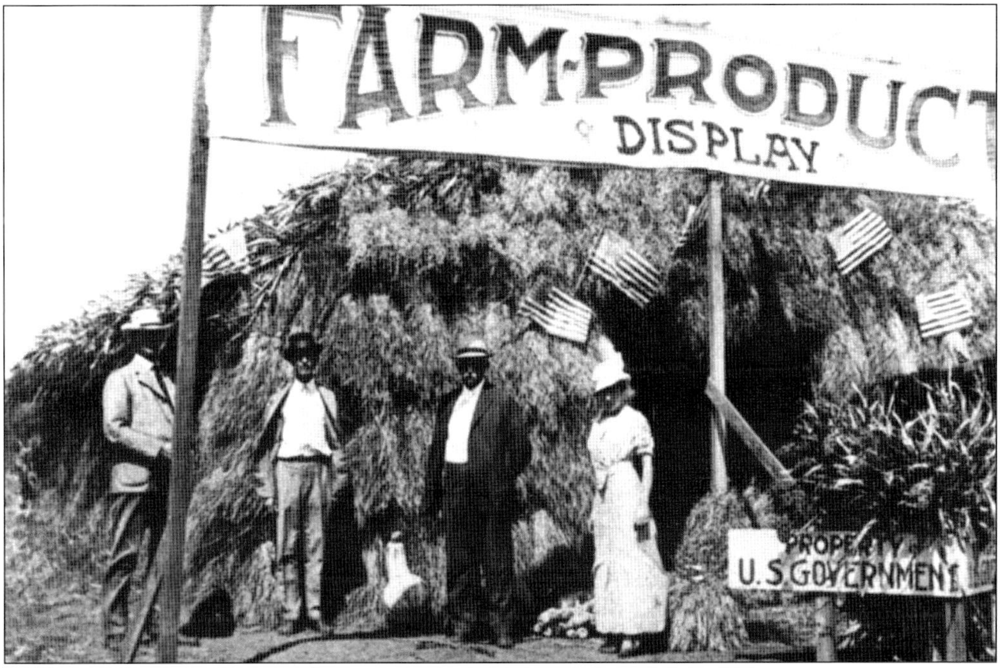

Imogene Neely, at far right above, was the first home demonstration agent for Nolan County. Seen here on September 7–8, 1915, she stands in front of her first display as agent. During this weekend event, Neely demonstrated how to can using tin cans as well as glass mason jars. On display at the Pioneer Museum is an example of this type of canning done by Norma Hackfeld Backhaus.

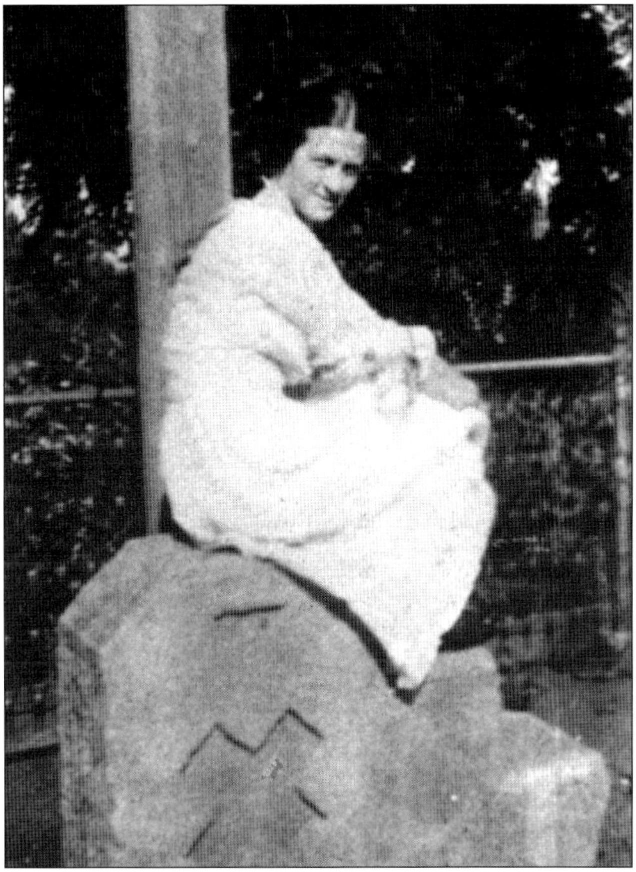

Margaret Hamner Newman, pictured in front of the Newman home on James Street in about 1919, is seated on a courtesy step, which is now on display on the front lawn of the Pioneer Museum. Courtesy steps were placed on people's lawns and throughout town to allow ladies to mount their sidesaddled horses in a slightly more elegant manner.

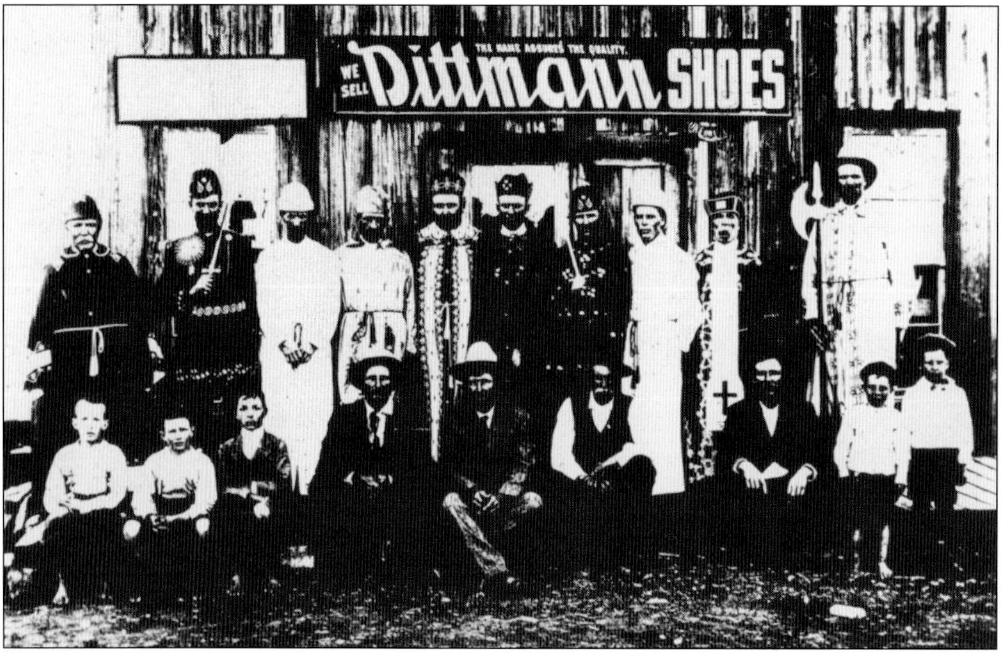

Woodmen of the World, a fraternal benefit society, operates a large privately held insurance company for its members. Seen here meeting at Dora in the early 1900s, the Sweetwater chapter of Woodmen of the World once had its headquarters on the site that became the Commercial Hotel. Included in this picture are Jim Ensminger, Pleas Dunlap, R.M. Dunlap, and Joe Brownfield.

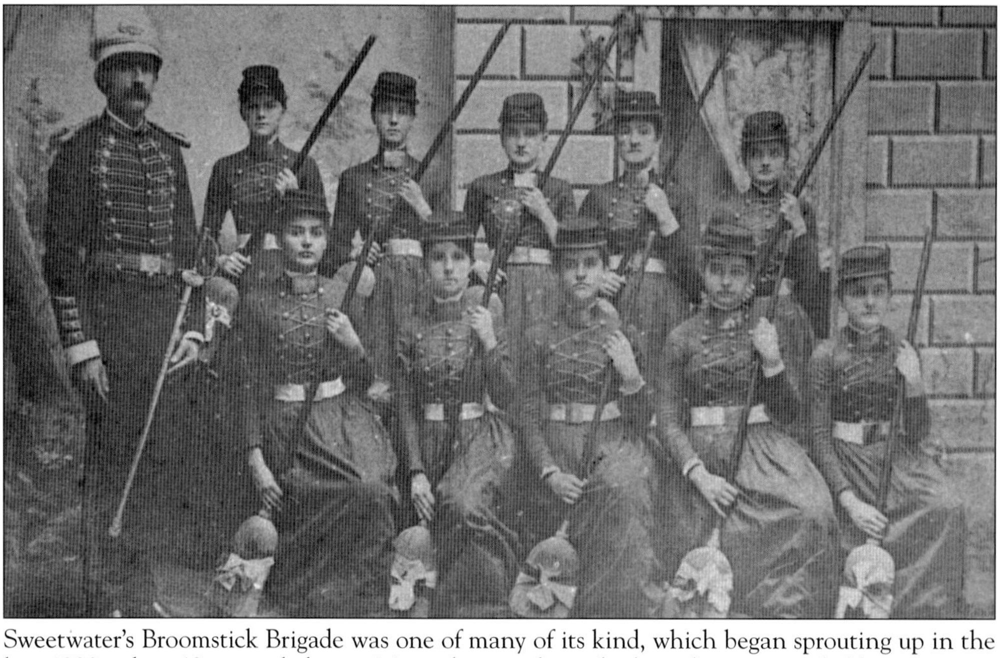

Sweetwater's Broomstick Brigade was one of many of its kind, which began sprouting up in the late 1880s when 12 young ladies in Massachusetts formed a brigade, commanded by a captain, and demonstrated their broom-handling abilities in a public drill. These teams performed like their male counterpart drill teams, and the fad spread; drills were often performed as fundraisers and for parades.

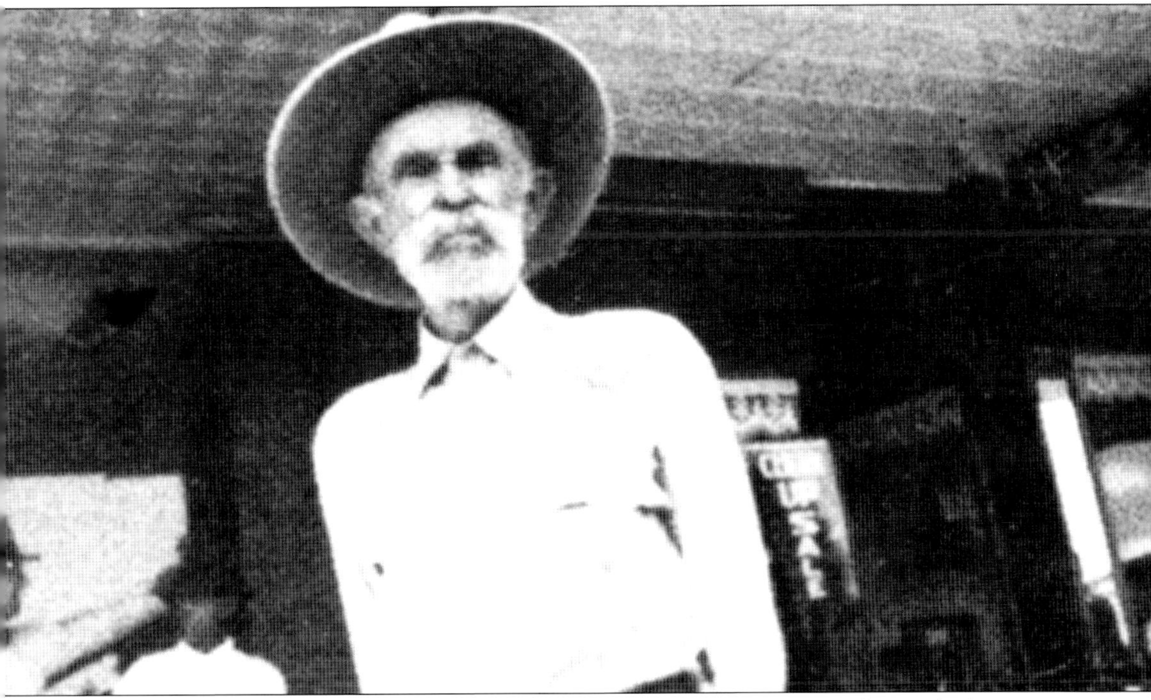

W.H. Boyd came to Nolan County in 1881; he was 84 years old in 1892. In 1868, his outfit threw in with Charles Goodnight, who was bringing the remains of Oliver Loving back from Fort Sumner, New Mexico. In 1860, Goodnight and Loving, hearing of the need for cattle in Fort Sumner, joined together and began a drive to the fort, on what became known as the Goodnight-Loving Trail, where they sold beef to the Army for $12,000 in gold. In the spring of 1867, the two began their third drive, which was slowed by heavy rains and Native American threats. Loving went ahead of the herd, and being impatient, he traveled during the day, which brought a Comanche attack. During the attack, he was gravely wounded; he died of gangrene due to this wound.

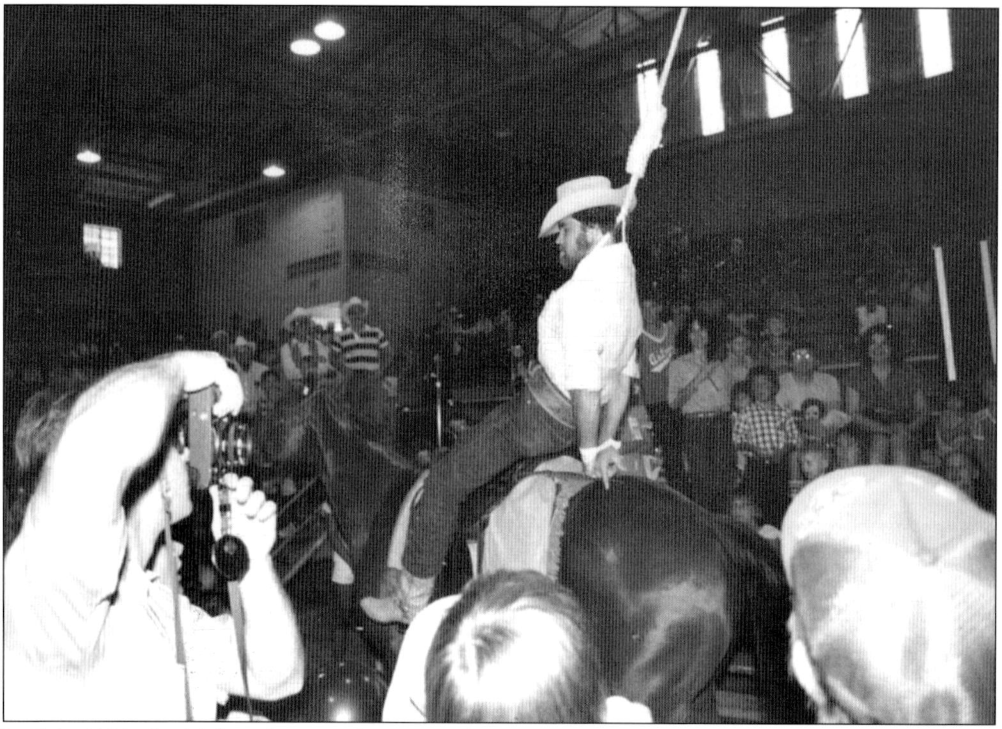

In July 1981, the Nolan County Centennial Committee celebrated the 100th birthday of the county by way of a Pioneer Days Festival. The festival included events such as a parade, as seen below; a barbecue by the Sweetwater Chuck Wagon Gang; art exhibits; walking tours; a saloon; various children's events; and the reenactment of a Wild West hanging on the corner of First and Oak Streets and again in the coliseum, as seen above. The event ended with a historical tour of Nolan County beginning on the west side of the square. Members of the Nolan County Centennial Committee included Franzas Cupp, Nelson Dressler, Mary Cook, Genevieve Dunlap, Russell Haney, Edith Hughes, Mildred Shuff, and Marion Tiehen.

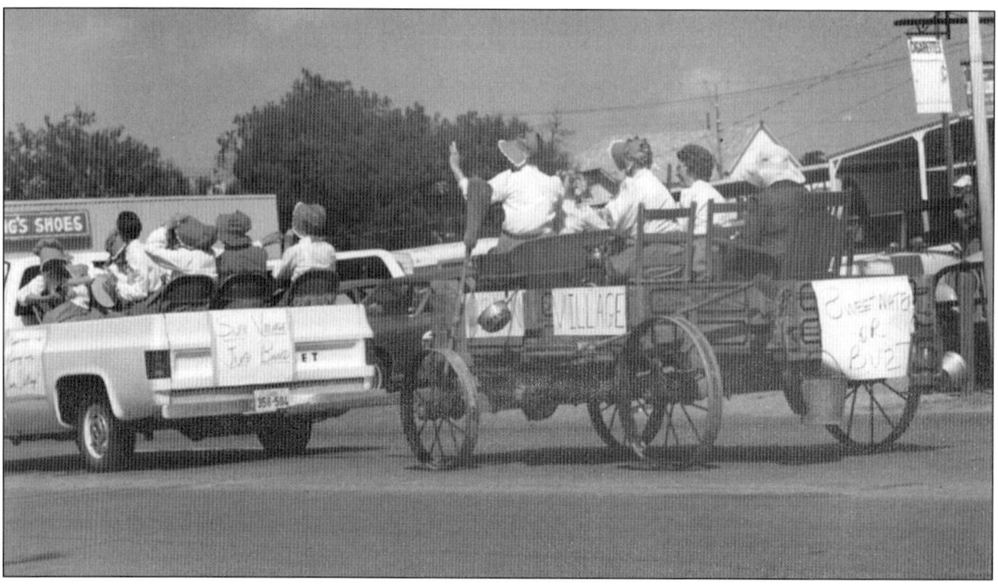

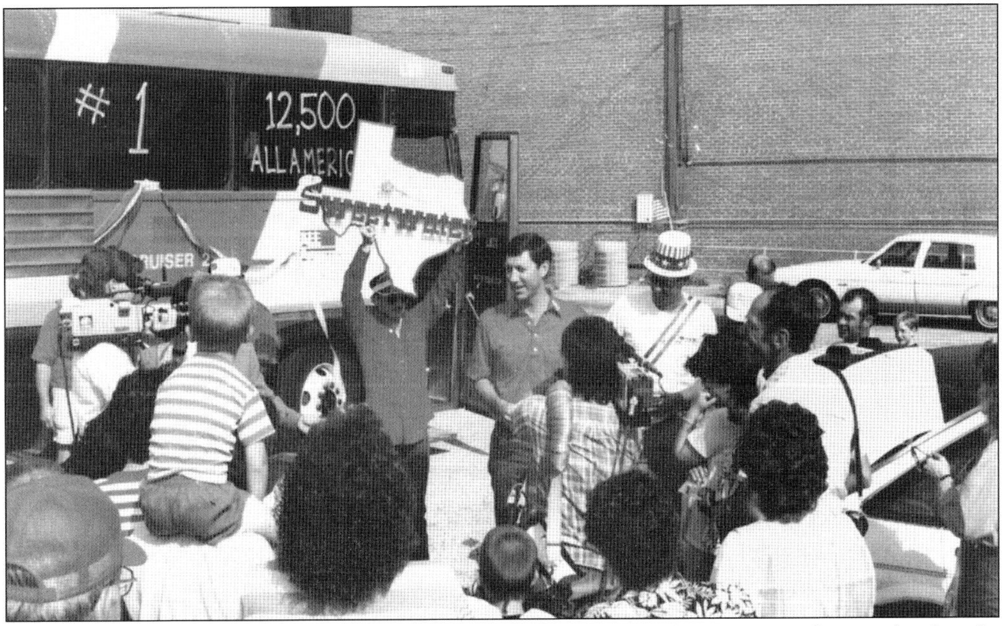

The actions and inactions of citizens in the late 1970s led to many of Sweetwater's historic landmarks being bulldozed to make room for a bank and a courthouse, and in 1981, the city commission entertained demolishing the Municipal Auditorium. At the same time, the city suffered the oil crash and, in 1986, tornados that destroyed half the city. Due to citizens' efforts, the city stopped and reversed the architectural destruction, the economy slowly began to recover, and everyone together helped to rebuild neighbors' homes lost in the natural disaster. These actions in 1988 earned Sweetwater the All-America City Award "in recognition of progress achieved through citizen action." Shown here are citizens on their way to pick up the award and former mayor Rick Rhodes accepting the honor.

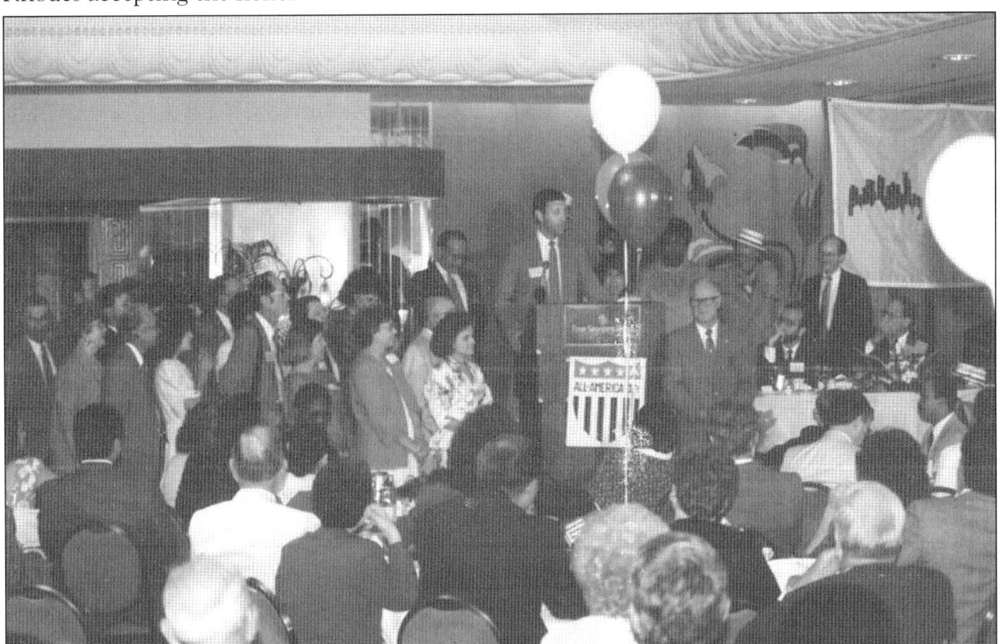

BIBLIOGRAPHY

Bradford, Louise. *A History of Nolan County, Texas*. Dissertation. University of Texas, 1934.

Monday, Travis. *Best of Museum Musings, Volume 1: True Stories About Nolan County, Texas and the Surrounding Area*. Raleigh, NC: Lulu Enterprises Inc., 2004.

Nolan County Historical Commission. *Nolan County First One Hundred Years, Sesquicentennial Edition*. Dallas, TX: Taylor Publishing Company, 1985.

Sweetwater Junior Historians. *Early Days Nolan County*. Sweetwater, TX: Sweetwater High School, 1975.

INDEX